The First and Second Italian Wars 1494–1504

Harry Lime in *The Third Man* (1949 British motion picture, directed by Carol Reed)

> *In Italy, for thirty years under the Borgias, they had warfare, terror, murder, bloodshed, but they produced Michael Angelo, Leonardo da Vinci and the Renaissance. In Switzerland, they had brotherly love, they had five hundred years of democracy and peace – and what did that produce? The cuckoo clock.*

Movie script, page 178, line written-in by Orson Welles, playing Harry Lime who was also performing as Cesare Borgia in Prince of Foxes (1949 American motion picture made in Italy based on Samuel Shellabarger's novel of the same name).

The First and Second Italian Wars 1494–1504

Fearless Knights, Ruthless Princes and the Coming of Gunpowder Armies

by

Julian Romane

Pen & Sword
MILITARY

First published in Great Britain in 2020 by
Pen & Sword Military
An imprint of
Pen & Sword Books Ltd
Yorkshire – Philadelphia

ISBN 978 1 52675 051 8

Printed and bound in the UK by TJ International Ltd, Padstow, Cornwall.

Pen & Sword Books Limited incorporates the imprints of Atlas, Archaeology,
Aviation, Discovery, Family History, Fiction, History, Maritime, Military, Military
Classics, Politics, Select, Transport, True Crime, Air World, Frontline Publishing,
Leo Cooper, Remember When, Seaforth Publishing, The Praetorian Press,
Wharncliffe Local History, Wharncliffe Transport, Wharncliffe True Crime and
White Owl.

For a complete list of Pen & Sword titles please contact

PEN & SWORD BOOKS LIMITED
47 Church Street, Barnsley, South Yorkshire, S70 2AS, England
E-mail: enquiries@pen-and-sword.co.uk
Website: www.pen-and-sword.co.uk

Or
PEN AND SWORD BOOKS
1950 Lawrence Rd, Havertown, PA 19083, USA
E-mail: Uspen-and-sword@casematepublishers.com
Website: www.penandswordbooks.com

Contents

Acknowledgements

Many hands take a manuscript and turn it into a book. I thank all those who made this book possible. I want to thank Phil Sidnell for his support and help. I offer profound thanks to editor Irene Moore. Her meticulous observations are most appreciated. Further, I am very grateful for the professional work of Matt Jones and the staff of Pen & Sword.

Internet Archive is a most remarkable site. There, I found old books for which I searched for literally decades suddenly becoming accessible and downloadable. Whereas once I handled fragile pages with only the greatest care now, I can enlarge and read texts printed hundreds of years ago without fear of damaging the book or missing meanings in the documents.

Above all, this book is possible because of the patience and support of my wife, Judith O'Dell.

North Italy.

South Italy.

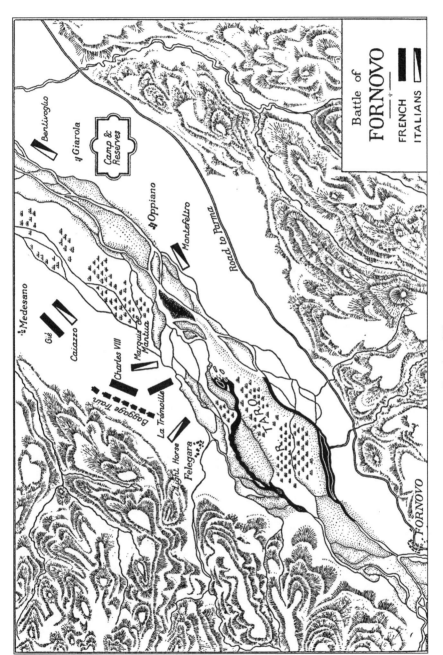

Battle of Fornovo.

Foreword

A Tale of Arms and Men

Fearless Knights, Ruthless Princes and the Coming of the Gunpowder Armies is a tale about fighting men and the transformation of society in Western Europe that shaped the world. We look at a mere decade, 1494–1504. In the swirl of events, our tale tracks the process of developments in the maelstrom of this time. In these ten years the nature of power and wealth changed: before 1494, the world's high civilizations were about equal in power and wealth; after 1504, Western European states were set on their trajectory to dominate the planet. True, this process took centuries and involved the spread of Western European technology across the face of the world, but it was in Italy, during this decade, that the process reached the tipping point.

I wish to be clear: this book is not a discussion of intellectual concepts and fine points concerning the relationships of society, ideology and economics: not at all. War is not a game of chess; it is a drama of the human heart. This is a chronicle of violence and passion, of ambition, achievement and death, of defeat and victory.

What this Book is About

My narrative covers this decade, following the course of military operations with a description of political involvements. We see these events from the perspective of the Italian commentators of the time, as refined over generations of historians reinterpreting these events for their readers. We start with the Kingdom of France after the accession of King Charles VIII (1483) and follow the path to the Italian invasion (1494). The military operations of this French invasion lead to southern Italy and then north again, where the French and Italian forces fight the Battle of Fornovo (1495).

After Charles returns to France, his new Kingdom of Naples is over-thrown by the Great Captain, Gonzalo Fernández de Córdoba, who found a way to defeat the French forces (1495–98). Before he can respond, King Charles dies unexpectedly, a most interesting occurrence (1498). Louis XII becomes King of France and invades Italy again (1499). He sweeps through Milan and supports Cesare Borgia's efforts to centralize the States of the Church (1499).

Here, Cesare Borgia enters the narrative. He is a unique military leader, neither a trained soldier of some military organization nor an aristocrat of a settled principality. As the son of Pope Alexander VI, he received a commission to remove the independent lords who had usurped Church control in the Ecclesiastical States. This operation was called an *impresa*. Using a variety of forces, Cesare began to build a new state, the Duchy of Romagna, administered from Rome and dependent on the house of Borgia. The swift return of the Sforza to Milan interrupted Cesare's *impresa*. Louis XII reacted quickly and recovered Milan, but found his relations with the Swiss badly damaged. The *impresa* resumed while the French retake Naples because of a deal Louis made with King Ferdinand of Spain. However, Ferdinand double crossed Louis, returned the Great Captain to southern Italy, and decisively defeated the French in the Battle of the Garigliano (1493).

My narrative is followed by seven appendices. Each essay covers a topic which further explains the narrative.

1. Important writers contemporary with the Italian Wars: I briefly describe the works of Phillip de Commines, Niccolo Machiavelli, Francesco Guicciardini, Pietro Bembo and the Loyal Serviteur.
2. Italy in 1490: here is a summary of Italian history that relates to my narrative, organized by the areas of north, central and southern Italy.
3. Money and Banking in Western Europe in the Later Middle Ages: this essay recounts the main events that, combined together, pro-duced the new world of money.
4. The Development of Gunpowder Weapons: from origins in China, the technique of explosive powder travelled throughout the world.
5. Military Organization: I give an outline of the tactical and opera-tional military forces of France, the Swiss and the Spanish. Of par-ticular importance is the development of new style infantry units made up of lightly armoured, heavily armed soldiers, some of whom used arquebuses.

6. Pope Alexander VI in the eyes of Church historians: we look at Pope Alexander in current Catholic Church thought.
7. Poison in the Renaissance: an intriguing subject, much discussed then and ever since.

The narrative and appendices tell how the process of military undertakings changed into a world-transforming manner of fighting. Alone, the military innovations do not seem particularly impressive but as part of a growing financial-banking society, they allowed the spread of European power and influence in an unprecedented way.

Why Read this Book

There are many fine books on the Italian Wars. This account is different from others because I draw together a series of nearly simultaneous operations along with their logistical foundations and means of payment. The keys to success in these wars were tactical innovations which meant new weapons, the concepts for their use and the money to pay for them. Charles VIII marched through Italy because he brought a new type of artillery train, mobile and powerful. Of particular significance are the campaigns of Cesare Borgia in the Romagna. Falling between the French in the north and the Spanish in the south, military historians have given little consideration to Cesare's campaigns. This is unfortunate because here is the origin of many innovations, both tactical and financial.

His campaigns demonstrate the emergence of those advantages of the European armies: their ability to satisfy financial needs with other peoples' money, which is to say, with borrowed funds. This was unprecedented in the world of the time and generated a very different style of warfare. Equally important are the campaigns of the Great Captain, Gonzalo de Córdoba, an imaginative innovator who applied his own ideas in southern Italy. He developed a tactical approach and operational style which was the beginning of modern warfare. Here is the actual emergence of the so-called 'Military Revolution'.

Chapter 1

Medieval Winter, Renaissance Spring

Autumn had come to Castle Bayard and France in the second half of the fifteenth century. Not the autumn that comes once a year with its gold, red and brown kaleidoscope of colours, but the autumn of age, rich with overgrown landscapes of well followed paths and fragile, brittle forms in baroque profusion, silhouetted against a cloudy grey sky. For centuries, French society had revolved around the mounted man at arms, the chevalier. He lived in the countryside, in a house that was also a collection of barns, stables and workshops. This house was fortified with watchtowers, strong gates and high walls. The house was the centre of a farm, with villagers attached to the estate who worked the fields and kept the animals. The main product of the estate was at least one chevalier, an armoured horse soldier, skilled in fighting.

The chevalier and his brothers provided the military strength to maintain authority in the land. Being strong, independent-minded men, the real authority that they respected was the strongest sword. Ambitious for personal and family power, they recognized the king and God as ideals but would fight for a minor slight of honour. The towns that lay scattered across the land, behind well-fortified walls, feared the chevaliers but understood how to profit from the horse soldiers' estates and wealth. Here, the townsmen manufactured or imported fine tools, weapons, clothing, along with tasty spices, exceptional wines and salt. Alongside the castles and the towns, stood the churches. Here were the fortresses of Christ, whose salvation came from a hierarchy of clerics, men perhaps not as strong as the chevaliers but smarter, whose origins were often the castle, sometimes the towns and, now and again, the villages.

The chevalier estates dominated much of Europe north of the Alps. To the south, spread a different land. Centuries-old Mediterranean towns spread across the river lands and coasts of Italy. Manufacturers, merchants and bankers ran these towns often in rivalry with popular leaders threatening social upheaval or aristocratic landowners threatening military despotism. For over 300 years towns joined together in shifting leagues, either supporting or opposing different sides in the wars of emperors and popes. These positions solidified into the Guelphs and Ghibellines: the Guelph supported an independent papacy and built squared crenellations on their fortifications, and the Ghibellines supported the emperor and built scalloped crenellations. The questions about papal power involved the medieval church, an institution that involved just about everything.

The Holy, Apostolic and Catholic Church centred in Rome was overshadowing Western Europe during this time as it had for centuries. From parish priest to town bishop, up through city archbishop, culminating in the deacons, priests and bishops of the city of Rome (these are the cardinals), the medieval church was the continuation of the civil administration of the Roman Empire in the west. At the apex of church administration sat the *Pontifex Maximus*, the High Priest of Rome, the Bishop of Rome, Successor of Peter, Holder of the Keys to Heaven and Hell, Vicar of Christ Almighty, Servant of the Servants of God, the Holy Father, His Holiness the Pope. Of all things sacred, Mother Church was the judge.

Secular matters fell to the emperor. Chosen by the people and crowned by the pope, the emperor oversaw public policy in *Res publica christiana occidentia*: a superlative ideal which had never worked out. The line between secular and sacred being very blurry and quite broad, popes and emperors had a lot to disagree about, along with the very real questions of who got to control vast amounts of wealth and for what purpose. Moreover, the universal pretensions of the emperors were ignored by royal crowned kings, who began to maintain that kings were emperors in their dominion. And so, His Holiness had arguments not just with one emperor but with every king. This, as we know, produced a lively history with armoured horsemen, tall castles, gallant nobles, warrior bishops, all fighting for a myriad of causes. Thus, it had long been so.

But a new and different breeze had begun to waft through the lands. Petrarch (d. 1374) pictured his time as a world about to emerge out of darkness. Many people saw the start of a rebirth of the human spirit. Leonardo Bruni (d. 1444) wrote a history of Florence which portrayed the emergence of a new age, ending an age between the ancient world and the modern. In the new age, deliberative republican governments would oversee societies developing in all sorts of marvellous ways. Wonderful new ways of doing things had begun to appear and gained general acceptance.

Gunpowder

The Chinese invented what later was called gunpowder sometime after AD 900. Guns, first Chinese then Mongol, appeared by about 1250. The earliest record of gunpowder in Europe is in Roger Bacon's writings, 1267. The oldest confirmed evidence of guns in Europe comes from 1327. Gunpowder technology spread not only to Europe, but also to India and the Islamic lands and the different traditions fed on each other, allowing a wide-ranging development. The first substantial use of gunpowder weaponry in Europe was the development of large bombards which threw massive stone balls against high fortification walls.

Fabulously expensive to manufacture, equally expensive to move and operate, only the richest political organizations could afford the great cannons. The French used bombards to force the occupying English out of their forts, ending the Hundred Years War (1453). Sultan Mehmed II used great cannon to blow down the ancient walls of Constantinople (1453). Every ruler sought to buy cannon to destroy or at least threaten their enemies' castles. The great courts of Western Europe invested in new ways and designs for all types of gunpowder weapons. Smaller, more powerful cannon, easy to use handguns, more efficient fortifications, better command systems, all were open paths to military success for the bold innovator

Printing

As European development in metallurgy grew, a new business emerged which combined the quick production of malleable metal 'typeface', oil-based inks and the agricultural screw press to mass produce a permanent page of text. Initially, these businesses printed broadsheets, single page, printed on one side, which contained a single message such as a church indulgence. The idea was then to sell the broadsheets. The innovations associated with the invention of printing were connected with the efforts of Johannes Gutenberg and date to his printing of the Bible, 1450–1454. The immense importance of the printing business is difficult to understate. Looking at the incunabula printed before 1501, we see a great diversity of printing styles and book formats as printers looked for the best ways to satisfy their customers' demands. By 1500 general formats became accepted, and books became much more common, spreading the practice of reading and the comprehension of complex ideas to a broad audience.

Sailing and Ship Design

Italy was the centre of many trade routes leading back to the east. Each main town had outposts in the eastern Mediterranean to which they shipped European goods and from which they brought back spices, fine cloths, metals and well-made goods. Lands near Italy imported these goods and most merchants made substantial profits. Further west, the kingdoms on the Iberian Peninsula saw the riches of the east in the hands of others. Aragon had staked out claims to southern Italy and Sicily, extending their routes further to the east. But Castile and Portugal were at the end of any route and poor besides.

In Portugal, Prince Henry, Duke of Viseu (1394–1460) valued learning. He established the original organization which became the University of Lisbon. He saw the possibility of finding an alternative route to the riches of the east. Herodotus told a story of how Phoenicians had sailed around Africa in three years. Prince Henry saw that the Portuguese could do the same in the opposite direction. He invested in ship design to send ships south following the African coast. Slowly, year after year, Portuguese ships sailed ever more south. Finally, Bartolomeu Dias rounded the southern tip of Africa in 1488. Ten years later in 1498, Vasco de Gama reached the Malabar Coast of India.

While the Portuguese struggled to circumnavigate Africa, an explorer thought he had found an easier way east. Christopher Columbus was a Genoese Italian from a small business family. Starting an apprenticeship with a merchant enterprise of important Genoese families, Columbus became a factor travelling to the eastern Mediterranean, the British Isles and Iceland. He set up his main base in Lisbon (1477–85) and sailed along the African coast. Columbus, his business compatriots and rivals looked west every day, sometimes wondering how far they needed to sail west to get east. They were not the first to think along those lines. What they did have, that no one had before, were newly available printed books so they could easily collate the information of millennia. Columbus studied the books, not as a scholar but as a master sailor. From his travels and discussions with sailors he believed that there was some land within three months sailing. He spent many years working on selling his plan to the court of Isabella of Castile and Ferdinand the Catholic of Aragon. After the joint monarchs conquered Granada, thus completing the *Reconquista*, Isabella financed an expedition under Columbus's direction. And so, with three old ships, a carrack, the *Santa Maria* and two small caravels, the *Pinta* and the

Nina, Columbus sailed off to go where no one had gone before – at least in recorded accounts.

Renaissance and Power

In the latter days of the twentieth century some have suggested that Columbus was no hero and initiated a great disaster. But the problem with Columbus was the problem with the Renaissance: men and women sought to change the world; using whatever tools they could find or invent, Renaissance people were driven, ambitious striving for all types of power. They stopped at nothing to achieve their ends, which was always to better mankind and themselves.

People love Renaissance art, literature and architecture, but often tend to forget the fact that the men and woman who were instrumental in the production of these things were hardly models of moderation and morality. Popes Alexander VI and Julius II, political bosses like those of the House of Sforza and d'Este, kings and emperors like Francis I of France and Maximillian of Austria, all of them were domineering amoral players in the games of power. Even when it came down to actual doing of things, Leonardo da Vinci was military engineer for Cesar Borgia and Michelangelo di Buonarroti designed fortifications for Florence.

The Good Knight

One of the few people to have a positive reputation as the Good Knight, Without Fear and Without Reproach was Pierre Terrail, seigneur de Bayard. For thirty-four years Bayard fought in the forces of the King of France. His career took him through much of Italy along with a campaign against Henry VIII. During that time he maintained loyalty and a sense of fair play, while supporting some of the more creative treasons and surprising underhanded manoeuvres in history. The reason that Bayard is so well remembered is that of a book.

Published at Paris in 1527, the account of *The Right, Joyous, Merry, and Entertaining History of Bayard*, was printed just three years after Bayard's death. The book is authored anonymously; he called himself simply the Loyal Servant. Research over the centuries has identified the archer and friend of Bayard, Jacques de Mailles, as the most probable author. Whoever he was, the author draws a portrait of a near perfect soldier, able and honourable. Like a painting by Botticelli, the figure of the man is idealized and magnified in an artistic context. The subject was attractive to begin with and the Loyal Servant turned an interesting, if somewhat typical life of a soldier, into a work of art.

In an age of Machiavellian princes, Thomas More wrote *Utopia* (1516). Amidst the chaos and carnage of an age of violent disagreement and change, some wanted to draw a positive picture, a suitable goal to attempt to achieve. Because the Loyal Servant wanted to show his contemporaries that there were still good people amid evil, he saved for us the story of a man who swam in the wreckage of war yet maintained honour and reputation.

Castle Bayard

The Estate Bayard had been in the hands of the Terrail family for generations. Centred on a fortified manor house of unimposing size and style, the estate was a well-managed and productive farm. Families of tenant serfs worked the fields, divided between serfs' lands and lord's land. The lord, his lady and children had the skills and knew the difficulties of the work and were not beyond lending a hand when necessary. The most important serf households supplied the assistance and service needed to run the house and land. The whole was a well-integrated community, recognizing rank but emphasizing consensus. One of the main products the farm produced were horses. Necessary to the warrior who held the manor, horses were also useful for farming and income. In many ways, Castle Bayard was a self-supporting horse farm which produced a mounted soldier who was so necessary to the state.

Pierre Terrail, a man at arms, began the construction of the manor house in 1404, during the reign of Charles VI, the Mad King. Local people knew the place as Bayard. The house overlooked the Grésivaudan valley, offering a magnificent view of the surrounding mountain ranges, the Jura and the Chartreuse. His son, Pierre II gained the title Seigneur de Bayard and so the house became a castle. Pierre II met his end in the Battle of Montlhéry (1465) between Louis XI and the League of Public Good, the alliance between Charles the Bold of Burgundy, along with the dukes of Bourbon and of Brittany.

Pierre II's son, Aymond, aged 45 at his father's death, became Seigneur de Bayard. He already had spent many years in the king's service as a man at arms and continued to do so. He married Helen Alleman, daughter of Henry II Alleman, Seigneur de Laval Saint Étienne and his wife, Jeanne de Beaumont, Dame de Saint Quentin. They had four children.

The story is told that when the old chevalier Aymond Terrail, Seigneur de Bayard was about 70 years old, he asked his children what life's task they wanted. The eldest desired to stay with his parents and manage the estate. The second was Pierre, about 13 years old who announced his desire to become a warrior like his ancestors, following the path of the Chevalier. Pierre's earnestness impressed his father who promised to place the young man in the house of a high noble so he could learn the skills needed for a noble horse soldier. This was in the year of Our Lord, 1489.

Page Bayard

Pierre's mother was closely related to Laurent Alleman de Laval, Bishop of Grenoble. Pierre called him uncle. The bishop, when he learned of Pierre's ambition to become a chevalier, promised to introduce the young man into a noble household where he would learn the arts necessary to an aristocratic man at arms. The bishop also paid for proper clothes and mounts for him. So it was, Pierre Terrail at age 13 or so, became a page at the court of Charles I, Duke of Savoy, son of Amédée IX and Yolande of France, daughter of King Charles VII. The court of Savoy was held in high esteem for its brilliance. Page Pierre learned arms handling, horsemanship, how to play the lute and important dance steps. In all of these, he excelled. Too soon, the young Duke fell ill and died (March 1490). The duke's wife, Blanche Palaiologina of Montferrat, became regent and no doubt continued the page's education, but the time had come for the young Bayard to move on.

In November 1490 Louis de Luxembourg, Seigneur de Ligny took the young Bayard as a man at arms. Pierre was a large and athletic youth, charming and personable. His horsemanship and particularly his skill of handling the temperamental warhorses earned him the nickname, *piquez*, that is, 'spur'. On the tilt-yard and in the melée, he not only handled his weapons well, but his sense of honour and justice was also well remarked. Louis de Ligny was a favourite of King Charles VIII, and his royal master found Spur highly skilled and enchanting. Besides impressing the high and mighty, Spur made a lifelong friend and companion, Pierre de Posquières, Lord of Bellabre.

The teenage youth was drawn to the athletic prominence given to tournament victors. His strength, endurance and horsemanship promised success, but he lacked the wherewithal to acquire the necessary equipment. He needed a couple of warhorses plus at least one palfrey, an armoured suit complete with replacement parts, proper court costume, along with swords, shields and lances. The story is that his mother's relative, Theodore Terrail, Abbot of Ainay, gave the youth the money to buy equipment. Since losers in the tournament had to surrender their horse and armour to the victor or the monetary equivalent, success at the tiltyards was profitable for some.

The young Bayard proved himself to be a formidable and chivalrous competitor. His surpassing skill on horseback and with weapons brought the attention of his lord, Louis Count de Ligny and Louis' friend, King Charles VIII. Bayard became a man at arms for the Count of Ligny, following in the count's retinue, and the count, being a favourite of the king, would become part of the royal entourage. Bayard was now a minor notable of the Kingdom of France.

Chapter 2

King Charles VIII's France

Charles VIII ascended the throne of France in 1483. His father, Louis XI, had rebuilt the French state, eliminating, or taming unruly nobles. The Hundred Years War had engulfed France since 1337. The English had managed to grab many provinces at times, but the French monarchy and state remained intact. The state began floundering in the reign of Charles VI, the Mad King (1368–1422). The question was who would manage the administration for the incapacitated king. The king's brother, Louis Duke of Orleans, struggled with his royal cousin, John the Fearless, Duke of Burgundy. The kingdom began to fall apart after the Duke of Burgundy had the king's brother murdered in 1407.

Henry V, King of England, had defeated the French army at the Battle of Agincourt (1415) and fought his way to Paris. Henry forced the Mad King to sign the Treaty of Troyes (1420) in which Charles recognized Henry as his heir and accepted Henry's marriage with his daughter, Catherine of Valois. At the same time, the murder of the Duke of Burgundy, John the Fearless, by partisans of Charles's son threw John's heir, Philip the Good, into an alliance with the English. Henry V died in the summer of 1422; his son by Catherine of Valois became Henry VI, King of England. The Mad King died in the autumn of 1422 and the infant Henry VI became King of France. English nobles ruled France, but none too well. To the north the House of Burgundy under Philip the Good expanded influence and power. To the south, Charles VI's son proclaimed himself King of France, but the English forced him to the south of the Loire.

Called the Dauphin Charles, many spread the story that he was not a son of Charles VI but the offspring of an adulterous relationship. His supporters, however, recognized him as Charles VII. The Anglo–Burgundian forces had worked their way south, slowly squeezing the Dauphin's dominion. The key to the Dauphin's Loire line was the fortress town of Orleans; if the Anglo–Burgundians captured that town, they would seriously weaken the Dauphin's cause. At that point, as the enemy invested Orleans, Joan of

Arc came to the Dauphin's court (1429). She led Charles to Reims where he was crowned King of France. He became Charles the Well-Served. Slowly, the French forces rolled back the English tide and undid the Anglo-Burgundian alliance. By 1453 the French had pushed the English out of their kingdom.

Charles the Well-Served died in 1461; he was succeeded by his son, Louis XI (1461–1483). The new king had fought against his father for years, joining the Burgundian Court. When he became king, he resolved to end the loose control of the great noble house. Weaving layers of plots and connivances, Louis XI earned his title as the Spider King. His strongest enemy, Charles the Bold, Duke of Burgundy, overreached himself in response to Louis' plots and met his death in the Battle of Nancy (1477). The Spider King snatched the Burgundian provinces he thought were his and so brought France under a centralized administration for the most part. Only Brittany eluded his grasp.

The Reign of Charles VIII Begins

Louis XI died in 1483. Three children survived him: the eldest at 22, Anne had married Peter of Bourbon, brother of the duke; the second was Joan at 19, married to Louis, Duke of Orleans, and the third was Charles at 13, now king, the eighth of the name. Ever since the reign of Charles V (1364–80), the royal majority was 14. But Louis XI believed Charles was too immature to run a nation and, on his deathbed ordered that his daughter Anne should hold guardianship of Charles. Anne of France, as she styled herself, took charge of the Regency. Anne reappointed Louis XI's officials who had demonstrated honesty and competence. She had two notorious officials prosecuted: death for one, exile for the other. Anne released prisoners Louis had locked up because they irritated him, allowed Louis' enemies to return and demanded honest, efficient administration.

Anne's sister, Joan was unattractive and deformed. Louis XI had forced her to marry Louis, Duke of Orleans, thinking that the marriage of Louis of Orleans to an impotent wife would end the Orleans line. Louis, who was heir to the throne, disliked Anne. He wanted to be regent and opposed her policy. He and other nobles raised a commotion, calling for an Estates General. Anne agreed and the Estates convened at Orleans in mid-January 1484 in the great hall of the bishop's palace. Organized in the traditional three estates, churchmen, nobles, and commoners, the composition of the Third Estate had changed; now the commoners were wealthier and more educated and many of these were critical of the nobles' monopoly of government. This change had escaped Duke Louis' notice.

There came a total of 284 deputies from all the provinces of France except Flanders. The main issues revolved around taxes and satisfaction of complaints. The assembled deputies accepted the imposition of Tallage (land tax) at the same rate as that of the time of Charles VII the Well-Served but warranted for two years only, along with a one-time gift of 300,000 *livres tournois*. While Louis of Orleans and his friends intended to embarrass Anne of France's administration, they found themselves threatened by the radicalness of some deputies of the Third Estate. Joining together with Anne's supporters, Louis pushed to have the session ended. Most of the deputies of the Third Estate did not want any trouble, some were bought off, the remainder were scared off and the session closed increasing the power of Anne's administration.

Anne of France and the Management of the Crown

Anne of France managed the kingdom from 1484 to 1491. Her main problems revolved around the intrigues of Louis of Orleans who continually tried to unseat her. Louis contacted Ferdinand of Aragon, Maximillian of Austria and even Henry VII of England to gather resources to overthrow Anne. Since Louis' accession to the French throne was possible, the neighbouring monarchs did not rebuff him but did not want to offend Anne either. Louis' main ally was the independent-minded Duke of Brittany, Francis II.

Brittany was the only major feudal polity that remained independent of the French crown and Francis II intended the situation should remain that way. The Duke's foreign policy assumed the fact that his daughter and heiress, Anne of Brittany, would marry bringing the duchy with her. Francis tried to collect four or five sons-in-law with his one daughter and managed to organize a formidable coalition of support. Louis of Orleans, to avoid Anne of France, settled in Brittany supporting Francis. Added to that, the young Charles VIII, still under Anne's tutelage, strongly supported Louis. Anne of France saw that war was the solution to her problem while Louis of Orleans was in Brittany.

Francis II managed the chaos of Brittany adroitly. His unruly vassals allied with Anne of France while he supported disaffected French nobles opposed to Anne. From 1484 to 1488, the French government waged the Mad War against Brittany. The French commander, Louis II de la Trémoille, loyally served Anne; he directed French forces in their efforts to undermine Francis. Using bribes, cunning treasons and underhanded dealings, Anne's agents unsettled Francis's rule. After signing a treaty recognizing Brittany's autonomy in 1487, French forces moved against the military access routes to Brittany, besieging Fougères, the route to northern Brittany.

War with Brittany

Francis decided the time had come to teach Anne of France a lesson in feudal manners. Alain d'Albert, in rebellion against Anne's administration, commanded 5,000 troops supplied by Ferdinand of Aragon. Maximillian of Austria sent 1,500 men and Edward Woodville, Lord Scales, brought 700 longbowmen. Since Henry VII of England refused to send any troops, the Bretons dressed 1,300 of their men in the cross of St George to make it appear that they were a unit of Englishmen. The Breton force consisted of diverse and contending units who did not trust each other, under commanders who often did not agree. Leading a host of mounted men-at-arms, archers and irregular infantry, Jean de Rieux, commander of Francis's army, marched to challenge the French forces. The French army commanded by La Trémoille was some 15,000 strong with some 7,000 Swiss mercenaries. A strong force of heavy cavalry headed the army, and a large train of the latest cannon brought up the rear. The army consisted of trained and disciplined fighting men who understood who commanded and who followed.

Commander de Rieux, after receiving reports from scouts, hid his forces behind a ridge about a mile south of Mézières-sur-Couesnon. The French, unaware of the position of the Breton forces, advanced in dispersed marching order. Scouts informed the Breton commanders about the approach of the French spread out along a narrow road. Commander de Rieux supported by Lord Scales wanted to charge the French immediately while they were scattered. The Lord d'Albert disagreed. If they charged the head of the French column, they would certainly throw the head of the French column back. But the French would only recoil on themselves, and then it would be the Breton army at a disadvantage. Instead, he ordered the Breton troops to deploy into battle order.

The point of the French forces emerged from the forest and immediately saw the Breton forces only some 800 yards ahead. A scout informed La Trémoille, who advanced his heavy cavalry to cover the deployment of his infantry and ordnance. The Breton and French forces faced each other, as the two sides manoeuvred into battle order across a rolling moor broken by a few granite outcrops. To the north and west, heavy woods bordered the moor which was bisected by a creek. To the north of the creek, the Breton army held a ridge crest to the north, with their left resting in woods and their right based on a fortified camp defended by artillery.

The French quickly deployed south of the creek once they saw the Breton army in position. La Trémoille placed his right wing, commanded by de l'Hopital, against the woods; his force was the centre; the Marshal de Baudricourt commanded the left wing. La Trémoille held a strong mounted force in reserve. Commanded by the Neapolitan Jacobo Galiota, recommended by Charles VIII for military acumen and experience, this force consisted of picked men, well armoured and mounted. The French placed their excellent cannon along their front and guarding their camp. Unless he made a serious mistake, La Trémoille was going to prevail in this battle. The French had more men, better-trained cavalry and superior cannon. The Bretons, not unmindful of this, kept a fifth of their force in reserve so, after a defeat, all might not be lost.

The artillery started the battle, first with a shot or two and then shot after shot as each side struck at the other. There were more French guns than Breton and the French forces were under better cover. The Bretons suffered under the exchange; if they did not move, they faced disintegration. Commander de Rieux ordered his right, men-at-arms supported by archers, to attack. Charging directly into the French lines, commanded by de l'Hopital, the Bretons pushed the French back a couple of hundred feet. As the French recovered, the Bretons lost impetus in the fierce melee and Lord Scales fell. The Bretons' right fell back.

While the struggle on the Breton right ran its course, in their centre the continuing artillery bombardment unsettled the German Landsknecht formation. Their commander withdrew the unit out of the line of fire. Jacobo Galiota saw the opening in the Bretons' line. He immediately launched his unit of select men-at-arms into the breach. Galiota fell in the attack, but his men swept through the Bretons' front and smashed into their rearguard and camp. Then, the Breton powder magazine exploded. Shooting flames followed by a deafening roar shattered the Bretons' morale.

Rieux and d'Albert turned and fled with the cavalry. The infantry fell to the French men-at-arms who cut them down, particularly those with the English cross of St George. The French counted 1,400 *hors de combat* and claimed 6,000 enemy dead and prisoners. Louis of Orleans had retreated to the woods and tried to resist the royal army but saw the wisdom of surrender.

The Prince of Orange hid among the dead but was discovered. The princes faced royal judgment, which was confinement in not very pleasant quarters; the nobles faced death for treason. Anne of France's forces had crushed Brittany. She ordered Louis of Orleans imprisoned in tight confinement at her pleasure, although the young King Charles VIII thought that was too harsh. She also confined Duke Francis II, but in a more open and pleasant place.

Times began to change. John Duke of Bourbon died in 1488. Madame the Grand, as Anne of France was called, became Duchess of Bourbon when her husband ascended to the coronet. She enjoyed her station as a duchess and found the regency tiresome. Add to that the fact that Charles VIII was getting older and would soon want power in his own right, Anne of France began to withdraw from the government.

King Charles VIII Rules France

The king was 19 and his friends and advisors now basked in his power. He released Louis of Orleans and brought him into favour. The first thing Charles wanted to be done was his marriage. As part of his father's agreements to partition the Burgundian lands, Charles was betrothed to the three-year-old Margaret of Austria, daughter of Maximillian, son of Emperor Frederick III and Mary, Duchess of Burgundy. She brought as dowry the Counties of Artois and Burgundy. As prospective Queen of France, Margaret lived at the French court.

A few months after his defeat and capture, Francis II of Brittany died falling off his horse and his 11-year-old daughter, Anne became Duchess of Brittany. To avoid being dragged into French power, she married, by proxy, the now widower Maximillian in 1490. Anne of Brittany would outrank Margaret of Austria by being her stepmother. King Charles, Louis of Orleans and Anne of France all agreed that this would place France between two Habsburg frontiers. They sent an army which occupied Brittany and Anne of Brittany agreed, with some persuasion, to marry King Charles. At the year's end, 1491, in an elaborate affair, Charles wed Anne. After marriage, Anne lived in the Clos Luce, a country house near the royal castle of Amboise. With his marriage, Charles took charge of the French government and did as he liked. Charles intended to marry Margaret to some French nobleman, but she became very unhappy and wanted to escape. Finally, Charles returned her and her dowry to Maximillian.

Married and independent, Charles began looking for achievements which would add lustre to his name and profit for his friends. He looked toward Italy.

Charles VIII Decides to Invade Italy

The actual process of decision-making in Charles VIII's court was complex and confusing. We can profit from the explanations of the memorialist Philip de Commines (1447–1511). He tells us that Charles's interest in the Kingdom of Naples started just after his coronation when he was 13. René II, Duke of Lorraine, came to the French court to satisfy his claims to the Duchy of Bar and the County of Provence. As Duke of Lorraine, René had inherited the coronet in 1473 when he was 22. During the Burgundian wars, René allied with Louis XI; he fought in the Battle of Nancy in which Charles the Bold died. After this Duke of Burgundy's death, Louis oversaw the distribution of the French part of the Burgundian territories, restoring Lorraine to René but withholding Bar. King Charles's court upheld René's right to the Duchy of Bar which the king granted for a sum of money, but he referred the question of Provence to a royal committee for examination. It revolved around the matter of who was heir to the holdings of the House of Anjou to which Provence was attached. After his mother died, René II inherited her title to the crowns of Naples and Jerusalem and had unsuccessfully fought in Italy to gain his inheritance.

The royal committee set a deadline of four years for a decision and in the meantime, Anne of France appointed René commander of 100 lances with a pension of 36,000 livres a year. During the four years, clerks of the County of Provence produced a will of King Charles I of Naples (1266–85) along with other wills of French kings of Sicily. These clearly showed that all the lands held by the House of Anjou belong to the King of France, including Provence, Naples and Sicily. As these papers moved through the royal court, the Kingdom of Naples rebelled against King Ferrante (Ferdinand I, natural son of Alphonso King of Naples, who succeeded to the throne 1458). King Ferrante drew on his connection with the Florentines and fought back. The rebel barons allied with Pope Innocent VIII and together, they offered the crown of Naples to René II. They even sent an escort for him to Genoa led by the Cardinal of Saint Peter ad Vincula (della Rovere).

The French court welcomed the offer, promised René II 60,000 livres and French support. René II, however, saw things differently – he wanted Provence. He had fought in Italy and knew that Naples was an unending morass. Moreover, even if he succeeded in securing the crown, he was sure Charles VIII would claim it. The four years were up, and the court discontinued his pension. René II demanded that they award him Provence or continue the pension. When the Court refused, René II left France in 1486, disgusted with the Royal Court. He never returned.

Meanwhile, the barons in Naples, with the intercession of the pope and Florence, agreed with King Ferrante. To settle their differences the barons agreed to come to Naples and negotiate with the king. They received solemn safe conducts, guaranteed by the pope, the Florentines and the Venetians but when they arrived in Naples, Ferrante seized and imprisoned them. A large number were executed, sewed up in sacks and dumped into the sea.

Chapter 3

The Collapse of Lorenzo's Peace

rancesco Guicciardini wrote a narrative of 'events which occurred within our memory', as he says. He starts his 'History of Italy' describing a time of profound peace, lasting some years before and after 1490. He went on, while the continued peace resulted from many factors, most politically astute observers at the time agreed that the master of the Florentine Republic, Lorenzo de Medici, exercising his skilful political acumen and application of power, did most to maintain the balance of power that caused the peace. Lorenzo did so because he understood that Florence was not particularly strong, although the city was rich, and any efforts of the other powers aggrandizing themselves would be at Florence's expense.

Besides Lorenzo, King Ferrante of Naples also worked to maintain peace. Years earlier, Ferrante had fought to expand his kingdom and increase his power. He now held sufficient power to preserve his realm from his enemies. It was said that there was a room in his residence with a large table in the centre around which sat numerous chairs, each holding the ceremonially dressed preserved body of a former enemy. Ferrante strove to hold the ambitions of his son and heir, Prince Alfonso, in check. This prince's daughter, Isabella, married the young Duke of Milan, Gian Galeazzo Sforza in 1489 when the duke was about 20. The problem was the duke's uncle Lodovico the Moor (so called from his complexion, or was it his disposition?) who was regent of the realm and had no intention of relinquishing power to his nephew, ever.

The king of Naples appreciated the fact that many of his subjects would prefer being connected to France rather than ruled by the House of Aragon. If the French came, they would sweep away his dynasty. Moreover, all perceptive observers noted the ambitions of the Venetians. The Turks were slowly absorbing Venice's eastern Mediterranean empire and the Venetians' solution was to expand their power in Italy. They already had a significant dominion in northern Italy, and they had the wealth and resources to generate money to establish Italian hegemony. For these reasons Ferrante desired peace.

In Milan, Lodovico the Moor, restless and ambitious, feared the Venetians' ability to advance west. Together with Ferrante and Lorenzo, the three powers checked any Venetian move. More important, Lodovico's position in Milan, regent for an adult duke, was precarious in the first place. Since the young duke was married to Ferrante's granddaughter, Lodovico was aware that the rulers of Naples would not mind seeing him removed, but to do that they needed an alliance with Venice. Any increase of Venetian power was a direct threat to Ferrante. The result was that both Lodovico and Ferrante saw Lorenzo as the keystone of Italian peace.

Many Italians felt shocked when news of Lorenzo de Medici's death (April 1492) spread throughout the peninsula. Lorenzo was only 44 when he died, but like his father, Piero the Gouty, he did not enjoy good health. Suffering from gout like his father, arthritis also caused Lorenzo great difficulty. While a diagnosis in terms of current medicine is not possible, Lorenzo was stricken with some sort of wasting condition. His death, unexpected by the uninformed, upset Florentine politics and Italian diplomatic relations, particularly that between Ferrante of Naples and Lodovico of Milan.

The new leader in Florence became Piero di Lorenzo de Medici, son of Lorenzo the Magnificent. Piero was the eldest of three brothers; he simply fell into power at the death of his father through the support of Medici partisans. Unlike his able and personable father, Piero was arrogant and undisciplined. As soon as he had secured his position, Piero reversed his father's policies without any discussion with important people in government or the Medici political machine. Rather, he followed the advice of Virginio Orsini, a relative of his mother, to attach himself to Ferrante of Naples in a secret compact. In part, this was directed against the pope's power in the lands of the church, but also some might see it as directed against Lodovico in Milan. The fact that the compact was secret, but not quite as secret as Piero hoped, lent credence to Lodovico's suspicions, already very active.

The New Pope

As this situation began to settle, in July Pope Innocent VIII died. Now the question of how well the new ruler of Florence would do, was compounded by the question of who would be the new pope. Innocent's death was not unexpected; the Cardinals in Rome had spent some time dickering over possible successors. On 6 August 1492, the twenty-three cardinals in Rome went into conclave. Innocent's nephew, Cardinal Lorenzo Cibo de Mari, looked toward a new pope who would follow Innocent's policies. Cibo supported the Genoese Cardinal Pallavicini, but Pallavicini was not as interested in the papal office as Cibo was for him. The French King Charles VIII and his court supported the Cardinal della Rovere. The French sent 200,000 ducats to a Roman bank to facilitate Rovere's election. But Lodovico the Moor and the Sforza did not want a pope in thrall to France. Cardinal Ascanio Sforza, Lodovico's older brother, organized an anti-French coalition. Sforza and Cardinal Raffaelle Riario, a relative of Rovere and Cardinal Camerlengo, pushed for Cardinal Borgia.

Borgia was Spanish and not involved in local Italian politics. Moreover, the new Kingdom of Spain demanded respect and a Spanish pope might relieve growing tensions between Spanish royal houses and their neighbours. The cardinal was an ambitious man, as all knew; he had collected very many church offices and benefices. As pope, he would need to divest these positions, and so many plums became available for distribution. Many in the conclave looked on with eager anticipation. Humbly Borgia begged the assembled cardinals for the papacy. Sforza and Orsini supported him. Promises of offices, benefices and money were suggested and accepted. Five cardinals resolutely opposed Borgia; these were the cardinals of Naples, Siena, Portugal, St Pietro in Vinculi (della Rovere) and St Mary in Portico. The conclave elected Cardinal Borgia pope and he took the style, Alexander VI.

Historian and statesman Guicciardini saw the new pope as an utter catastrophe and believed most Italians agreed. He went on, over forty years later, to state that Alexander VI was exceedingly able in his understanding of people and ability to manipulate them and he understood how to handle crises, but he also was crass, duplicitous, a stranger to truth, greedy, ambitious and, moreover, willing to use cruelty and barbaric methods to advance the interests of his children. And his children were no better than their father.

Regardless of Pope Alexander's qualities as a pontiff and ruler, the relations between Ferrante, Lodovico and Piero deteriorated significantly through their lack of good will. When a new pope received the triple tiara, ambassadors of Christian princes came to offer homage to him as Vicar of Christ on earth. Lodovico, so that all might see the solidarity of the Italian league formed by Lorenzo, suggested that their ambassadors should come to Rome together and allow one spokesman to speak for them all.

Previously, Innocent VIII set members of the league at odds by discussing matters with them one at a time.

Ferrante and Piero ostensibly agreed with Lodovico on the soundness of this approach, but Piero was put out by Lodovico's plan. Appointed as one of the ambassadors of the Florentine Republic, Piero planned on presenting a splendid, even ostentatious entrance into Rome. Included in the Florentine embassy was the Bishop of Arezzo, a noted humanist and master of rhetoric. The bishop was to speak for the Republic and had prepared an eloquent speech. The bishop was upset that under Lodovico's scheme, his talents could not shine, and Piero was not happy that his monumental show would sink into being just one part of a large group.

So, rather than come straight out and tell Lodovico he did not want to participate in the joint embassy, Piero convinced Ferrante to tell Lodovico that such a large and complex embassy would cause confusion and so the Italian powers should adhere to the old custom of individual embassies. Ferrante did tell Lodovico of this concern but indicated that the main objection came from Piero. Lodovico was most upset because his plan was known in the papal court and this rejection made him look bad. What bothered Lodovico was the growing evidence that Piero and Ferrante had a personal alliance and that he was not included.

Lodovico the Moor and the Peace of Italy

Another natural son of Innocent VIII, Franceschetto Cibo, had received some castles and their estates around Rome. After his father's death, he moved to Florence. Since Franceschetto had married Piero's sister, Maddalena, he was close to Piero and the Medici court. Piero convinced Franceschetto to sell the properties to Virginio Orsini for 40,000 ducats. King Ferrante of Naples was behind the transaction. Orsini was his vassal and Ferrante had lent him the money to buy the property. Because the House of Aragon had long been at odds with their northern neighbours in the Lands of the Church and the new pope was an unknown quality, Ferrante thought to protect his frontiers by having bases deep in a potential enemy's territory. Further, the king also feared that Pope Alexander VI was working in league with Cardinal Ascanio Sforza which is to say, with Ascanio's brother, Lodovico the Moor, and so Ferrante saw the property as a necessary protection.

But Guicciardini comments: 'It is certainly most true that wise men do not always discern or pass perfect judgment; often it is necessary that they show signs of the weakness of human understanding.' Ferrante should have considered, the historian went on, how much benefit he might gather from gaining a few castles against what harm could happen if the transaction soured. And soured it did!

First, Pope Alexander took umbrage at the thought that Ferrante and the House of Aragon had pre-emptively attempted to weaken his dominion. His Holiness was not a party to the transaction and declared it null and void because he ruled that any attempt to transfer property without his permission caused the property to revert to the Holy See. To add emphasis to his displeasure Alexander then strongly condemned both Piero de Medici and Virginio Orsini, claiming that they were conspiring with Ferrante to undermine the dignity of the papacy.

Second, and worse, Lodovico the Moor, who already held deep suspicions of Ferrante, had thought that Pope Alexander would always follow Cardinal Ascanio's lead. Finding that Ferrante was involved in the land transaction made him doubt Alexander's commitment to the Sforza cause. More, the fact that Ferrante and Piero de Medici were working together made him the odd man out. Lodovico set to work to bind Alexander to his cause. He kept reminding Alexander that Ferrante and his kingdom had been enemies to the dignity and property of the Holy See. He emphasized, however, that innocent as any of Ferrante's actions might seem, they were part of a design to undercut Alexander's power and dignity.

Then, Lodovico lent Alexander 40,000 ducats and a unit of 300 fully equipped and trained men-at-arms to be paid jointly. Lodovico sent to Ferrante a request that the King of Naples, in some way, smooth over Virginio Orsini's problems with the failed transaction and the pope's anger (no doubt, forgiving the money loaned). Lodovico's toughest action was reserved for Piero de Medici. He reminded Piero how his father, Lorenzo, had maintained the tranquillity of Italy by being a moderate and honest intermediary. And Lodovico told Piero that what made north Italy a tranquil land was the long-term alliance of Sforza and Medici. Piero was making a mistake, Lodovico went on, to forsake this alliance.

Lodovico's efforts to smooth things over only resulted in things getting worse. Ferrante saw Lodovico's suggestions as a sign of weakness. Instead of pulling Orsini back, Ferrante told him to take possession of the castles as soon as possible according to the contract. While Orsini organized the men to accomplish this, Ferrante informed Pope Alexander that Orsini was open to compromise. At the same time, Ferrante was telling Orsini to ignore any such offer.

Watching his whole alliance system collapse, seeing Florence joining with Naples, Lodovico saw his power seriously diminished. Beyond losing strong allies, now the wife of the Duke Gian Galeazzo, Isabella, daughter of Alfonso, son of Ferrante, was certainly pushing for the duke to receive power and remove Lodovico. Naples would continue to support Isabella and many people in Milan, unhappy with high taxes, looked to the young duke's accession to power. Lodovico saw he needed a whole new approach if he was to maintain himself in power. Other members of Lorenzo's Italian league were equally unhappy with Ferrante and Piero's understanding. Lodovico looked to Pope Alexander and Venice to make a new combination to set against Florence and Naples.

Pope Alexander lent an ear to Lodovico's entreaties but hoped to marry one of his sons to Alfonso's daughter. Ferrante was not opposed but soon Alfonso, who despised the Borgia pope, made it clear that the marriage would never happen. Ferrante's ally, Virginio Orsini, had gained a significant position in the church lands around Rome, which now was added to the holdings of the House of Colonna, all tied together in the Guelph faction opposing the pope. To these opponents, Pope Alexander's enemies in the church were added. The Cardinal of San Pietro in Vinculi, fearing for his life at Borgia's hands, put himself in self-exile, staying in his fortress of Ostia. He strongly supported the King of Naples. Alexander began looking more favourably on Lodovico's proposals.

The Venetian Senate was very sceptical of Lodovico's new combination, having been burned in the reign of previous popes and not about to trust the Borgia pope. The rising disunion and disruptions were most satisfactory to the Venetians, but how deeply they should involve themselves in the disagreements was a serious question. Lodovico personally lobbied individual senators and his persistence paid off. In April 1493 the parties signed a new defensive pact between the pope, the Venetians and the Duke of Milan (that is, Milan under Lodovico's direction). The pact ensured that the Venetians and the Duke of Milan would each send 200 fully equipped men-at-arms for the protection of the pope and to recover the lands held by Virginio Orsini. If need be, much stronger forces would expel Orsini from the papal lands.

In reality, Lodovico found himself more diplomatically isolated than before. The pact which formed the league of which he had been a member had the proviso that no member state would ally with any other state. Many princes began looking for an advantage, seeing the league's disintegration. Piero, Alfonso and the Colonna, allied with the party of the Cardinal of San

Pietro in Vincoli organized an armed coup to seize Rome and expel Pope Alexander. Ferrante, however, feared the rise of disorder and set to repair the damage caused by the storm over the Orsini castles

Guicciardini commented, 'Removing the cause of disruption does not always remove the effects of that cause; this is because it frequently happens that decisions are taken from fear seldom appear sufficient to the fearful.'

And here sat Lodovico the Moor. He did not trust either the Venetians or Pope Alexander and found himself at odds with Florence and Naples. His city of Milan was restless, and some of his most determined enemies lived in the city. Without considering what the results might be, Lodovico grasped at medicine that was more powerful than the disease, as Guicciardini said. Because he had no faith in his army and distrusted all the other Italian powers, Lodovico endeavoured to bring foreign armies into Italy. He schemed, plotted and attempted to buy French intervention in Italy.

Enticing Charles VIII

Lodovico and the House of Sforza had been friends of France ever since his father's time. He was sure he could draw the young French king with a powerful army into Italy, to do his bidding. But not to seem too obvious, Lodovico conferred with Pope Alexander, suggesting that with the French army in play, the pope could recover the lands the Aragon kings of Naples had taken and, moreover, carve out principalities for Alexander's children. The pope found common cause with the regent of Milan. With this understanding, Lodovico started a campaign to convince King Charles VIII to march through Italy, attack and conquer the Kingdom of Naples and exterminate their ruling family. That way, he would remove the threat of Naples' military might and gain a non-Italian ally to counterbalance the Venetians.

First, Ludovico sent messengers, ostensibly about other matters, to Charles. These 'tickled' (as Commines said) King Charles's fancy about his rights to the Neapolitan throne with images of glory and riches. These agents also spread around gifts to Charles's favourites. Then, as the second ploy, Ludovico sent a magnificent embassy to Paris. The ambassadors, high and rich nobles all, were to discuss the process by which the Duke Gian Galeazzo would do homage to King Charles for Genoa (which Milan did not strongly hold, nor did France have a substantial claim as suzerain). The leader of the embassy, Count di Cajazzo, was a cousin to the Prince of Salerno, who was in Paris as an exile from Naples for his part in the unsuccessful rebellion against Ferrante.

This prince had sounded out Charles's favourites and advisors about the prospects to be gained from an Italian expedition. So, when Count di Cajazzo arrived in Paris, he knew who to pressure. The king granted the ambassadors a public audience in which all pomp and proper ceremony played out. Then Charles invited the count into the royal closet for private discussions. There, di Cajazzo let Charles understand that Ludovico was offering substantial military aid, supplies and funds to allow Charles to avoid having to raise supplies and men on his own. Soon, the embassy left Paris to return to Milan, but di Cajazzo stayed behind. He now dressed as a Frenchman and dealt privately with Charles's favourites and advisors, freely spreading money around. This was how Philip de Commines, who was employed by Charles VIII as a diplomat and advisor at this time, saw the situation. Once he made the decision, Charles VIII explained that the expedition would be just the first step on a great crusade to retake Constantinople and then advance to the Holy Land and capture Jerusalem. Whether he believed this, or his advisors saw a crusade as a fine way to raise money, is an interesting question.

Many of King Charles's high officials and great noblemen viewed an expedition to Italy with scepticism. Mobilizing the necessary forces was expensive and marching them, their equipment and supplies into Italy was beyond expensive. Once there, they would face King Ferrante and his son, Prince Alfonso, both well-practised in the arts of war. The victory was nowhere near certain, and defeat would mean the loss of the whole investment with no gain and much loss. King Charles, 22 years old and thirsting for glory and fame, paid no attention to the older, experienced lords of his court. Rather, being in the hands of young admirers from low social backgrounds, he pushed for the recovery of his 'rightful' inheritance and the great glory it would bring to his reign.

Still, Charles wavered between determination and indecision. The vision of triumph, on the one hand, balanced the prospect of a rout on the other. But cupidity and ambition won. King Charles signed an agreement with Lodovico's ambassador in secret, telling no one but his cronies, the Bishop of San Malo and the Seneschal of Beaucaire. The secret terms were not revealed for months, not until the French were in Italy. First, Lodovico would loan Charles 200,000 ducats. Then, once the French king brought an army into Italy to conquer the Kingdom of Naples, Lodovico would supply 500 paid men-at-arms with all their accoutrements for Charles's army.

Further, Charles could bring or acquire as many armed ships in Genoa harbour as he wished. For his part, King Charles promised to defend the Duchy of Milan against any enemy (enemy of Lodovico, that is). As support for Lodovico, Charles promised to station a company of 200 lances at Asti, a city owned by the Duke of Orleans. Moreover, after the conquest of Naples, Charles would recognize Lodovico as Prince of Taranto, which he awarded to Lodovico on signing the agreement.

The Italians Consider How to Deal with the French Threat

A rumour without actual information swept throughout Italy. Each potentate looked toward the future with apprehensions of what the French might do, along with the expectation of future gain from what might fall out from their arrival. King Ferrante affected unconcern, pointing out how young and fickle was the French king. He boasted of his army and fortifications, saying he had no fears of the French. Ferrante also enjoyed pointing out that if the French were looking to reclaim old holdings, then the rulers of Milan were also their targets. Ferrante knew he was very unpopular with his subjects, who, if they did not like the French, did not like the House of Aragon any better. Most perceptive people understood that should a French army approach the kingdom of Naples, Ferrante's administration would collapse.

Secretly, Ferrante decided to approach the French and come to some understanding that would deflect their ambitions from Naples. His ambassadors were already in France on other business; to them, he sent Camillo Pandone who Ferrante had employed on other confidential French business. Pantone was granted a sinking fund to covertly bribe King Charles VIII's ministers to turn the king's attention elsewhere or find agreement for an act of submission.

Besides dealing with the French, Ferrante reopened talks with Pope Alexander to settle the Virginio Orsini affair by offering an agreement for marriage between his house and the Borgias. Ferrante did achieve an agreement with Pope Alexander, a child princess of Naples was betrothed to a child prince of Borgia, but they were too young to marry. The alliance was secret, Alexander promising to protect the Kingdom of Naples and Ferrante doing the same for the papal lands; as a result, Pope Alexander dismissed the units of men-at-arms sent by Venice and Lodovico.

More important, Ferrante opened talks with Lodovico the Moor because he appreciated that fear motivated the regent of Milan. He decided that

Lodovico's security was paramount. His granddaughter he would protect, but his grandson-in-law, Duke Gian Galeazzo, was expendable. Ferrante let Lodovico know that he would not oppose any step that he might take regarding official positions in the Duchy of Milan. Lodovico responded positively to Ferrante, saying how dangerous were King Charles's ambitions for Italy, yet also pointing out the long history of Milan's dependence on France. Lodovico gave assurances to Piero de Medici in Florence and Pope Alexander in Rome in his efforts to keep them asleep while King Charles prepared his forces. The fact that most observers at the time saw that the French danger to Italy was going to be just as fatal to the Sforza as to everybody else lent veracity to Lodovico's claim of not wanting the French to come. Lodovico did not see the coming French expedition in that same light.

Chapter 4

Charles VIII Invades Italy

Ferrante was satisfied with the results of his efforts to secure his throne. His alliance with Pope Alexander was particularly pleasing, but in just a few months Ferrante died (25 January 1494) and Prince Alfonso became king. His youthful enthusiasms and heedless demands for action were now gone, and the new king applied himself to defending his throne. The bastion he sought was the papacy; he worked with Pope Alexander to gain the papacy's recognition of his right to Naples. In a consistory on 18 April Pope Alexander faced down the opposition, ignoring protests and threats from French cardinals who said they would appeal to a council. The pope announced his firm intention of recognizing Alfonso as King of Naples. In June Alexander's legate celebrated Alfonso's coronation, but rather than securing the peace of Italy, Pope Alexander's endorsement of the House of Aragon worked to destabilize the situation further.

In facing down many cardinals in the April consistory, Pope Alexander continued to embitter his rivals in the church. In particular, Cardinal della Rovere ended his reconciliation with Alexander and retreated to his castle in Ostia. With Alexander in the east and Alfonso in the south, Rovere found his position on the mouth of the Tiber untenable: both Alexander and Alfonso could easily crush him between themselves. The cardinal decided that the best solution to his difficulties was in France so on 23 April Rovere secretly left Ostia and travelled to France, to the royal court in Lyons. Weeks later the Venetians were still speculating what the cardinal would do when in fact he was telling Charles VIII how weak the Italian armies were and how hollow their defences.

For months, King Charles's ministers and advisers had brought objection after objection to the Italian expedition: the funds were not available, especially because Charles's endless rounds of tournaments, entertainments and parades of pomp and display cost more than the royal revenue supported. Alfonso, King of Naples, was much stronger than his enemies said; the expedition would extend into the Italian autumn and winter and the French soldiers would contract illness. King Charles ignored it all.

What worried the French king was if, when he and the flower of French Chivalry were out of the country, France's neighbours would invade. The two most threatening potentates were Ferdinand the Catholic, King of Aragon, together with his wife, Isabella of Castile, rulers of the rising Kingdom of Spain, and Maximillian of Habsburg, emperor-elect. Charles had a particularly delicate problem with Maximillian; he had married Maximillian's bride by proxy, Anne of Brittany, at the same time repudiating Maximillian's daughter, Margaret of Austria, with whom Charles was betrothed when both were children. Besides the personal affront, Margaret had brought important parts of Franche-Comte and Artois as dowry which the French never returned. King Charles opened serious negotiations with both monarchs. For Ferdinand, the French surrendered the land of Roussillon to the crown of Aragon. The more difficult settlement was with the emperor-elect. In the end, the Treaty of Senlis (1493) exchanged the dowry lands for – from Maximillian's point of view – more vulnerable lands in Burgundy and Picardy.

Thus, his frontiers secured, Charles faced his court with the firm intention of marching into Italy in 1494. He put his trust in Galeazzo di Sanseverino, ambassador of Milan, who eloquently enthralled the young king with tales of great chivalric deeds. Then came Cardinal della Rovere who told Charles that he had only to appear in Italy with his army and all would welcome him, helping him drive their common enemies out. Nothing was going to change Charles's decision.

In June King Charles appointed Gilbert de Montpensier to be Captain General of the Royal Army. The transports were in the harbour of Aigues-Mortes; the troops and cannon were ready. Louis, Duke of Orleans, travelled to Genoa to take command of the fleet. The Bailli of Dijon was in Switzerland to recruit some 4,000 pikemen, 1,500 of which would join the advance guard and the remainder march to join the Duke of Orleans. On 22 August King Charles left Lyons for Grenoble; there the king left the government in the hands of his lieutenant general, the Duke of Bourbon. The army loaded the baggage on mules under the direction of the local muleteers and began the march over the mountains. On 3 September King Charles spent the night on Italian soil. The invasion began.

The Invasion Begins

King Charles and his commanders thrashed out the details of the Italian expedition during March and April 1494 while they were in Lyons. Their plan was for two separate forces, one advancing down the peninsula and the other sailing from Genoa, combining at Naples. Together, both forces would include 1,500 lances and 12,000 foot, divided between the two armies. Information soon came, telling of Alfonso's mobilization, raising questions about Lodovico the Moor and his brother Cardinal Ascanio Sforza's commitment to the French cause and concerns about Pope Alexander's pivoting around different alliances. The French king demanded more troops. Now the French fielded 1,900 lances, 1,200 mounted archers, 19,000 foot and contracted for some 2,000–3,000 Italian infantry. French resources being limited, the royal command decided to maintain a fleet of 50 ships and galleys which could carry only about a fifth of the necessary troops.

The main force would take a land route. The fleet would carry the artillery and their manpower along with sufficient forces to protect them. The total for the royal army was 22,100 fighting men, however, the host was much larger. Each man-at-arms, a lance, consisted of an armoured chevalier, two or three mounted archers, an armourer, cook and washerwoman. Each man needed a horse and there were extra warhorses for the Chevalier and at least a couple for each archer, plus a few more for the helpers. Even if the mounted archers were part of the armed workforce, still, each fighting horseman accounts for at least three others. And, we need to consider the numbers of people following the army: baggage handlers, suppliers, casual labourers and various entertainers. The whole mass was very large, spread across the landscape like a swarm of locusts. Even if they were well behaved, they were a problem and their behaviour was never good.

While King Charles attended to his forces, King Alfonso of Naples prepared to repel, or at least delay, the French. He re-hired the old Nea-politan *condottiere*, Roman Baron Fabrizio Colonna and the Milanese exile Gian Giacomo Trivulzio. He added Niccolò Orsini da Pitigliano to his stable of mercenaries. The Ottoman Sultan, Bayezid II even offered 20,000 crack Ottoman troops to block the threatened French crusade. With his forces, King Alphonso set out to derail King Charles's advance. Using Genoese exiles, he attempted to bring insurrection against Lodovico's regime in Genoa, hoping to block Charles's forces using their port. If he could hold the port for just a few months, he might delay Charles's invasion for a year, possibly breaking up the whole scheme.

As the plot against Genoa proceeded, Alfonso launched an attack on the Duchy of Milan. His son, Prince Ferrandino, led an advanced guard of 240 men-at-arms north to the Romagna in mid-July. King Alphonso followed with a large force, but when the king was passing by Rome, Pope

Alexander demanded that Alfonso cover Rome with strong forces as part of his duty as a papal dependant. Alfonso decided to stay on the northern borders of his kingdom, south of Rome with 300 men-at-arms while his Grand Constable Virginio Orsini would stay in the vicinity of Rome to the south with 200 men-at-arms. So, the strike toward Milan was just an armed reconnaissance expedition.

News from France about troop movements caused all states to hire mercenary soldiers and repair their fortifications quickly. Suddenly, Italian rulers understood that the whole fighting force of France was about to descend on Italy. There had been no disturbance like this since the days of the Hohenstaufen, or indeed, the Gothic invasion a thousand years before. This coming event shook Lodovico the Moor who had encouraged the French King to march to Italy. He permitted Charles to use Genoa as a naval base to ship troops and supplies to Italy, but he thought that the French king would come with a few hundred men-at-arms; that Charles would play at the Italian chess board wars, under Lodovico's direction. A few castles here, a town or two there would change hands; Charles and Alfonso would come to some agreement, honour would be satisfied and Charles would go home, all of this to Lodovico's profit. Instead, King Charles was coming across the Alps with the whole of the French armed host. What started as a clever idea as a threat became in reality, a nightmare.

Lodovico in Milan waited for the French, pledged loyalty to King Charles while looking for a counterweight to their strength. In Florence, tradition and business looked to France but Piero de Medici had tied himself to Alfonso. Charles had sent envoys to Florence to request free passage and supplies. Popular opinion approved of allowing Charles's army passage, but Piero had pressured the government to refuse the French king's request. Charles dismissed the Florentine ambassadors and expelled the agents of the Medici bank, but not the rest of the Florentine establishments.

Both kings, Charles and Alfonso, sent envoys to the Republic of Venice, attempting to entice the republic to join their respective alliance. The Venetians carefully considered their options. The French, with their military power and crusading zeal, caused more concern to the Venetians than the Neapolitans because of how the Turks would respond to the French advance into the Mediterranean. The Ottomans might respond to any crusading zeal by retaliating against the Venetians. If, on the other hand, the Venetians supported the Kingdom of Naples then King Charles could ally with Maximillian and threaten Venetian holdings in the north of Italy. The Venetians decided on strict neutrality.

Pope Alexander could not claim neutrality because he had already committed himself when he recognized Alfonso as King of Naples. The situation he faced, however, was not beyond his double-dealing skills. The pope had convinced Alfonso to provide estates for some of his children. The pope depended on Prospero Colonna to protect Rome. Cardinal Ascanio Sforza and his brother, Lodovico, arranged the joint Milanese and papal *condotta* for Prospero. Neither the pope nor even Prospero knew that Lodovico collected Prospero's pay from the French, who thought that Prospero was working for King Charles.

In late May, Prospero and Fabrizio Colonna took over Cardinal della Rovere's fortress at Ostia. Since della Rovere was associated with King Charles, the French did not appreciate this move. Lodovico suggested that the Colonna declare for the French, but because the Colonna estates and family members were in reach of King Alfonso, the Colonna refused. At the same time, Pope Alexander tried to convince the Colonna to adopt him as their leader, while at the same time trying to convince Alfonso to attack them.

This tangle of interests and motives is what confused Alfonso's attempts to launch his offensive north. This is why he had to leave his strongest forces covering Rome. In late May French forces began concentrating in the Piedmont. In Genoa the French raised money and equipped a transport fleet. In late June Louis of Orleans with Neapolitan exiles arrived in Genoa at the same time as Alfonso's forces, commanded by Genoese exiles, approached the city. The French and Milanese troops, including 3,400 Swiss infantry under Antoine de Baissey, ensured the failure of rebellion.

In late August, the news came that King Charles was crossing the Alps. The Neapolitan fleet, based in Livorno with Piero de Medici's permission, again sailed towards Genoa to intercept and disrupt the French supply lines. Giulio Orsini, with 4,000 men including many Genoese exiles, landed at Rapallo south of Genoa on 3 September. The fleet withdrew once the troops settled into position. When Louis of Orleans found out about the Neapolitan effort, he organized a thousand-man strike force of Swiss infantry and sent them by sea to contest the landing. This advanced force dug in and waited for the arrival of another 2,000 Swiss infantry accompanied by Genoese and Milanese sword infantry. The Swiss began skirmishing with Neapolitan troops who advanced into the field separating the sides. A stream on one side, hills on the other bounded the field, confining the forces in such a way that precluded the deployment of the great Swiss squares. The Swiss allowed the Italian infantry to engage the

Neapolitan troops. As the sides engaged, the French fleet bombarded Rapallo. The Neapolitan infantry suddenly broke and fled the field. Some Neapolitan high officers found themselves abandoned and surrendered. The victorious Swiss infantry killed the wounded and prisoners, then they sacked Rapallo.

The French Dominate Northern Italy

King Charles marched over the pass at Montgenèvre and entered Asti, a holding of the Duke of Orleans, on 9 September. Lodovico Sforza and his wife Beatrice née d'Este, with great ceremony came to receive Charles in Italy, bringing Ercole d'Este, Duke of Ferrara with them. The French and Italians decided to advance as soon as possible, Lodovico providing more money to facilitate Charles's movements. Lodovico was concerned that when the winter came, the French would decide to stay in Milanese lands. Unfortunately for all concerned, King Charles fell victim to smallpox and had to remain in Asti for a month recovering, while his army camped and enjoyed beautiful Italy. Charles's scouts, however, had explored routes of advance and the French decided they would march to Naples down the length of Italy, through the most productive lands to keep supplied and picking up their artillery already transferred by ship to Genoa.

As the French prepared to march south, in the Romagna, Prince Ferrandino prepared to threaten Milan, to distract the French. He reinforced his men-at-arms with troops of the mercenary commanders Trivulzio and Orsini, who led a mixed group of Neapolitan, Florentine and papal soldiers. The French and Milanese detached a force to counter the Neapolitans. These were led by Béraut Stuart d'Aubigny with French soldiers and Gianfrancesco da Sanseverino, Count of Caiazzo, with soldiers of Milan. But neither army moved against the other. Between the French-Milanese and the Neapolitan armies were the lands of Bologna and Imola-Forli. Giovanni Bentivoglio held Bologna and Caterina Sforza ruled Imola-Forli. Both were allied with Milan but held their lands from the pope. Neither declared for either side.

The French decided not to wait any longer. On 19 October the French-Milanese forces invested the town of Mordano in Imola. While there were Neapolitan troops in the garrison, Ferrandino did not come to relieve the town. The Count of Caiazzo requested surrender, telling the garrison commanders that the French, and particularly the Swiss, fought like mad dogs. The garrison commanders refused. In a matter of hours, the French drew up their guns and blasted away at the fortifications and soon the cannon fire broke breaches in the walls. The French–Milanese storm carried the town. The French and Swiss troops killed everyone they found, soldiers, civilians and the mass of local refugees. That the invading French could successfully assault any fortification and then would slaughter the people within sent shock waves through Italy. All the defensive sites in Romagna folded. Bologna under Giovanni Bentivoglio fell into line with his Milanese allies and Caterina Sforza quickly came to terms. Ferrandino's Florentine and papal troops dispersed, and he withdrew with his men-at-arms to Cesena.

After King Charles recovered from his sickness in Asti, he ordered his soldiers mobilized and resumed his march. The town of Pavia was on his line of advance where Charles spent a night at the castle. There resided the Duke of Milan, Gian Galeazzo, Charles's first cousin (their mothers were sisters, daughters of Louis II Duke of Savoy). The duke was ill, had been ill for years according to Lodovico. At 25 years of age, his infirmity was ascribed to overindulgence with his young and beautiful wife, Isabella of Naples, daughter of Alfonso now King of Naples. When King Charles came to the Duke of Milan's sickbed, he wished the young duke to recover his health. At the king's side stood Lodovico. Charles knew that only the sick young man stood between Lodovico and the Coronet of Milan. The Duchesse Isabella surprised both Charles and Lodovico when she threw herself at Charles's feet, begging him to protect her husband, her infant son, her father and his kingdom. Charles mouthed platitudes about protecting the duke and his family but indicated that the enterprise was too far along to stop.

Lodovico had found himself in a difficult spot. The invasion he had done so much to bring about was threatening to swallow him. Their massive army with artillery the likes of which no one had seen before, was an overwhelming force. The French army's dedication to the arts of war endangered Lodovico's hold on Milan. He had not come to this opinion all at once; he had already arranged with Maximillian that he and his heirs would receive the Coronet of Milan if the young Gian Galeazzo should die and, suddenly but not surprisingly, the young duke died. This was on 21 October, just a few days after King Charles had visited him by his bedside and pledged French protection.

Lodovico, who was accompanying the king through the duchy, left him and hurried to Milan where the nobility of Milan requested Lodovico assume the coronet, displacing Gian Galeazzo's young son, Francesco.

King Charles recognized Lodovico as Duke of Milan, but there was more to his position than just surface appearances. The Sforza title to Milan was not particularly strong but they had held the city for about fifty years. Gian Galeazzo had as strong a title as any Sforza. However, Lodovico's claim was simply that of a Sforza usurper. The older ruling family of Milan, the Visconti, whom the Sforza had displaced, had a primary claimant in the person of the current Duke of Orleans, Louis, King Charles's heir.

The French March Begins

Charles joined his main force at Piacenza on 18 October. He held meetings with his commanders about how to proceed, particularly about routes to Naples. The commanders and the king decided on the western route through Tuscany, south to Rome and then on to Naples. The king ordered Gilbert de Montpensier to lead the vanguard over the mountains toward Tuscany. The French had tried to secure the agreement of the Florentines for free passage and supplies, but they had so far refused, so the French entered Tuscany as Florentine enemies. The first Florentine fortress on the French road was Fivizzano. Gabriele Malaspina, Marchese di Fosdinovo, had a claim on the fortress. He undertook to point out the fortress's weakness to the French troops who stormed and took it. The Marchese's men joined the French in a harsh sack, killing all the Florentine defenders and many inhabitants. Most of the remainder were sent to Lyons for ransom. The violence of Fivizzano's sack scared the rest of the forts in Lunigiana into surrender.

Some days later, the French approached the updated Florentine fortress of Sarzana. Lodovico encouraged Charles to assault the fortress, thinking that it would stymie the French advance for weeks or possibly halt it completely. But this was not to happen because of events in Florence. Piero de Medici was seeing his power eroding. He had allied with Alfonso without considering what Florence needed if the city was going to oppose the French king. Nothing was prepared nor were the fortresses ready. The Florentines found their businesses disrupted by the French king and there was very little profit to be had from Alfonso. Paolo Orsini's cavalry supported by 300 Florentine foot marched to reinforce Sarzana. A force of French men-at-arms routed this force, killing many and taking most of the rest prisoners. Piero went to the French camp because he would get nowhere in Florence. He knew he would have to come to terms with King Charles. Piero surrendered Sarzana, along with Pietrasanta, Pisa, and Livorno to the French for as long as the French expedition lasted. He ordered the castellans to do this on his authority. A greater capitulation was beyond Charles's imagination. When Piero returned to Florence, the *Signoria* declared him a rebel and he fled.

Charles now continued through Tuscany. Lucca invited him to enter their city. Once there, he requested a substantial loan and custody of the fortress of Montignano. He got the loan and left the fortress. Ambassadors from Siena came promising Charles free passage through their lands, followed by ambassadors from Florence on 8 November, as King Charles marched toward Pisa. The French had entered Pisa a week before when Montpensier had marched in, welcomed with happy demonstrations by the populace. When King Charles came, the people received him with great joy, hoping that the king would grant them liberty from Florentine control. Charles and his advisors, seeing this as a fine move to weaken the ambivalent Florentines, readily agreed. The Pisans immediately expelled the Florentine officials at Pisa. Ever playing the double game, Charles expressed regret about that event.

Florentine ambassadors had already promised King Charles entrance to Florence. This essentially revoked Piero de Medici's alliance with Naples and demonstrated that his influence was at an end. Charles entered the city as a victorious commander. With some 10,000 crack troops, he demanded the Florentines remove the gates through which he would march and make a breach in the city wall. He would parade through the city streets.

At the head of the French column drums sounded the march enlivened by tunes played on fifes echoing through the narrow street, Via San Frediano. First came companies of Gascon halberdiers, crossbowmen and archers, all marching shoulder to shoulder. Then the Swiss, led by flute players dressed in close-fitting particoloured hose and doublets, yellow and red, black and white, each man with the white cross of their confederation on front and back. There were pikemen, thousands strong, carrying a forest of fifteen-foot pikes with standards and unit flags. Interspersed at the heads of units, came officers with personalized headgear, topped by great plumes. Next, came the commanding officers of the infantry in their fine armour and trappings, de Cleves, de Nevers, de Lornay and the Bailiff of Dijon, to the continuous rolling of drums. They were followed by companies of foot guards in cloth of gold hose, marked by a golden chain on each man's neck, dressed in the royal colours, violet and white, units of halberdiers and long-swordsmen.

As the heavy infantry passed, loud trumpets sounded and great drums beat the march as another formation approached. The *compagnies d'ordonnance*, the king's horse came. The companies of Ligny and other noble lords in their best trappings paraded down the streets. Here were the Bayards, the Bellaires, and the Tardieus, each mounted on a great warhorse with shining armour and colourful surcoat on man and beast. There were 800 lances, each accompanied by three or four mounted archers equally well equipped, bearing escutcheon shields and waving banners, in all 5,000 mounted men. After the lancers came the Royal Scottish archers: big, strong men in coats of mail and gold embroidered hacquetons, arm guards, steel caps, bows and quivers, swords and daggers. Following the Royal Scots, rode their officers, de Crussol, Claude de la Chastre and George Cockburn, armed and armoured men.

Then, amid great fanfares of trumpets, 200 gentlemen of the royal guard in white and violet accompanied by their pages and lackeys on barbed horses, passed by followed by the king's retinue of courtiers and pages. At last, surrounded by a double row of footmen, rode King Charles on his favourite horse, Savoy, a black Bressian, with but one eye. His full armour was embossed with gilded figures and gems; his large white hat, decorated with black plumes, tied under his chin with colourful ribbons, held a golden crown. In his hand, Charles carried a great lance. Over his head, high Florentine magistrates carried a silk canopy. The grand equerry rode before him holding the great Sword of State. After the king and his guards came high ecclesiastics and other worthies, followed by the long baggage train. As the cavalcade passed, the Florentine crowds cheered *Viva Francia*!

The truth was clear: the French king's soldiers marched ready for battle and the king carried a lance, symbolizing that the city fell in battle. The Florentines received him with wary respect, worrying that his troops might turn to plunder. Charles understood, however, that a reluctant ally was preferable to a bitter enemy and his troops maintained acceptable behaviour.

Chapter 5

The March South to Rome

King Charles struck a deal with the Florentines. Florence accepted French occupation of their main fortresses until Charles returned to France and Charles agreed to return all Florentine holdings, taken from them since his arrival, including Pisa. The Florentines gave Charles a loan of 120,000 florins and allowed two French agents attendance at any official meeting regarding France or Naples. But his request for the Florentines to reinstate the Medici was refused, although they did agree not to arrest their persons or confiscate their property. In return for making the deal, Charles restored all the Florentines' previous trade privileges. The parties signed their agreement on 25 November. The king resumed his march south three days later.

The French commander, d'Aubigny, with his vanguard advanced from the Romagna into Siena. A little later, Charles arrived with his main force from Florence. The Sienese welcomed the king but refused to allow him to occupy their ports and denied him a 30,000 ducat loan. Charles did not care, all he needed was free transit across their territory. Soon, the French left Siena after installing a garrison in the city and entered the lands of the Papal States.

As the French pushed south, Ferrandino had withdrawn from the Romagna and concentrated his men near Rome. He hoped to gather enough forces to deter King Charles. Rome, however, was not in a proper condition to support a vigorous defence because the main supply route up the Tiber was blocked. In September, Prospero Colonna and a cadre of French agents had infiltrated della Rovere's (the Cardinal St Pietro in Vinculi) fortress at Ostia and began blocking the route to Rome. As the French marched south to Bracciano, Charles detached de Ligny's company and other men-at-arms to a total of 500, along with 2,000 Swiss infantry under Yves d'Alègre, and sent them to reinforce the garrison of Ostia. For support, the French also held the *condotta* of Fabrizio and Prospero Colonna. Once they had secured Ostia against any possible attack, the French forces were to support King Charles as he approached Rome. It was in Ostia that Bayard, a member of de Ligny's company, became acquainted with della Rovere, Prospero Colonna and made an enduring friendship with Yves d'Alègre.

Ferrandino's efforts to halt the French advance on Rome was bound to fail. To urge him along, King Charles sent him a safe conduct for himself and his men to pass through the Papal States. Moreover, Pope Alexander ordered him to leave Rome. Outmanoeuvred, Ferrandino publicly rejected the safe conduct; still, he had to leave Rome. Ferrandino marched his army out of Rome through the Gate of San Sebastiano during the last days of 1494. At about the same time, Montpensier marched the French vanguard into Rome through the Gate of Santa Maria del Populo.

Charles Enters Rome

In the fading light of evening, 31 December, came the main French army, led by drummers and torchbearers through the Gate of Santa Maria del Populo, parading down the muddy street. First came great bodies of Swiss, marching beneath their standards in dignified and perfect step. Their short coats were multi-coloured, revealing their muscular limbs, their officers wearing high plumed hats. They had short swords at their sides and carried long ashen pikes. Some of these soldiers carried halberds, long staffed axes to strike or thrust. Along with every thousand infantry, there were a hundred arquebusiers, who fought in close formation; their commanders and front rankers had helmets and shoulder guards; the rest had no armour. Behind them came 5,000 Gascons, crossbowmen who appeared shabby next to the Swiss.

The cavalry followed riding in companies, the nobility of France in silken doublets, plumed helmets and gold collars – 2,500 men-at-arms carrying stout fluted lances with heavy points, paraded along the torchlit streets, riding massive horses with manes docked and ears clipped. After the heavy cavalry, the light cavalry rode by – 5,000 light horse, each with a great wooden bow, helmet and cuirass. All the horsemen wore their captains' devices embroidered on their doublets.

King Charles's royal guard of 200 elite noble men-at-arms came next, each holding on his shoulder a large iron mace, mounted on massive warhorses, dressed in gold and silk. The king was surrounded by his royal guard of Scottish crossbowmen 100-strong with 300 more crossbowmen following. Charles was entering Rome as a conqueror just as he had in Florence, wearing armour and carrying a lance. On either side of the king rode Cardinals Ascanio Sforza and Giuliano della Rovere. Companies of foot and horse, armed for war, not display, followed the royal procession through the streets.

Interspaced in these formations, came the guns. Thirty-six artillery pieces, just a part of the total brought to Italy, all mounted on wooden wagons easily pulled by horses. Most of the guns were cannon, eight feet long, 6,000 pounds of bronze which fired iron balls the size of a man's head. Next came culverins, half as long with smaller shot, then falcons, smaller still, with shot the size of an orange. The larger guns were mounted on wagons with four axles, one of which was detachable to set the gun ready to fire on two wheels. The smaller guns rode on single axles.

While Charles's army marched into Rome by torchlight, Pope Alexander hurried from his papal palace to the Castel Sant'Angelo accompanied by his court, along with cardinals Battista Orsini and Ulivieri Carafa of Naples. His Holiness had good reason to put stout walls between the French and himself. Rumour and sound information had spread into Rome regarding just what the French King intended to do to the Borgia pope. The Cardinal San Pietro in Vincoli and his allies counselled the king to call for a church council to remove the impious Borgia and Pope Alexander had sent legates to Charles when he was in Viterbo, imploring him to bypass Rome. In turn, Charles sent his envoys to the pope, demanding free passage and supplies for his army and his investiture with the Neapolitan crown.

Alexander would have none of that, especially after his enemies snatched Ostia from him. On 9 December Alexander arrested and confined Cardinal Ascanio Sforza and Prospero Colonna. This accomplished little: the Colonna forces refused to relinquish Ostia and maintained their blockade of Rome. Alexander, never one not to find some path to his objective, had Prospero sign a *condotta* and sent him on his way. Lodovico pressured King Charles to demand Ascanio's release. All of this added to Alexander's appreciation of King Charles: here was a man with whom he could do business.

Indeed, Charles's collection of cardinals, San Pietro in Vincoli, Ascanio, the Colonna, and the Savello, all begged Charles to remove Alexander not only because he was corrupt, immoral and a thief, but also because, they said, King Charles could never trust the duplicitous, treacherous Borgia. Charles more clearly saw where his interests were. In Rome, Charles set up his headquarters in the Palace of San Marco (now, the Palazzo Venezia), mounting his cannon around the building as a warning to those who might dispute his position in the city. During his negotiations with Alexander in Castel Sant'Angelo, Charles had twice to move his cannons to face the castle walls, to punctuate his terms. But he had no intention of harming his Holiness; most of Charles's Privy Council had received gifts, and the promise of more from Alexander and Charles saw no reason to disappoint his friends when someone else was paying the bill.

Charles was satisfied with his expedition so far. He might have moved against Pope Alexander but, much better, he used Alexander's vulnerability to extract as much from him as possible. The pope conceded free passage and gave supplies to the French army. Once the parties reached an agreement, Pope Alexander returned to his palace. To publicly display their concord, His Holiness received King Charles in St Peter's Basilica. Following tradition, the Most Christian King genuflected to His Holiness, kissed his feet and was then raised by the pope to kiss his cheeks. The French received and garrisoned the main fortifications, Ostia (which he already held), Civitavecchia and Terracina.

Moreover, Alexander gave his captive Ottoman prince, Djem, to Charles to facilitate Charles's coming crusade. But Alexander kept the ongoing subsidy from the Ottoman sultan to keep Djem in custody. Further, Alexander gave Charles his son, the Cardinal of Valencia, 19-year-old Cesare Borgia, as a hostage. However, His Holiness deferred the question of investiture of the Kingdom of Naples.

On to Naples

The French success was obvious to all. From September of 1494 to January of 1495, Charles had advanced the length of Italy to Rome without hindrance. Everywhere the French either threatened or bullied their way past fortresses and cities. King Alfonso saw his strategic situation as hopeless. The skilled and effective military commander decided, even before Charles left Rome, that he could not win. When Alfonso heard of Ferrandino's retreat into the kingdom, found out there was a French-inspired rebellion in the Abruzzi, and that Pope Alexander had come to terms with King Charles, he panicked. In Naples, crowds cheered for French success and booed Alfonso, old King Ferrante and Prince Ferrandino.

The rumour spread that Iacopo, Alfonso's chief surgeon saw it – old King Ferrante's ghost which said that Iacopo must convince Alfonso not to resist but yield to the French! Only thus might he save his line from utter destruction. Alfonso, said the apparition, must accept blame for the many murders of notable Neapolitans he secretly convinced Ferrante to order. In a panic, Alfonso decided to flee. He abdicated the throne and loaded four light galleys with treasure. He sailed this little fleet to Sicily, to Mazari, a small town given to him by King Ferdinand the Catholic. His son, Ferrandino became king, but without a treasury and without a hope of repelling the French.

As January passed, King Charles had sent his vanguard southward, to Montefortino, a village in the Roman *campagna*, subject to Jacopo Conti, a Roman baron. Conti originally supported the French, but a personal feud with the Colonnas pushed him into the Neapolitan camp. He held the castle at Montefortino and refused to surrender or allow free passage. The gunners wheeled up their cannon. In a few hours, the artillery had wrecked the castle. The soldiers then put all the inhabitants to the sword except for Conti's three children and a few who found refuge in the citadel.

King Charles left Rome on 28 January. When he came to Velletri, the news that Alfonso had fled came. At the same time, the Cardinal of Valencia disappeared. The fortress of Monte San Giovanni dominated the land route from Rome to Naples. Charles, so successful at pushing his way through Italy, simply marched for the pass and its fortress. Held for the Marquis of Pescara, the fortifications were strong, occupied by 300 foreign foot supported by 500 trained militia. The site should hold the French for days if not weeks.

The French quickly invested the fortress. King Charles dispatched envoys to Monte San Giovanni demanding surrender. The Neapolitans seized the envoys, cut off their ears and noses and sent them back to the French camp without a word of explanation. Quickly, the French wheeled their cannon into firing positions. A few shots shattered the fortress walls at some points. The French foot was given a generous ration of wine and marshalled for the assault under the eyes of the king. Commander la Tremouille led the column surging up the hill and stormed the fortress. Suddenly, the pennon and royal standard appeared in two different breaches. The garrison fled the fight and the fortress fell in an hour. But the fight did not end as French foot soldiers hunted the garrison in tunnels and rooms, taking the hapless Neapolitan soldiers and throwing them over the parapets onto the pikes of those below, or just slaughtering them where they were found. Nine hundred Neapolitan soldiers lay dead while the French pillaged castle and town.

In the wars in the north, such actions were not unknown nor unexpected. To the Italians, such things were unheard of atrocities. In their chess board wars, their mercenary soldiers might be on one side or another.

Such slaughter did not happen: this event shocked the Italians. Bayard was there and he received a share of the booty. It was the archers and pikemen who killed the unfortunate Italian soldiers, not the king's chevaliers, but war was war as far as he was concerned. The result was spectacular. Neighbouring fortresses surrendered as soon as the French came into view. As was said at the time, King Charles was greater than Caesar; he conquered before he was seen.

Ferrandino hoped to pull his kingdom together. He marshalled fifty squadrons of horse and 6,000 foot. All were picked men under experienced commanders. He chose to block the French advance by occupying San Germano, a fortified position in the Liri River valley just to the north of the monastery of St Benedict at Cassino. Protected in the rear by high mountains, the position faced the Liri leaving little room to deploy heavy forces. The fortress was known as one of the strategic keys of the Kingdom of Naples. Before Ferrandino arrived, the French van appeared commanded by the Marshal de Gie with 300 lances and 200 foot.

When scouts brought word that the French were approaching, the Neapolitan troops, who knew of the dreadful results of defeat, feared more for their families, their lands and their lives than fighting for King Ferrandino. The men abandoned San Germano, even leaving behind eight large cannon. Disappointed, Ferrandino ordered his army, what remained of it, to hold Capua, the old and well-fortified town on the Volturno. The French forces, rightly believing they had nothing to fear, advanced in dispersed order. Each lance, with his companions and helpers, moved through the countryside without colours or orders, as if on a journey instead of a march, searching for plunder and entertainment. Often, in the evening, the French would occupy a village left by the Neapolitans in the morning.

Ferrandino put his best commander in charge of the troops in Capua, the *condottiere* Gian Giacomo Trivulzio, and worked with him to find the best troop placements. Helping them, Virginio and Niccolo Orsini were there with their crack troops. Suddenly the Queen Mother, Joanne I sent a message to Ferrandino. Come to Naples, she demanded, only the king could control the ongoing rioting! Reluctantly, Ferrandino, with a few friends, rode toward Naples. The king pledged he would return the very next day.

Once Ferrandino had left, Trivulzio sent an envoy to the French, requesting safe conduct. A safe conduct pass quickly returned to Capua. Trivulzio and a group of important Capuans travelled to Calvi where King Charles had just arrived. Trivulzio stood forth in full armour, appropriately greeting the king. He came, he said, in the name of the people of Capua and his soldiers. They were loyal subjects of King Ferrandino. While there was a chance of victory, they all would fight for him. Now, there was no hope and they requested terms. In the discussion of terms, Trivulzio said that he was working on King Ferrandino's instructions. He enquired about terms for Ferrandino – was there a possibility of settlement? King Charles accepted Capua, Capua's citizens, and Trivulzio on generous terms, but for Ferrandino the best he would get from Charles was honourable and comfortable retirement in France. While Trivulzio was away, soldiers plundered the royal quarters in Capua carrying away horses and goods, after which the men-at-arms dispersed. Seeing the tumult and knowing Trivulzio went to see the French, Virginio and Niccolo Orsini with their men marched to Nola, part of the holdings of Virginio.

Ferrandino and a few followers returned to Capua late the next day. About two miles from the city gates, armed Capuans blocked his way. Amazed, Ferrandino demanded to know what this was about. One of his officials told him that, since he had abandoned Capua, his commander went over to the French, soldiers had plundered his quarters, Virginio and Niccolo had left and the city was defenceless in the face of the French army. The city would submit to the conqueror. Ferrandino, tears in his eyes, begged them to change their minds but actually he suspected the rest of his kingdom would soon follow and soon the town of Aversa and even Naples sent envoys to Charles.

Ferrandino quickly returned to Naples. He immediately summoned an assembly of Neapolitans to the square in front of the massive New Castle, his residence. The king announced to his subjects: the city should surrender to the French; he was going into exile, but he would be back. After he entered the castle gates, the crowd began to plunder the stables nearby. Incensed, Ferrandino rode out of the gate with his guards toward the crowds who quickly dispersed. With that, he returned to the castle after ordering all ships in the harbour to be sunk or burned.

Inside the castle, while he was preparing the court's evacuation, Ferrandino suspected some of the 500 members of the German garrison were plotting to make him a prisoner and sell him to the French. The king informed the guard's officers that the men could have everything stored in the castle. While the guards divided up the spoils, Ferrandino freed most of the many prisoners in the dungeon, collected the dowager Queen Joanne, former wife of King Ferrante, her daughter and his uncle Federigo, along with their court members. The party left by a postern gate, boarded light galleys and sailed away from Naples.

The king sailed across the bay to the island of Ischia. Once landed, the commander of the powerful fortress dominating the island refused to admit the party and their guards allowing only the king and one follower to enter. Ferrandino agreed. Once the king and his one follower entered the castle, they violently seized the commander and convinced him of the error of his ways. After the royal party had left Naples, the city sent envoys to King Charles who accepted their surrender. Charles also sent Ligny with 200 horse to Nola where they found Virginio and Niccolo Orsini with some 400 men. The Orsini surrendered to the French and were confined after they and their men were relieved of their belongings.

King Charles in Naples

The French soldiers infiltrated Naples without difficulty, preparing the city to receive King Charles. The king entered the city on 22 February. Escorted by just a few guards, he wore hunting clothes and carried a hawk instead of a spear, mounted on a mule instead of a warhorse. Ferrandino sent envoys to negotiate a settlement, but Charles refused and Ferrandino sailed off to Sicily. The two castles in the city still in Ferrandino's hands did not hold out long. The German garrison that held the New Castle put up resistance to French efforts at entering but refrained from counterattacking. They willingly agreed to discuss terms. The terms agreed, each soldier could leave with as much as he could carry. The provisions in the castle's magazines were immense and Charles allowed his people to distribute them among his followers. The Castle of the Egg sits in the sea just off the shore. Charles's cannon damaged the walls but could not make a breach. But after a few days, the garrison sent word they would surrender the castle if they could leave without hindrance if not relieved in eight days. And so, they did.

With Naples secure, Charles's men advanced into the countryside to subdue resistance to the king's rule. Delegations from most of the important towns and castles met these advanced parties with pledges of loyalty. Some more distant places, however, remained in the hands of Ferrandino's followers. The French did not consider the reduction of these strongholds worth any effort. The crusading project remained an idea but with far less attraction after Charles understood that the Holy Land was much further away than he thought and Constantinople, while closer, was still far away. Suddenly Prince Djem died and the crusade evaporated.

Three months passed. King Charles ruled Naples with tournaments, banquets, pageants and celebrations. The French nobles received estates, titles, heiresses and lordships, displacing their previous occupants. The Lord de Ligny and Bayard's company tracked down fugitives from the former court. Near Nola, they captured Virginio Orsini and the Count of Pitigliano. Charles was very pleased with Ligny's accomplishments since the beginning of the Italian campaign. The Lord de Ligny received the young and beautiful Princess of Altamura in marriage and so became Prince of Altamura, Duke of Andria and Venosa. The French were truly enjoying themselves. Contrasted with life in Flanders and northern France, small cold houses and homely women, slabs of beef and pork with hearty beer, leaden skies and rainy weather, the Italian south appeared like a fantasy paradise.

The Neapolitans, who received the French as an improvement over the Aragonese now began seeing them as just more bloodsuckers. The lesser nobility, managing most agricultural production found themselves squeezed more than before. However, what was worse than restive petty nobles and peasants was the emerging chaos rising to engulf the French royal forces. Actual French forces were merely a few tens of thousands with a matching number of camp followers; the Italians were many more. King Charles's triumphant march was spectacular but, following the collapse of Italian diplomatic balances, shattered the whole scheme of chess-board wars. Now the combatants were out for blood. Even more of a problem, the double-dealing of every player had finally so clouded the overall picture that no player knew where he stood.

As spring moved into summer, King Charles's house of cards was tumbling down. The original selling point for many participants, the crusade to Jerusalem, evaporated. The other main selling point, loot, was on everyone's mind and in good measure was accomplished. The Italian wonderland was beautiful but home beckoned. Questions about how family and crops were doing, how estates and lawsuits were coming along, became more important to nobles and soldiers. Commanders began making preparations for a return march home by summer's end. Perhaps they might have to fight their way through, but that did not give them pause. Indeed, they might depose Lodovico on the way.

Chapter 6

The Holy League Arises to Fight King Charles

Before he even decided to invade Italy, King Charles sent envoys to the Most Serene Republic of Venice. Asking for Venetian support, Charles's envoys promised that even if the Venetians chose neutrality, they would remain friends of the French. The Venetians announced that the French did not need their help, but they would accept any lawful result the French might accomplish. Then the French began to pass through Italy like a thunderbolt. The Venetians sent envoys to Charles to ensure their interest when Charles was in Florence. His answers were equivocal. While maintaining their neutrality, the Venetians received Lodovico's envoys suggesting an anti-French combination. As Charles advanced south, the Venetians watched the French overwhelm Tuscany, the Papal States and Naples. If the French had met a reverse in any of these endeavours, the Venetians let Lodovico know they would join him in opposing the French, but the French did not find any reverses.

These discussions did not go unnoticed. Charles disliked and distrusted Lodovico, which is why he was so pleased when Gian Giacomo Trivulzio offered his services. Trivulzio was the leader of the Milanese Guelphs. King Charles granted him a company of 100 lancers and gave him an ample salary to support the force. Further, Charles did not grant as he had promised, the title and lands of Prince of Taranto to Lodovico, saying that he did not have the lands in hand. Quite perturbed with the French, Lodovico passed orders to his governors in Genoa telling them not to release the twelve war-galleys being equipped for Charles, nor give the French any armed vessels. Charles, whose fleets found the Mediterranean weather difficult, became wroth because he could not assault the isle of Ischia.

Lodovico's growing hostility to the French was obvious to everyone. Charles's successes frightened the Venetians who saw him as attempting to build an Italian hegemony. Pope Alexander had had enough of the French king and Emperor Elect Maximillian feared the French success in Italy would lead to their challenging imperial pretentions, particularly in Northern Italy. Charles, however, did not realize his most determined opponent was the King of Aragon, Ferdinand the Catholic. Charles had negotiated a treaty with Ferdinand, surrendering Roussillon, thinking he was buying a free hand in Italy with this concession. In the treaty, Ferdinand did say he would not oppose Charles in Italy. Charles neglected to take to heart the statements Ferdinand inserted into the text that Charles's claims must demonstrate legal title, that there be no prejudice to Holy Church, nor to His Holiness, nor His Holiness's rights of a fief in the Kingdom of Naples.

Once he occupied Roussillon, Ferdinand sent word to the court of Naples, that they could expect his support and Ferdinand's Kingdom of Sicily was open to them in extreme situations. He also sent word to Pope Alexander, asking His Holiness's protection for the House of Naples. Since Ferdinand's marriage to Isabella of Castile in 1469, facilitated by the Spanish Cardinal Borgia (now Pope Alexander VI), the royal pair worked to build the Kingdom of Spain. Trade interests of eastern Spain passed through Italy and so Ferdinand was very concerned about what went on there. As King Charles invaded Naples, Ferdinand sent a fleet to Sicily with 800 light horse and 1,000 Spanish foot.

After the fall of Naples to King Charles, envoys of the Spanish sovereigns began to discuss terms of an anti-French combination with the Venetian Senate and the Sforza in Milan. In April 1495 in Venice, a congress of ambassadors formed the Holy League which included Pope Alexander, Emperor Elect Maximillian, the Sovereigns of Spain, the Venetians and the Duke of Milan. The league intended to protect members' lands from any encroachment by an unspecified outside power. In actuality, the confederates were agreed that Charles would not keep the Kingdom of Naples. In secret articles, Ferdinand promised to aid Ferrandino to recover his dominion. Already, turbulence swelled in the Kingdom of Naples. Aragonese interests in Calabria invited Ferrandino to base his operations in their province. Authorities in Sicily prepared to support Ferrandino's efforts while the Venetians prepared to attack the French holdings on the east coast of the kingdom. The Duke of Milan prepared to attack the French holding at Asti where Louis of Orleans remained with only a few troops. Moreover, the confederates promised to raise money to defray the war costs of Spain and the Emperor Maximillian. They wanted to add Florence and Ferrara to their league, but neither polity was able to disentangle their interests from the French. Still, the Holy League planned to cut short King Charles's career of conquest in Italy.

That the French king was going back to France was no secret. That the French intended to be a determining factor in Italian politics was also clear.

Every Italian power saw their basic interest threatened by King Charles; the Italians formed the first European alliance of divergent states that united against what they saw as an over-powerful enemy. The league authorized the collection of an army, and their military commanders discussed the best way to decisively break the French. The logistics of holding together a large army was hard, particularly if that army had a long march to meet the enemy in the south of Italy. Since King Charles was going back to France, the confederate commanders planned to stay in richer northern Italy and catch Charles's army in transit, defeat his soldiers and capture King Charles.

The French March North

Information about the establishment of a massive coalition in opposition to the French in Italy came in many ways to the French in Naples. Charles and his advisors called together a council to consider their best options. Such a large and powerful alliance had never been seen. Best, they decided, to return to France; there, in a secure base, they could deal with whatever problems the combination made. The question, however, was how the French could hold Naples while at the same time advance north to Asti in the teeth of the Confederates. The French had to divide their forces: second line troops would remain in Naples, half the Swiss, and 800 French lances, along with 500 Italian men-at-arms belonging to Prospero and Fabrizio Colonna. Charles had granted the Colonna large estates and rich offices, and he believed they would fight for their own. The best soldiers would accompany the king on the march north. The king appointed Gilbert de Montpensier as viceroy of Naples with the command of many French lords who were now the owners of rich estates. Charles promised his officials in Naples that he would send reinforcements and money after he returned to France.

But, before actually going to war, the spring in Naples was beautiful; Charles had no intention of being forced out of Naples by some Italian threat. Instead, the French enjoyed themselves. Charles spent the spring managing the business of government. In the morning he held audiences and met with his counsellors and in the afternoon he enjoyed Neapolitan pleasures. King Charles showed concern toward the people of the Kingdom of Naples, but French arrogance and condescension irritated many. On 12 May the king made a ceremonial entrance into the city on his warhorse, Savoy, wearing royal robes, crown, orb and sceptre. He rode under a canopy held by four Neapolitan nobles, surrounded by his commanders. The parade ended in front of the cathedral where King Charles took an oath to govern well but he was not crowned because he had not received Pope Alexander's investiture.

Charles left Naples on 20 May. He had already sent some contingents north. With him marched some 800 lances, 200 royal men-at-arms, Trivulzio with his 100 lances, 3,000 Swiss infantry, 1,000 French foot, and 1,000 Gascon foot. Charles instructed Camillo Vitelli and his brother to join him in Tuscany with 250 men-at-arms. Some of the king's advisors suggested that Charles and part of his army go north in ships, but there were not enough ships and the king felt it would be wrong to show weakness in front of the new league. The king intended to march straight into whatever they had planned because he was confident the French soldiers would push their way through.

Charles was hoping to put further pressure on Pope Alexander regarding his investiture with the crown of Naples. In truth, Alexander had no intention of meeting him. With most of the cardinals, his guards and the contingents of troops sent by Venice and Milan, he left Rome for Orvieto on 27 May. On 1 June Charles entered Rome peacefully, declared that he was upset that the Pope had left and stayed only two days. Charles withdrew his garrisons from the papal towns of Terracina and Civitavecchia but held on to Ostia. As he continued his journey northward, he returned by the same route he had come.

The French marched north as a victorious army. His best men-at-arms surrounded the king, his tough Swiss infantry followed and interspersed in the formations were his treasured cannon along with the plunder of Italy in the baggage train. Each soldier had his bag of goods there. By 13 June the army reached Siena. The Sienese welcomed King Charles; they requested him to appoint a French noble to work out differences between the ruling administration and their opponents. Charles appointed Louis Count de Ligny to deal with the problem but Ligny chose one of his officers, who knew about the difficulties in Siena to stay behind, and he followed Charles on his continuing march. Ligny's officer did what he could and followed the French army on 1 August.

Information that the French finally decided to leave Naples came to the Confederate force. Emperor Elect Maximillian had invested Lodovico with the Duchy of Milan with all due ceremony and pomp; then the Duke of Milan paid homage to Maximillian. The Confederates agreed on how to distribute the expense of their large forces, with Venice providing many men-at-arms, Lodovico bringing 2,000 German heavy infantry and arming ten galleys to protect Genoa. Lodovico saw the Confederates' forces as sufficient to stop Charles's march and then carry the war into France. He directed his commander to besiege Asti with 700 men-at-arms and 3,000 foot. While these troops were preparing for the siege, Lodovico sent envoys to Louis of Orleans at Asti. The newly invested duke proclaimed that Louis should never make any claim to Milan, that he must surrender Asti to Lodovico's commander, stop bringing troops from France and send back to France those troops already in Italy.

Louis of Orleans ignored Lodovico's commands. When news had come to Louis that the Confederates had allied, he ordered Asti's fortifications refurbished and requested forces from France. After Lodovico issued his demands, Louis took the offensive. His troops took fortified sites, pushing Lodovico's troops back. Lodovico's men withdrew into a fortified base near Asti where they were safe from attack, but unable to attack the French. Louis had collected 300 lances, 300 Swiss foot, and 300 Gascon foot. King Charles ordered Louis to stay on the defensive protecting Asti while Charles marched towards him.

Louis was never one to pass up an opportunity. When two important men of the town of Novara came to him and asked him to take over their town because everyone there was fed up with Lodovico's corrupt administration, Louis could not resist taking this town for France. He mobilized a strong force, setting out at night with the Marquess of Saluzzo. They crossed the Stura on a bridge of boats and easily took Novara. The Milanese retreated into the citadel, but on the fifth day, the citadel commander told Louis that he would surrender if not relieved in a full day. The French raided Milanese lands and found support for Lodovico weak.

While Louis was dealing with Novara, Lodovico's commander, Sanseverino, collected troops in Vigevano behind which Lodovico himself assembled his army. Because he was now allied to the Venetians, Lodovico withdrew his eastern garrisons to concentrate against Louis. The Venetians even sent him 500 light horse. At that time, Louis thought to surprise Vigevano and sent 500 men-at-arms against the town. But Sanseverino had crossed the River Tesino on a bridge of boats: Louis' men-at-arms suffered heavy losses. When Sanseverino offered battle to Louis, mindful of Charles's orders, the French withdrew back to Novara. King Charles remained concerned about the situation around Asti.

The French had left Naples on 20 May and reached Pisa on 19 June. In a month the French marched north through the route that took four months to march south. They had left garrisons in Siena and Tuscany. Florence was ready to receive Charles, but because Piero de Medici was with him and Florence was filled with soldiers and armed citizenry, the French decided to avoid difficulties. Charles marched to Pisa, passing by Florence to his right. As he marched to avoid Florence, Girolamo Savonarola came to King Charles. The charismatic priest requested Charles to restore the Florentine fortresses he held. Charles equivocated, on the first day saying yes, on the next day, no. Then Charles said his oaths were not binding because the Florentines were not trustworthy, but he left saying that he needed to think about it.

Once in Pisa, Charles had to decide if he was going to satisfy the Florentines and restore Pisa to their control thus making enemies of the Pisans. Charles had given his word to the Florentines, but his commanders, especially Ligny, pointed out that holding Pisa and Livorno would ensure communications from France to Naples. To decide these important questions, the king and royal council met. Also, information came regarding the concentration of the Confederate army near Parma. All agreed that it was prudent to keep the Florentines happy, their money was so very good. On the other hand, if the French met reverses, they thought it better to have Pisa on their side instead of Florence, because the Florentines were sure to turn on them.

Word spread through the Pisans that the royal council was discussing their fate. People began demonstrations in front of where the French royal council was sitting, begging for salvation from the wicked Florentines. The demonstrations spread throughout the city; Pisans approached French nobles, officers and soldiers, begging them to save Pisa from the Florentines. The Pisans were convincing; men, high and low, came to Charles. They said,

'For honour and glory of the honour of France,
For comfort and satisfaction of his soldiers,
Who were ready to lay down their lives for him,
He should not deprive the Pisans of that benefit he gave them.'

The soldiers also said, if money was a problem, they offered their collars, plate, pensions and pay. These dramatic pleas impressed Charles. His mind made up, he informed the Florentines that he would give them what they wanted when he was safe at Asti. Charles also allowed the Pisans to hire a force of 600 well trained French infantry. When the Florentines complained to Charles, he told them that he would handle the matter once he was in France.

Soon, French reinforcements arrived in Pisa by ship. These included 120 lances and 500 foot. King Charles sent them to join the force facing Genoa, along with his fleet of seven galleys, two great ships and two small ships. Charles left Pisa on 22 June after he was sure his local garrisons were safe. When the French army started their march from Pisa, the force was only some 10,000 strong plus, of course, the numerous camp followers, sutlers, soldiers' women and so forth. While the French army was not large, the men were the most professional and proficient in the French royal forces.

They took a route to Pontremoli which then began the ascent up the Apennines. The French had a supply station at Pontremoli where they had stored provisions for the trip over the mountains. The advanced guard under Marshal Gie arrived at the town. With the marshal was the *condottiere* Trivulzio, who convinced the town people to dismiss their garrison of 300 soldiers and surrender on condition of safeguard for property and lives. But the Swiss foot had not forgotten that when the army was marching south, they were involved in a brawl in which Pontremolians had killed 40 of their number. As soon as the Swiss foot entered the town, they plundered, burned and put the inhabitants to the sword. Unfortunately, the French supplies burned with the town.

North from Pontremoli the route ascended switch-back trails, little better than mule paths. Most armies would either find a different way north or abandon their cannon and as much baggage as possible. Not this army: with the Confederate forces massing ahead, King Charles and his men pushed forward. Their cannon symbolized victory and each soldier had his plunder in the baggage train. The men started to climb, dragging all their guns and loot with them. The Swiss, in disfavour because they burned the supplies, stripped off their finery in the July heat and harnessed themselves in shifts of 100 or 200 to each gun. Working to the music of their fifes and drums, yodelling group to group along the twisting path, they dragged the cannon up the hills. The noble men-at-arms removed their armour and shoved and hoisted cannon wheels. They broke rocks and built bridges. The ascents were hard, descents harder still. Exhausted, hungry, sore, dishevelled, the army, cannon and camp followers strove to reach the boulder-strewn valley of the Taro.

The Italian Confederates

Near Parma, the forces of the Confederates readied themselves to attack the French. Here, 2,500 men-at-arms, 8,000 foot, and 2,000 Venetian light horse sorted themselves out into battle formations. Venice hired some three-quarters of the soldiers; the remainder were Lodovico's. The Venetians appointed as governor general of their troops, Francesco Gonzaga, Marquis of Mantua, a young and valiant prince *condottiere*. With him, as Venetian Proveditors (the Governor-General could not act without the agreement of at least one Proveditor) were Luca Pisano and Marchione Trevisano. The Duke of Milan awarded command of his troops to his favourite, Count Gaiazzo. The count was not well experienced in war, so supporting him, Lodovico appointed Francesco Visconti, head of Milan's Ghibelline faction, as Commissary.

The Confederate war council had considered marching to Rome and stopping the French there. But Pope Alexander requested they remove their advance force after he had decided to leave Rome. Then the Confederates decided to remain in the north. They thought King Charles would sail home from Pisa with his best troops and leave a large garrison in Pisa. When the news came that the French marched out of Pisa, heading toward the Apennines, they thought he was headed toward Alessandria to reinforce Louis of Orleans. Just a little later, word came that the French were marching straight through the mountains, the Confederates decided to trap the French on their route down the valley of the River Taro.

The Italian army planned to confront the French near the village of Fornovo on the banks of the River Taro, where the road came down from the mountains. Arriving in the area before the French, they camped near the east bank of the Taro at Ghiarola. They built a well-entrenched camp with ditches and palisade at a spot where they blocked the road to Parma, believing the French were heading there to join an anti-Milanese faction. The land around the river was broken with scrub forests, small open areas, and low but steep banks along the flow. Beyond the immediate flood plain stretched an open plain. The Marquis Gonzaga was not confident in the strength of his infantry in the face of either French cavalry or Swiss infantry. Furthermore, he had only a few guns and those were not as manoeuvrable as the French. Gonzaga saw his men-at-arms as his best hope. If he could hit the French hard enough on his first charge and they panicked, the Italians would win. He planned on allowing the French column to march along the roadway following the other side of the rocky bed of the Taro from where he would place his ambush, striking the long French flank.

The Italian Confederates' camp was on the right bank of the river, on the opposite side from the main road, north of Fornovo. They laid their guns to bear on the road and fortified the camp parameter. In the camp were some 2,400 men-at-arms, mercenaries of Venice, Milan and different Italian lords; 2,000 light cavalrymen and mounted crossbowmen along with 600 stradioti Venice had raised in their Balkan holdings. Their infantry was a mix of German pikemen and foot crossbowmen, a total of about 10,000 men.

Once the French were spread out on the road past their camp, the artillery would begin the battle. The Italian order of battle was complex with nine separate formations with their commanders. Governor General Gonzaga was supreme commander of the Venetian troops but could only co-ordinate with the Milanese commanders. When Gonzaga ordered deployment, he directed placement, but actual tactical efforts were in the hands of the formations' commanders.

On the far-right wing of the Italian battle line, were units of light cavalry consisting of mounted crossbowmen under Alessio Beccacuto and half the Venetian *stradioti* under Pietro Duodo. They were to cut across the head of the French column and bring it to a halt. The main striking force of the right was the Count of Caiazzo's Milanese troops: 600 men-at-arms supported by 3,000 German pikes. Once the light horse blocked the French column, Caiazzo's men were to hit the French vanguard. In the centre, Marquis Gonzaga marshalled his strongest formations. His retainers and followers, 500 men-at-arms, were his main force with 500 mounted crossbowmen and 4,000 pike infantry supporting his heavy cavalry. The left wing's spearhead was 500 Venetian mercenary men-at-arms under Fortebraccio de Montone. He would attack the French rearguard.

The Italian art of war, developed over generations of strife, had become stylized, emphasizing personal bravery and skill, but neglecting teamwork in combat. Rather than massing all their forces for a co-ordinated attack, the Italians attacked with sequential relays, first one formation, than the second formation in turn. Behind Caiazzo's right-wing force, Annibale Bentivoglio and Galeazzo Palavicino led a formation of Milanese men-at-arms; behind Gonzaga's centre, Antonio of Urbino was with a mix of troops from the Marches and the Papal States; behind the left wing was Gambara of Brescia and Benzone of Crema with their mix of troops. Two companies of men-at-arms and a large number of irregular infantry covered the Italian camp.

When the Italians had approached their chosen site, the mile-wide Taro valley broken by trees and rocky outcroppings was dry. That evening the army encamped, their commanders met and decided on their deployments and methods of attack. Later that night, the heavens opened – rain, thunder and lightning hit the valley. Soon, a swift torrent swept along the Taro riverbed, making the rocks slippery and turned the sand to mud. In the morning, the river remained passable but only with difficulty. It was 6 July 1495.

Chapter 7

The Battle of Fornovo

The French

King Charles and his army marched in a long column through the mountains, carting their artillery and impedimenta along a single track which they improved as they passed. Marshal Gie led the vanguard, marching about a day ahead of the main body. The vanguard arrived at Fornovo where they stopped to wait while the main body brought the artillery down the slopes. Marshal Gie saw that there was a considerable force down the road from Fornovo. The marshal sent a trumpeter to the Italian camp. He proclaimed: 'In King Charles's name, the French army requests free passage for himself and his forces. They will hurt no one. They will pay reasonable amounts for provisions. They only want to return to France.' At the same time, Marshal Gie sent a party of horse to scout the Italian army.

The Italians anticipated this move. They sent a formation of irregular light cavalry, known as *stradioti* to intercept the French scouts. The *stradioti* killed several of the scouts and, in Turkish fashion, they cut off their heads; the rest of the scouts fled back to their camp. As the *stradioti* approached the camp, the French fired falconets and arquebuses. The *stradioti* seized a Swiss under-officer and returned to the Italian camp. Gie worried that the Italians would attack immediately. He sent word to the main body to hurry and began to construct defensible positions. By the next day, the vanguard backed up into the hills and formed a strong position. The Italians meanwhile were waiting for the arrival of more forces.

That same day, the French main body arrived at Fornovo. They immediately began constructing camp but had to remain under arms because the Italian light horse kept annoying them with sudden but elusive attacks. Then, late that night, came the heavy rain. In the thunder and flashes of lighting, the French leadership considered their options: if they couldn't talk their way past the Italian army, then they must have victory. Surrounded by enemies in a hostile forest, a defeat would mean destruction. But the French had met no real resistance in their Italian adventure and held the

Italian fighting men in contempt. The French men-at-arms exalted in the coming fight, joyous at the coming sporting event, a life and death battle. D'Ars, Bayard, and de Ligny's company were to accompany the king. The only possible disappointment they faced was that the Italians might simply give way.

In the morning of 6 July the king discussed their options with his officers and advisors. The storm in the night turned the river from a quiet, sedentary stream into a torrent; not a major obstacle but full of slippery rocks and muddy bottoms. The sky remained cloudy, and further storms threatened. The bad news came that Louis of Orleans was not coming because he was involved with Sforza's forces who pinned him down at Novara. The good news was that the troops were confident and eager. Still, if the French might avoid combat, the march back to France would demonstrate their might. King Charles had the well regarded, experienced Philip de Commines send a letter to the Confederate camp for the Venetian Proveditors. The letter was an appeal for peace and free passage. Previously, Commines had dealt directly with the Venetian Senate and knew the Proveditors. The Confederate commanders considered the communication. The Venetian officials wanted to deal with the French. They all agreed to send the French request to Lodovico, but the preparations to assault the French had already begun.

The French avoided the right bank of the Taro and marched along the river, part of the soldiers on the river bank and part on the brow of the hill along the bank because the left side was too narrow to hold the force as they moved north. The French deployed opposite the Italians. In the north, the van under Marshal de Gie was the strongest formation with 350 men-at-arms, 200 mounted crossbowmen, now ordered to fight on foot, and 300 foot crossbowmen. Supporting them was a great square of Swiss pikemen, 3,000 strong, under the command of Engelbert of Cleves and the Bailli of Dijon. Light cannon protected their right flank. In the centre, under the direct command of Louis de la Tremouille, there were 300 men-at-arms, supported by about 2,000 French infantry. Here was King Charles, surrounded by his guards and de Ligny's company with Bayard. The rear held some 300 men-at-arms and some 2,500 infantry under the Count of Foix. The rear also covered the baggage trains which followed behind the armed formations. The French forces were some 9,000, facing some 14,000 Italians.

Seeing the French deployment almost complete, ever the diplomat Commines went to find King Charles to ask if he could again attempt to find a peaceful solution to the impasse. He found the king mounted on his great charger Savoy. King Charles, in full armour, radiated confidence and good cheer. Charles told Commines that Savonarola told him that God leads him. The armed and armoured men-at-arms around the king, de Ligny, Bayard and others were joyous and excited for battle. The commander Tremouille was more than ready for the attack. He rode back and forth, exchanging a word, a gesture, a laugh. Hilarity spread among the soldiers. King Charles told Commines to try and see if he could make the Italians see reason and allow the French to pass, but as the diplomat and his retinue set off, the valley echoed with the slow booming of cannon. Approaching the enemy camp, de Commines' troops found themselves behind already advancing Venetian men-at-arms and quickly turned around. Racing back to the French side of the Taro, Commines realized he may have already lost some of his followers – the battle had begun.

Combat

The morning had dawned with a stormy clouded sky. When the day progressed, the Italian artillerymen directed their guns at the French van and opened fire. At the same time, the storm came. Wind, rain, thunder and lightning swept the battleground, drenching cannon and men, horse and foot. Alessio Beccacuto pushed his mounted crossbowmen and Venetian *stradioiti* under Pietro Duodo across the Taro through the French light cannon and arquebus fire. The Count of Caiazzo's Milanese troops, 600 men-at-arms supported by 3,000 German pikes, followed.

The three formations of Italian horse had to ford the slippery river bed and muddy banks crowded with tree trunks, roots and shoots and had difficulty threading their way across in tight formation. Beccacuto's mounted crossbowmen drove across the French route, with Duodo's *stradioti* swarming beyond the crossbowmen, headed directly for the French baggage trains. The Italians sent the stradiots to raid the French baggage to distract the French from the attack coming in front. They swarmed over the trains, grabbing horses, armour, loaded mules and sent them back across the river. This was easier than the Italians expected because the baggage was only lightly guarded. Trivulzio had advised the king that any forces used to guard baggage were lost to the effort to win the battle. Of course, people moved their really valuable goods elsewhere.

As the Italian light cavalry crossed to the north of the French, Caiazzo's Milanese horse charged toward Gie's men-at-arms but their formation, disrupted by the river crossing, disintegrated. French men-at-arms charged into the Italian horse, pushing them back across the Taro. The German infantry, in formation and at the ready, charged toward the French forces. Marshal de Gie released his Swiss pikemen who crushed the Germans, slaughtering most of them, dispersing the rest. Rather than let the fight get out of control, the French marshal recalled his troops and put them in battle order to face a new threat. This was Bentivoglio's body of men-at-arms. Bentivoglio was to support Caiazzo, but he and his formation had bolted so Bentivoglio waited for the battle to resolve itself while Gie kept Bentivoglio under observation.

The battle was decided in the centre. King Charles had posted much of his strength in his van: he was sure they would fight well. Mounted on his warhorse, surrounded by his faithful men-at-arms, with his best formations of heavy horse in support, he faced the advancing formations of Italian horse as they began to cross the Taro. Gonzaga led the Italian formation of men-at-arms, his retinue and closely allied troopers. As they crossed the river, the steep river banks, tree roots, trunks and shoots everywhere broke his ranks of horsemen. The supporting Italian foot held back as the horses strove to cross the river, then struggled themselves to get across. Some made it, disordered and broken up, and others failed to cross.

Gonzaga brought some order to his men-at-arms and led them against the French horse. Giving the signal, King Charles charged the enemy at the head of his formations of horse, being among the first to engage the Italian men-at-arms. Intermixed, all the horsemen of the Italian centre struck at the French simultaneously creating a massive melee. After the collision of the horse, the men-at-arms fought with swords, broken lances and poniards. Brave men fell. The horses fought for their riders, kicking, biting and pushing back and forth. The French point, the king at their head, broke into the Italian mass, but the Italian numbers overwhelmed and pushed the French back. An Italian formation, a company calling themselves the Broken Lances, young gentlemen all, hit the French point hard. Gonzaga and his heavy cavalry sought to capture King Charles, which would be a victory for sure. The Italians did seize the Bastard of Bourbon, but Charles held his own, fighting alongside his best horsemen. The king was in trouble. He made a vow to St Dennis and St Martin for salvation while his faithful soldiers covered him.

Having made his vow, Charles restored his strength and launched back into the fray. That the king was in danger became clear to other French formations of men-at-arms. They charged forward, smashing into the flank of the Italians. An Italian commander, Ridolfo Gonzaga, uncle of the Marque, tried to rally his men. He lifted the visor of his helmet to call for order when a Frenchmen struck him in the face with a dagger. Ridolfo fell from his horse into the milling mass of French and Italian men-at-arms and was trampled. The Italians' cohesion broke; the line of horsemen turned and fled the field, casting away their beautifully painted lances. With the horsemen giving away, their infantry followed, soon accompanied by the whole of the Italian centre, back across the Taro River and down the road to Parma.

King Charles, exhausted by his efforts, let his men-at-arms pursue the Italians. As they rode away, he was left alone with only a gentleman of the bedchamber, Anthony des Aubus, as a companion. A small troop of Italian horse, avoiding the French advance, came upon the king and his companion alone. They saw easy plunder and attacked. Charles had caught his breath. On his magnificent warhorse, Savoy, he danced around his attackers, utterly confounding them. Very soon, the commotion attracting his soldiers' attention, his men-at-arm drove off the Italians.

The Italian left, composed of Venetian horse under Fortebraccio, briskly moved against the French rear under the Count of Foix. The two sides clashed in a melee but nowhere near as intense as the fight in the centre. In the raging storm, when the Italian centre collapsed and fled the field, Fortebaccio's formation turned and followed the centre, closely followed by their support. In the Italian right, the same thing happened when the soldiers saw the panic in their centre and left. When the battlefront broke, the *stradioti* plundering the baggage grabbed what goods they could and bolted back to the Italian camp.

The Marquise of Gonzaga and his following would rather risk their lives rather than honour. Many of their friends were dead or wounded in the fight. They had to withdraw across the river in the face of the French fury. King Charles urged his men forward, killing and overthrowing Italian horsemen, slaughtering their infantry. They took no prisoners nor stripped the dead. The king and the men repeatedly yelled, 'Guignegate! Guignegate!' (This referred to a village in Picardy near Terouanne where the French men-at-arms won a battle but then lost it because they broke ranks to plunder). Once the Italians withdrew across the Taro, King Charles called his commanders together. They could see masses of people milling about the Italian camp and moving north on the Parma road. The king wanted to attack and smash the Italian forces, but Trivulzio and Francesco Secco both told the king that the Italians were broken and their men and carts fleeing down the road. They continued, the river was still rising and both men and animals were wet, cold, and tired.

When the Marquis de Gonzaga returned to his camp, he found panic and disorder. Each person, soldier or commoner, seemed to be working to save himself and his baggage. As soon as he entered the camp, he demanded the soldiers return to order. Other commanders announced that the French were more disheartened than themselves. Both sides claimed victory, but in less than an hour, the French had lost some 200 men, and the Italians some 3,000, including 300 men-at-arms. The amount of bloodshed shocked the Italians while the rain continued to fall.

Later that Day

The battle which had lasted but an hour or so had ended and the results elated King Charles and his companions. They surveyed the bloody banks of the swirling river in the battle's aftermath; friends and relatives collected the few bodies of the dead and properly prepared them for their return to France. Practised surgeons and medically skilled soldiers tended to the many wounded with stitching, bandages and various healing compresses. While the men-at-arms did not recover booty from the dead while the fighting lasted, now came the time for profit. Hundreds of weapons, trappings and suits of armour, not to mention loose horses were there for the collecting. Many beautifully wrought lances, gaily coloured, if too light for French taste, were there for the taking. Any of the *stradioti* who made an appearance soon discovered their error.

The French had repelled the Confederate army, opened their road north and still had their plunder and cannon. King Charles saw only the victory. There was no reason why more French nobles and soldiers need to die facing this fancy horde of overdressed cowards. The king called together his paladins, awarding gifts for outstanding fighting. Among those honoured was the Chevalier Bayard, whom the king had known for years. He had accompanied Charles in that first charge of the centre, as part of de Ligny's company. He had two horses killed under him during battle, finally fighting on foot. King Charles awarded him 500 crowns and took possession of an Italian banner which Bayard had wrested from a mounted formation when he was fighting on foot. (A crown was France's version of the Venetian ducat and the Florentine Florin but with a lower weight of gold.)

Across the swift flooded river, Francisco Gonzaga marshalled his troops back into battle order. The commanders of the Confederate army feared that the French would charge their camp's fortifications. In the rain, the ability of the artillery to fire was questionable. Soldiers and camp followers struggled to put the earth ramparts into battle condition. Word came forth from the high command: the French were more hurt and disorganized than they were. The Marquis Francisco Gonzaga even proclaimed a victory, a position he maintained for the rest of his life. He argued that if they had killed or captured King Charles, the whole French expedition would have collapsed. And, even though this was not achieved, still the French retreated from the position. Nevertheless, all of the participants on the Italian side understood just how shocking and disruptive had been the French fury.

The Following Days

That night, the French marshalled their forces, made the artillery ready and organized the wagon trains. Before dawn, the army pulled out, heading down the high road to Piacenza. Since they did not sound trumpet fanfares when they broke camp, Gonzaga later claimed the French sneaked away and thus conceded defeat. Of course, striking tents, loading wagons, getting men and horses ready for the march is not done quietly, so if the Confederates didn't know that the French were leaving, they weren't keeping an eye on them. After all, what else were the French going to do?

The Confederates stayed in their camp all that day, binding their wounds, preparing their dead. The high river and swift current appeared too much for their army to overcome, so the commanders said. At sunset, Count Gaiazzo took 200 heavy horse, crossed the river and galloped after the French on the road to Piacenza. Late at night, they found the French camped for the night. The Italians made their presence known, harassing the French that night and the next day. But the French had recovered from the battle and were in good order. The young French men-at-arms enjoyed sparring with Gaiazzo's men. Local Guelphs received Trivulzio and readily sold the French whatever they needed. The rest of the Confederate forces finally followed Gaiazzo, but they avoided any combat. The Venetian Proveditors refused to allow any more fighting in the name of the Serene Republic.

At the end of the second day, the French reached Piacenza on the Po River. Just to the west of Piacenza, the tributary river Trebbia flowed north into the Po. The French established their main camp on the west bank of the Trebbia. Between the east bank of the Trebbia and the town of Piacenza, a distance of a couple of miles, the French posted 200 men-at-arms, a strong force of Swiss infantry and the heavy artillery to secure their camp. That night, the rains came again, causing the Trebbia to rise, cutting communications between the two parts of the French forces, but the Confederates did not attack as they might have done. Instead, Count Gaiazzio marched into Piacenza to secure the town.

King Charles had had enough of wandering around northern Italy. The following day, he pulled his forces across the Trebbia, concentrating his army on the west side of the river. He decided to press the march forward, to Asti. As he marched off, Count Gaiazzo brought 500 German foot from Piacenza to harass Charles's forces. But, again the Venetian Proveditors refused to allow their men-at-arms to attack the French. When the French reached Vercelli, they found a newly arrived large body of Swiss infantry who joined them. Lodovico, besieging Louis of Orleans in Novara, saw his advantage in denying the French supplies. He expected Charles and his army to head for Asti and prepared accordingly.

Lodovico detached a formation of heavy horse and 2,000 infantry to sweep the country between Charles's army and Asti. They removed all supplies, either having them transported into secure fortifications or destroying them. King Charles's supplies became very short. The French continued to march toward Alessandria and Lodovico's forces concentrated on clearing out supplies on that route. But after King Charles reached a certain point, he turned and marched towards the mountains and, with his funds still ample, supplies. In eight days he and his force reached Asti. King Charles entered the town as the victor. He encamped his army, planning to relieve Louis of Orleans in Novara and settle with the north Italian powers.

When the French entered Asti, Gonzaga had reached the area of Novara about the middle of July. The troops which Charles had dispatched toward Genoa came back to him. They were not able to break Milan's hold on the port. The Milanese were pressing the siege of Novara. The news came to Bayard that his cousin Germane, Barachim Alleman, and his uncle, Charles Alleman, were killed there. King Charles had to make decisions.

Chapter 8

King Charles's Italian Adventure Ends

Battle at Novara

After King Charles reached Asti, there remained the problem of Louis of Orleans, still besieged in Novara. Duke Louis had sent messages, telling Charles that without reinforcements, he would need to surrender. After Louis had seized Novara, the Venetians sent some troops to support Lodovico. The main Milanese force had reached Novara on 1 July. They set up a base at Lumellogno where they could cut Novara off from supplies and waited for the Confederate army coming from Fornovo. The Confederate force arrived on 17 July, pushed away the outlying French forces and invested Novara. Louis had expected easy pickings but now found himself besieged by Gonzaga, Marquis of Mantua. The French were in trouble. Novara's fortifications were old and with very few cannons. The French garrison of 8,000 men was outnumbered by four to one. Food was short and dysentery common. The problem worsened when the Confederates diverted the canals which ran near the town. The water-flow turned the mill wheels that made flour; without water they had to make flour with pestle and mortar. Louis enforced rationing for the town population and garrison, but food was significantly short of what was needed.

Within a month, the besieged were in distress. The muddy streets were full of dead and dying men. Duke Louis was ill but still rode around Novara and stood night duty like all of the soldiers. He ate only iron rations, sending what food he could to the hospital. He hoped Charles would come soon. The besiegers were at an advantage but their problem was that they could not make a decision on how to implement their superiority. Lodovico wanted to let famine break Novara but since the town was his, he wanted as little damage as possible. The Venetians, who were paying the Confederate army, were spending more than 100,000 ducats a month and their camp was exposed on three sides to danger: from Asti, Vercelli and Novara. Also, the sickness that spread inside Novara hit the besiegers. The German pikemen were unruly and the *stradioti* plundered at will. The Venetians wanted to end the siege as soon as possible.

In early August, the French managed to bring four carts of corn and twenty-eight cattle into Novara. The Venetians demanded the investment tightened up and the town assaulted. On 3 August Lodovico arrived at the Confederate camp accompanied by representatives of Spain, Naples and Venice. An assault came on 15 August, capturing and burning some suburbs. On 26 August the Confederates learned that a relief was coming, 1,500 troops under Coligny and La Palice. The Italians ambushed and repelled the French, killing many and capturing the supply train. Ten days later, the Confederates took the Monastery of Saint Francesco, closing one of the main gates to Novara. The next day, Louis' forces withdrew from all their extramural positions. The fight for Novara reached stalemate.

For three more months from July, August and into September, neither the French nor the Italians were able to achieve a decision. Charles waited for more money and reinforcements to overwhelm Lodovico and the Duke of Milan did not want to risk an attack. Louis of Orleans remained in Novara, almost out of provisions, anticipating that King Charles would come and relieve him. Not until September did large numbers of Swiss infantry arrive. By then, more wet weather dampened Charles's ardour and he saw the coming of winter. He decided the time had come to strike a settlement with Lodovico. If the war was stretching French resources, surely Lodovico felt the same pressure.

Already, on 26 August, King Charles had signed a treaty with the Florentines' envoys in Turin. Charles received a loan of 70,000 florins and 250 Florentine lances paid by Florence, to support the French in Naples. In return, he again promised to return the Florentine fortresses he occupied. Louis of Orleans saw that he was going to get no help from King Charles. He slipped out of Novara on 22 September. Three days later the French garrison surrendered and were accorded the honours of war. The survivors staggered out, only some 5,000 from the original 10,000. Most were severely weakened, only some 500 or so were able to bear arms. Even worse than this defeat, from Louis' point of view was the knowledge that King Charles had no interest in pressing Louis' claim to the coronet of Milan. Without Charles's support, Louis could do nothing.

Louis was right. King Charles made peace with Lodovico by promising to withdraw and drop any claim to Milan. In return, Lodovico promised to support Charles's claim to Naples and allow the French to use the port of Genoa for shipping supplies to Naples. The French and Milanese signed the agreement at Vercelli to the strong complaints of the Venetians and Spanish. With the making of peace, King Charles and his soldiers marched toward France and home. Queen Anne and his sister, the Duchess of Bourbon, greeted him when he arrived at Lyons. The court moved on to Paris where Charles fulfilled his vow made on the field of Fornovo to St Denis and St Martin. After the celebration, King Charles the Victorious began a tour of his kingdom.

The Collapse of Charles's Kingdom of Naples

When he pulled out of Naples Charles took all the money he could raise during his stay, as well as the best troops and all the artillery. He left Gilbert de Montpensier as viceroy. Commines described the viceroy as a man of integrity but of little prudence or energy. Stuart d'Aubigny was constable and responsible for Calabria facing Sicily. They had no money and little prospect of raising large amounts. The French had plundered well and there was very little left. The French had managed to alienate even the old Angevin faction who joined with many other nobles to open communications with Ferrandino in Sicily. According to secret reports, the Neapolitans would prefer to have a government of the Turks or the devil to the French.

The Spanish and Venetians knew the French king was pulling out of Naples and was going to march north. Rather than worry about Lodovico's problems with the French marching north, Ferdinand the Catholic decided to push the French out of the Southern Kingdom. Ferdinand had already provided sanctuary for former King Alphonso and King Ferrandino in his kingdom of Sicily. His agents had long dealt with the Venetians, putting no obstacle in their paths to occupy Naples' Adriatic ports. Ferrandino supported by Spanish troops and Venetian ships still held some ports, Brindisi, Gallipoli and Ortanto among others. Soon, a Venetian fleet of twenty-four galleys came from Corfu.

Just a few days after King Charles marched out of Naples on 24 May 1495, Spanish troops crossed from Sicily to Calabria. Besides soldiers, Ferdinand sent his talented commander, Gonzalo de Córdoba. This commander was a younger son of a Castilian noble who devoted himself to Isabella of Castile in 1468. He fought for Isabella in the three-sided civil war under the direction of Alonso de Cárdenas, Grand Master of the Order of Santiago. Then followed the ten-year war with Granada in which Gonzalo excelled in this war of ambushes, sieges and skirmishes. Isabella was well pleased with her commander, calling him the Great Captain. King Ferdinand assured King Ferrandino that Gonzalo and his troops would put Naples back in his hands. In return, Ferrandino surrendered to Ferdinand some towns in Calabria, including Reggio. Having landed at Reggio, the Spanish troops joined with Ferrandino on 26 May, bringing a force of 600 light horse and 5,000 foot. Many Calabrians welcomed Ferrandino's return, coming to join his small army. From Reggio, the force marched a short distance north along the coast into the hills, to the small town of Seminara where they planned to set up camp. The town admitted them without resistance.

The French constable, d'Aubigny, was kept informed about the Aragonese moves. Quietly, the French began concentrating in Calabria. The Aragonese were intent on establishing a secure base. They sent out neither scouts nor spies. The French worked hard at not alerting them. The Swiss garrisons and local French lords marched to d'Aubigny. They collected 100 men-at-arms and 1,200 Swiss. Suddenly, on 21 June Ferrandino and Gonzalo saw the French coming towards Seminara through the valley below the town. Commander Gonzalo recommended caution, knowing that his light horse could not face the French men-at-arms nor would the local militia stand up to the Swiss. Ferrandino scoffed, quoting 'Fortune favours the bold'. They drew up their army along a small stream in the valley.

The Spanish light horse were veterans of the war for Granada. They were very good fighters, but their tactics followed those of the Moors of Spain and North Africa. They struck, withdrew, turned and struck again. They could not, and had no intention of, meeting fully armoured men-at-arms in close combat. But the Italian militia knew nothing of these tactics. When the French heavy cavalry crossed the small stream, their formation became somewhat disordered. The light horse manoeuvred around and, in formation, hit the French horse hard. They disrupted French ranks, but then they turned and withdrew to reform.

The Calabrian militia saw the Spanish cavalry withdraw, thought they were defeated and fled the field. The Spanish infantry found themselves deserted and they quickly retreated to Seminara. The Swiss infantry swept away any troops who intended to face the oncoming French. King Ferrandino rode his horse into the mass of retreating foot, trying to stop the rout but his horse was killed and he found himself on foot facing the onrushing enemy. A former page and friend of his, Giovanni di Capua, rode up and gave Ferrandino his horse and faced the French to allow him to escape. The French cut down di Capua.

The Spanish commander Gonzalo withdrew his command to Reggio where he set up camp. Rather than try to attack the French directly, he began developing a different method of confrontation. His forces would not successfully face the French in large engagements, so Gonzalo began developing a tactical system of small engagements, 'little war', that is, guerrilla combat. Using small units in a hit and run tactic, de Cordova intended to grind down the French until they left.

King Ferrandino fled to Palma and set out on a boat to Messina. Despite defeat in Calabria, his popularity remained strong in Naples. With the aid of the Spanish and Venetians, he soon commanded a sixty-ship fleet, supported by twenty supply boats, with a hundred or so men-at-arms and a strong-box with a hundred ducats. He sailed toward Naples. Captain Ricajenso, an admiral of great experience, directed the fleet which sailed along the Italian coast toward Naples. Each city the fleet passed, one after another, raised Ferrandino's flag. As the fleet sailed slowly up the coast, Ferrandino's supporters in Naples attempted an insurrection, thinking they were going to catch the French unaware, but finding the garrison at arms occupying important spots, the uprising faded away. The fleet stayed near the bay of Naples for three days waiting to see Ferrandino's flags breaking out. Seeing nothing, they sailed for Ischia. A small boat came to Ferrandino's fleet carrying representatives from Naples' underground. They begged the king to land as soon as possible. The French administration would soon crack down on Ferrandino's faction in the city. They promised they would support him if he came.

Ferrandino and his fleet sailed back to Naples on 6 July 1495, the day of the Battle of Fornovo. The ships approached the shore at Madalena, outside the walls of the city. The French viceroy, Count of Montpensier, had enough information to know that Ferrandino was coming and decided to hit the Aragonese as soon as possible because if Ferrandino did successfully land, the Aragonese faction would seize Naples and his forces could do little. Montpensier pulled almost all the French troops out of Naples to oppose the landing. The Aragonese faction in the city was amazed that the French left the city and resolved to seize the opportunity. They flew to arms, rang the bells and took over the city gates. Lining the walls, people cried out, 'Ferrandino!' The faction in the city signalled the fleet by hoisting a white sheet.

The French found themselves locked out of the city. They were between a hostile city and the fire of the royal fleet. Unable to face the arrows and shot from the fleet, Montpensier marched his soldiers along the wall and over a high and difficult height to reach the gate near the New Castle. As the French marched away, Ferrandino rode into Naples on horseback with his armed followers parading along with him. Ladies threw flowers and sweet-scented water, nobles ran out into the streets welcoming the royal party and embracing their king. All the while, Neapolitans worked on improving the city's defences.

Ferrandino's troops and young nobles in the city, under the command of the Marquis of Pescara, rushed toward the New Castle. They erected barricades in streets facing the piazza in front of the castle. Montpensier deployed his men-at-arms in the piazza and attacked into the city. As the French began to force their way in, Neapolitans shot at them with crossbows and arquebuses causing heavy casualties. At sunset, Montpensier withdrew his forces into New Castle. The French had to leave their horses in the piazza, about 2,000 of them. In the next few days, the French artillery in the castle swept the piazza and nearby buildings. Soldiers sallied out to surprise the Neapolitans unexpectedly. They secured the New Castle and settled down to endure a long siege.

Just after Ferrandino secured Naples, Prospero and Fabrizio Colonna rode into the city with their retinues. They left their French employers because, they said, they found Virginio Orsini and Count Pitigliano insufferable. In reality, many speculated that the Colonna had received rich estates from the French and with a timely change of sides, they might keep them. With Ferrandino establishing his rule in the kingdom, Capua, Aversa, Mondragon and other towns declared for him. Gaeta took up arms for the king, but the French garrison crushed the uprising and pillaged the town.

The French remained in control of both the New Castle and Egg Castle. The two castles are about a mile apart and the French tied them together, easily done since both fortifications sat on the bay. The French also constructed a line of strongpoints protecting a land route from one to the other castle, from the Tower of St Vincent of Egg Castle up to the Pizzifalcone hillock, down to the Royal Gardens and the Croce monastery, over to New Castle. The French fleet huddled under the castles comprised four light galleys, a small galliot and a galleon. Montpensier was ready for an extended siege, hoping to hold out until a French relief force came.

Ferrandino wanted the French to leave the two castles. He had siege lines built that blockaded the French strongpoints and the Spanish fleet patrolled the bay, cutting supplies. The Aragonese began pushing against the French positions: they fortified the hippodrome, took part of the Pizzifalcone hillock but not the French-occupied fort on top. From the heights, Ferrandino attacked the Croce monastery. French artillery repelled the attackers. The Marquis of Pescara suggested to Ferrandino that they could gain the monastery by a stratagem. Pescara kept communication open with his former slave who now lived in the Croce monastery. Often, the marquis came to the monastery's wall to talk with this man, who was a Moor. He fixed a time with the Moor for when he would bring men into the monastery to open a gate for Ferrandino's troops. At night the marquis and his men placed a ladder on the wall. Pescara mounted and as he was about to go over the wall, an arrow pierced his throat, killing him on the spot.

The French Attempt to Save their Kingdom

King Charles was very concerned about his men in Naples. When he had reached Asti, he ordered a relief force to sail to Naples. Commander d'Arban organized a fleet carrying 2,000 Gascon and Swiss infantry along with supplies for the castles. As the fleet sailed toward Naples, the Spanish fleet of thirty ships and two large Genoese ships met them. The French fleet turned and sailed back north. The Spanish gave chase and captured Gascon ships, but the French fleet made port in Livorno. Once landed, most of the troops left the ship, made it to Pisa and found other employment.

After the failure of the relief operation and waiting three months, Montpensier agreed to a treaty with Ferrandino on 4 October: the castles would surrender if not relieved in two months; the French could then march out with their arms and property and would have free passage out of the Kingdom of Naples. To enforce the treaty, Montpensier delivered four hostages. Cut off from communication with the French forces remaining in the kingdom, Montpensier had no information about d'Aubigny's efforts to succour him, but d'Aubigny knew of Montpensier's plight. Deciding to send a force to Naples, he collected all available troops, containing Gonzalo's offensive with a minimum of soldiers. He put the troops under the command of an energetic young officer, Precy. In September, Precy marched his troops from the Basilicate north to relieve Montpensier.

Messengers sent to tell the besieged in Naples that help was on the way were all captured by the Aragonese. Ferrandino hastily drew together a large but mostly untrained army and sent them south to contest the French advance. At Eboli, twenty miles or so from Salerno, Precy found himself facing some 12,000 Aragonese troopers while he had only 3,000 Swiss infantry and some men-at-arms and most of those were local supporters of the Angevins. On 2 October, Precy advanced across the small stream which separated the forces. The Aragonese commanders, confident in their numbers, spread their troops in a wide arc, planning to capture the whole of the French formation. Again, French military superiority showed.

The Swiss smashed through the Aragonese line and the men-at-arms chewed them up. Messengers sent to announce the victory to Montpensier were again all captured.

Precy knew of Montpensier's agreement with Ferrandino; he endeavoured to avoid that eventuality. But, unfortunately for the French, as they marched north from Eboli, they found another Aragonese army facing them at Sarno. These were the practised, experienced troops of the Colonna, with Prospero at their head. Chasing after local militia with 3,000 men was one thing, trying to cross swords with the Colonnas' tough men was quite another. On 10 October Precy turned about and withdrew back south, leaving supplies, cattle and some cannon for Prospero to collect while he retreated. The French had lost Naples.

Ferrandino, thinking the war was almost over, sent the Spanish fleet to sea. But Montpensier still had his small fleet. Surreptitiously he loaded booty, guns and 2,500 troops on board and sailed away to the French base at Salerno. He left 300 men to hold each castle. Ferrandino was enraged at what he saw as bad faith: Montpensier broke his pledged word by simply leaving without surrendering the castles. He threw the hostages into unpleasant confinement. The New Castle eventually offered to surrender if the hostages were released and the garrison was allowed to depart. On 8 December they left the New Castle. Finally, Egg Castle surrendered on 17 February 1496.

With the removal of the last French hold on the city of Naples, 'the standard of Charles VIII was thrown down as easily as it had been raised'. All the important towns quickly recognized King Ferrandino. The French retained only footholds here and there. Within a year of his conquest, Charles had lost the Kingdom of Naples. A desultory war continued as the French under Montpensier tried to make up for lack of resources by persistence. As June passed into August the French forces, starved of money and success, collapsed. Montpensier refused to leave his men and died of want and disease with them.

Disease stalked both sides; Ferrandino died on 7 September 1496. His uncle, Federigo, succeeded to the throne. Neapolitan troops, Spanish leadership and ships, and Venetian forces slowly cleared out the last of the French. On 18 January, Taranto surrendered, ending all French occupation of the Kingdom of Naples.

Chapter 9

King Louis XII

C harles's tour of his kingdom displayed his great success but as the winter came, so did bad news. In December 1495, the king's three-year-old son, Charles Orlando, died of measles. When Charles had married Anne of Brittany in 1491, she was about 15 and very unhappy with the forced marriage. Soon, however, she became pregnant and Charles's unwavering attention and concern for her wellbeing won for him her affections. The child was named after Charles and the great hero Roland at the insistence of Anne's family. The child was beloved by his parents and his death was devastating to both. Charles's spiritual advisor told him to grieve privately so he might support his queen. She was in the throes of despair and there was even fear for her life, but she slowly recovered.

The politics of the matter were not good. Now Louis of Orleans was heir apparent. Soon, the death of Charles of Angoulême left his son, Francis, as heir after Louis. Charles of Angoulême named Louis of Orleans as guardian of his children but Francis's mother, the 19-year-old Louise of Savoy, did not trust Louis and disliked him. She objected to his supervision of her son and daughter so vociferously that the issue came before the Royal Council. By their decision, Louis became honorary guardian, while the actual guardian remained Louise. Some, including Louise of Savoy, had probably seen the complex pattern of death churning around Louis' ambitions.

Charles still hoped for an heir. Queen Anne was again delivered of a son, which the couple named Charles, but the infant died after five weeks. A little later the Queen had a stillbirth. In 1498 King Charles was now 28 and more mature. The loss of children and his personal relations with those close to him led him to examine and change his life, becoming a more conscientious ruler and a better person. He began to reform the royal administration.

One of Charles's efforts was to reform Louis, Duke of Orleans. In 1496 Charles intended to invade Italy again to save his Kingdom of Naples. Louis collected a large force at Lyons for the invasion. He requested a meeting of the Royal Council to plan the campaign. There, Louis said that he would only go to Italy with his forces if King Charles ordered him and if he could attack Lodovico. King Charles denied his requests, although he did say he would never order someone to go to war if he did not want to go. Because of this, Charles had to postpone a major expedition even though his hold on Naples was crumbling. Louis had developed a powerful dislike for Charles; nevertheless, he still had to deal with the king at the many social events of the aristocracy. Especially because Louis and Charles were former carousing companions, Charles enjoyed chiding Louis about the way he treated his wife, who was Charles's sister. Louis' problematic marriage was known to all. Louis XI had compelled Louis of Orleans to wed his deformed daughter, to provide for her and to make sure Louis of Orleans would not have an heir.

One of the motivations driving Louis' constant rebellions was to free himself from the web his father-in-law had woven around him. His crippled wife, Jeanne, was pleasant and forgiving but Louis saw himself locked out of power, hindered in his claim to the coronet of Milan and deprived of an heir. At court, Charles expected Louis to bring his wife to dinners, balls and tournaments. Louis tired of wandering around the court, followed closely by Charles's deformed sister. To escape the royal court, he assumed his duties as royal governor of Normandy. Louis appointed his friend, Archbishop George d'Amboise, as his lieutenant general. Soon, royal lawyers began questioning Louis' administration of Normandy and started an investigation of d'Amboise. The archbishop initially managed to convince the investigators that there was nothing amiss, but the investigations dragged on and on.

In April 1498 Louis and Archbishop d'Amboise were in residence at Louis' Chateau of Blois. They were expecting royal officers to come and arrest both of them soon. Suddenly, a royal official rode into the courtyard. Louis' men scattered, expecting an arrest warrant for the Duke of Orleans. Louis strode up to the official, who gasped out, 'Sire, the king is dead! Long live the king!'

The Death of King Charles VIII

The king died on 7 April 1498. After Charles had finished his tour of the kingdom, he went on to Lyons to prepare his new Italian expedition. In early spring 1498 the court moved to the royal chateau of Amboise. On 7 April, Palm Sunday eve, at midday, he took his queen by the hand and led her out of her chambers, to a place on the grounds she had never been, a tennis court set up in the dry moat. To get there they passed through an old neglected gallery. On entering, it is remarked, that the king hit his forehead against a lintel. Charles was not knocked unconscious nor inconvenienced for long; then he watched the matches for some time and talked with his gentlemen and others. Suddenly, he fell backwards and lost the ability to speak. This happened about two in the afternoon. They put the king on a crude pallet of straw in the dry moat, near the tennis courts. There he stayed while people came and went. A couple of times the king spoke, calling upon the Virgin and saints to assist him. At eleven that night, nine hours later, he cried out again and then died.

As the years went on, the story was told of how the big-headed dumb king hit his head on a stone lintel and then had some sort of brain haemorrhage which killed him. He did it to himself! But in most cases, these are not the symptoms of a brain haemorrhage. The swift onset of the malady is curious. Even more interesting is the nine hours of waiting for something to happen. That the collapse might be from a stroke is possible, but there are other more probable causes of Charles's demise. Beginning about 1450, a science of assassination started to spread in Italy and moved north. Rather than the swift slash with a sword or an arrow in the dark, poisons became the weapon of choice. The increased interest in the natural world generated a wide pharmacopeia of poisons. All sorts of 'preferred' compounds became available to the sophisticated assassin: hemlock, belladonna, foxglove, arsenic and strychnine. The Borgia are credited with the effective use of cantarella (whatever that was). The elaborate clothing and bulky jewellery provided easy delivery methods.

Indeed, poison was suggested as a cause of Charles's death. But the principal person of interest was, by this death, now King of France. The suspicion is obvious: just before he visited the tennis game, someone gave Charles an orange. It had come from Italy and had a strong, unusual taste and smell. The specific symptoms that Charles experienced are consistent with strychnine poisoning. This would explain the sudden collapse and then the nine hours that Charles lay dying. The unusual part of the account of Charles's death is the fact that he was left on the ground in or near the moat where he had fallen.

Why, as was usual then and now, was he not carried into the castle and placed in a more comfortable place? If someone had injected strychnine into the orange, then muscle spasms, arching and breathing problems would follow Charles's collapse on the ground. He would writhe constantly. Knowledgeable people would understand what they were seeing but to do anything about it would only expose them to similar fates. So, in the long run, it was better to let Charles stay where he was with a few witnesses rather than bring him into the castle where stories would spread if this speculation is right. No wonder that Louis and the Archbishop d' Amboise expected an arrest; that would mean that their plot had failed and was detected. But, of course, if there was such a plot, it did not fail.

King Louis XII of France

Charles VIII's death shocked the court and kingdom. With him died the direct Valois line which had ruled France since 1328. Louis was a cousin, a member of the cadet branch of Valois. The poison rumours quickly spread and, beyond Louis of Orleans, suspicions pointed to Lodovico, Duke of Milan or the Venetians. But everyone knew that the person of interest was Louis. Machiavelli pointed out that Louis was disqualified from being king because of his dereliction and defection from the royal government. However, Louis' claim was clear: next in line was Francis of Angoulême, three years old, and after him, Charles of Bourbon, nine years old. There was no alternative. As Commines said, 'Everyone ran to the Duke of Orleans.'

Despite the discussion, on 16 April, the French court proclaimed the Duke of Orleans, 'Louis XII, by the grace of God, King of France, Sicily and Jerusalem and Duke of Milan.' The new king received the crown at Reims on 27 May 1498. Louis was 35 years old when he became king. His personal experiences were very different from the cloistered and pampered prince who usually ascended thrones. Harsh imprisonment, failed efforts, commander of armies, fleets and besieged castles, allowed Louis a wide experience of dealing with all sorts of people. He had a free and easy manner with everyone. The great nobles made fun of Louis' tendencies toward 'commonness', but he did not care. Tall and lean, he liked boiled beef and wine. His face was weather beaten from much outdoor activity, particularly hunting. He suffered bouts of malaria.

When it came to management, Louis was well grounded. He understood money, spending when necessary, cutting expenditure when possible. Moreover, Louis spoke directly and clearly. He extended trust rather than suspicion in his dealings. When Ferdinand the Catholic heard that Louis complained about two times when Ferdinand had lied to him, he laughed and said he had lied to Louis at least ten times. What this tells us is that Louis knew how to handle difficult people. Of his early actions, none was better than when he forgave the officers of state and army, all of whom had defeated his armies, chased him down at one time or another, and confined him in custody, saying, 'It is not honourable for the King of France to avenge the quarrels of the Duke of Orleans.'

Louis XII was an excellent administrator and popular king. He balanced royal resources and so was able to raise revenues and lower taxes at the same time. His ambition, however, remained to gain the coronet of Milan. He held the Sforza as usurpers and traced his claim to his grandmother, Valentine, daughter of Duke Gian Galeazzo Visconti (reign 1395–1402). King Louis looked forward to a new Italian campaign, saying, 'We've got the men, and we've got the money too.'

Affairs in Italy at Louis' accession: The Problem of Pisa

After King Charles left Italy, others saw opportunity in the chaos that the French created. Ferdinand the Catholic, the Spanish sovereign, had many connections in Italy. He dealt with Lodovico, supporting Milan against the French; he aided the Venetians in their quest for bases in southern Italy, and he expected the assistance of the Spanish Borgia pope. He saw profit from fishing in the pond of Italian troubles. Also, despite Spanish diplomatic recognition of Federigo as king of Naples, he let it be known that he had a strong claim on the crown of Naples by the fact that his uncle, Alfonso I of Naples, was also Alfonso V of Aragon. And many important people in Naples preferred Ferdinand as king. The Spanish sovereign found his claim particularly useful in negotiations with the French. Some ideas floated around, such as partitioning Naples between the French and Spanish or trading French claims on Naples to Spain in return for Spanish Navarre going to France. Nothing ever came of these ideas, but they kept the pot stirred.

Emperor Maximilian saw an opportunity to reinforce imperial power in Northern Italy. He had struggled for years with the imperial princes over money and prestige. If he could prevail in Italy, he might improve his power in Germany. Lodovico wanted investment as Duke of Milan, and he paid Maximilian well for the title. Then the new Duke of Milan promised support for imperial policy if Maximilian came to Italy. Of course, should Maximilian come, the French would need to deal with him as well as Lodovico. Maximilian was well aware that the imperial princes were not interested in any Italian adventure. Their cold response to his speeches before the Reichstag demonstrated that. So, he raised his vassals and personal following and came to Italy. He was led to believe the both the Milanese and the Venetians would raise men and funds for his expedition, but this did not happen. Rather Lodovico told him to defend western Milan by convincing the Italian rulers allied with France to withdraw from the French and join the Italian allies. Maximilian knew enough about the different powers to understand that this was an empty errand. Instead, he turned to the Pisa-Florence imbroglio.

The war between Pisa and Florence dragged on year after year. In the late 1490s, the wrangle had become the focus of attention in Italy. *Condottieri* captains came and went, collecting payment from all sides. Some blamed the continuing war on the mercenaries who refused to fight, but were simply extending the difficulties to give themselves employment. Still, the Pisans hated the Florentines and refused to surrender their city and liberties. Their passion impressed many of Florence's leaders, but The Republic would not let Pisa go. Maximilian decided if he could resolve this conundrum then he would advance imperial authority in Italy.

Both Milan and Venice were interested in holding Pisa, hoping to weaken Florence. The Pisans would accept either power as overlord, but they refused Lodovico's terms and the Venetians saw Pisa as too far away to permanently defend. Maximilian went to Pisa, bringing forces by land and sea, reinforcing Milanese and Venetian troops defending the city. Pisa's allies began to besiege the Florentine held port of Livorno. The French intervened, their fleet landing reinforcements and food. After the Genoese fleet succumbed to a storm, Maximilian withdrew and returned to Germany in December 1496.

Lodovico withdrew his troops from Pisa when Maximilian left. However, the Florentines were unable to attack with full force. Civil upheaval involving Savonarola and struggles for a new constitution drained their energies. In 1497 Spain and France signed a six months truce which included Pisa as an adherent of Spain. When the truce expired, the Venetians brought strong reinforcements to Pisa. The following summer the Florentines executed Savonarola and established a new constitution. They prepared to renew the war by appointing the *condottiere*, Paolo Vitelli, as captain general. To counter the Florentines, the Venetians sent Niccolo Orsini with strong forces to the Casentino valley in the hills. They took Bibbiena, helped by Medici followers in the town. Paolo Vitelli and his brother, Vitellozzo, pushed their forces into positions blocking supply lines to the Venetian forces.

The Venetians were paying a heavy price for their involvement with Pisa. Concerned with a rising Turkish threat and the new French king's plans to take Milan, the Venetians accepted Ercole d'Este's offer for arbitration. After the Venetians withdrew their troops, the Pisans refused to accept the suzerainty offered to Florence because they did not trust the Florentines. Now Pisa stood alone. The Florentines ordered Paolo Vitelli to take the city. The *condottieri* invested Pisa and began an artillery attack against the walls. In August, the guns blew open a breach, but Paolo Vitelli wanted to make more breaches so he would lose fewer soldiers. His Florentine employers were increasingly impatient. After some days, Vitelli selected a specific day for the assault. Came the day, there was no assault; it seems Vitelli and all his soldiers were sick. He lifted the siege in early September which enraged the Florentines. They believed Vitelli had taken bribes from the Pisans. They ordered him arrested, taken to Florence, tortured and executed. Florentine efforts to recover Pisa were at an end for the time being.

Louis XII Prepares for War with Milan

On his accession to the throne, Louis had two particular objectives: one was his desire to divorce his wife and marry Charles VIII's queen, Anne of Brittany, which needed a papal dispensation and the second was adding Milan to his families' holdings. Pope Alexander's son, Cesare, at 23 years of age, no longer wanted to be a cardinal of the church. His Holiness saw in Louis' marital problems opportunity to advance his son's new career as a secular lord. Cesare wanted to marry Carlotta of Naples, daughter of King Federigo of Naples and his first wife, Anne of Savoy. The 18-year-old Carlotta was living in France, where she grew up under the direction of Queen Anne of Brittany. Cesare came to France in October 1498, just after he resigned from the College of Cardinals, bringing Louis' dispensations for divorce from Jeanne and marriage to Anne of Brittany. But Carlotta refused to marry the Borgias' son. She was supported by Anne who then allowed her marriage to Count Guy XIV of Laval. The French monarch created Cesare Duke of Valentinois and found an acceptable substitute for his wife in the 19-year-old Charlotte d'Albert of the House of Navarre. The young lady was beautiful and rich and taken with the dashing Cesare. The Duke of Valentinois signed the marriage contract in May 1499. As a part of this deal, the Borgias agreed to assist Louis' conquest of Milan and Naples.

While he worked toward resolving his situation, just as King Charles secured French borders before he went to Italy, so Louis began dealing with France's neighbours. In only a few months after Louis' accession, Maximilian had launched raiding parties into former Burgundian lands which he claimed. They were readily driven off by local forces. Louis sent diplomats to Philip the Handsome, Maximillian's son who ruled in the lands inherited from his mother. Philip's holdings were wealthy and in close commercial ties with France. He was open to negotiations with King Louis. In August 1498 Louis and Philip agreed to a treaty in which Philip renounced any claims against France he might have for Burgundy and Picardy and agreed to do homage to Louis for Flanders. In return, Philip received three cities in Artois. This cut the ground under Maximilian's claims. Louis followed his dealing with Philip by agreeing with the English King Henry VII to renew the Treaty of Étaples in July 1498. The disagreements with Spain remained, but Ferdinand did agree to an understanding that France and Spain would have the same enemies in common, but would never be enemies to the pope.

Having secured his kingdom, Louis looked for allies in Italy to oppose Milan. Venice had had enough of Lodovico. By July 1498, the Venetians were ready to join with France in a war to rid Italy of the obnoxious Milanese duke. This resolution, not shared by all in the Most Serene Republic, including the doge, was proof positive of how badly Lodovico had scared and hurt his former allies. Differences were needing a settlement. What about Pisa? Louis desired to help Florence recover their lost subjects; the Venetians favoured Pisan independence. And just how much Milanese land was rightful for Venice? The Venetians wanted lands on both sides of the Adda but Louis saw that as excessive. Louis wanted 100,000 ducats from Venice; the Venetians thought he should pay his way; Louis responded with the fact that if he were to come, he would have to tell the French that the expedition was paying for itself.

Irritation with Lodovico overcame all. Both sides pressured Pisa to accept Ercole d'Este's arbitration. Venice would gain Cremona and the lands east of the Adda and would pay France a subsidy. More, the Venetians would field 1,500 men-at-arms and 4,000 infantry, attacking Milan from the east. Louis could get Genoa. In return, France would give strong support if the Turks attacked Venice while the war against Lodovico was in progress. The agreement was completed at Blois on 9 February 1499. It remained secret for weeks.

King Louis also made agreements with Milan's western neighbours. The young Duke of Savoy, Filiberto, easily moved toward an alliance with the French. He would have 200 French lancers and a subsidy to pay them while he would supply 600 light horse and 2,000 infantry. Free passage through Savoy was guaranteed. The Marquis of Saluzzo, a comrade in arms with Louis at the siege of Novara, received 100 lances; the regent of Monferrato, 50 lances and 2,000 mounted crossbowmen. As news of these arrangements filtered back to the Duke of Milan, he made efforts to counter them, but he did too little too late.

King Charles had launched his expedition to Italy in the hope that everything would fall into place. Commines was astonished that Charles did as well as he did, considering the disorganization of resources and lack of planning. King Louis had no intention of leaving much to chance. Louis announced that Italy, particularly Milan, would pay for the war. In money matters, King Louis was astute. Some said he was avaricious, but that is often the cry set against those who demand to get what they pay for and who dislike wasting money. He straightened out the account books, collected what was owed, paid only valid bills and cut needless expenses. In April 1499 the king announced he had sufficient resources at hand to pay for two years of war. As part of the financial overhaul, he reorganized the French army. He formed strong companies of heavy cavalry, opened negotiations with the Swiss cantons and agreed to pay them a grant of 20,000 livres and in return was allowed to recruit as many Swiss infantry as he could pay. He also recruited thousands of French infantry. Louis appointed Ligny and d'Aubigny as his commanders and kept as commander Trivulzio who remained in Asti, raiding Lodovico's supporters. In May 1499, the French army was to concentrate at Asti, ready to attack Lodovico.

Chapter 10

Louis XII Takes Milan

Lodovico's Tribulations

D uke Lodovico struggled to find allies. His only firm ally was King Federigo because the Neapolitan king saw that his realm was also threatened by the French, but he was unwilling to weaken his defences to help Lodovico. The duke thought to entangle Maximilian into the defence of Milan by convincing him to attack Venice. After all, from 1493 to 1498, he had paid about a million ducats into Maximillian's treasury for various reasons. The duke also acknowledged Milan was under imperial suzerainty and so deserved imperial protection. Unfortunately, Maximilian's experiences in dealing with Lodovico was disappointing. The imperial potentate sent no aid, rather he implemented some weak diplomatic efforts to dissuade King Louis. To keep the Venetians busy, Lodovico sent word to the Turkish sultan that he would provide money for a war against Venice. Lodovico even told King Louis that he would send tribute to France to avoid war.

The duke should have put his money into his army. He did not retain any first-rate commanders because he feared they might overthrow him and his army was disorganized and ill-trained. Lodovico's son-in-law, Count Caiazzo, Galeazzo da Sanseverino, led an impressive force on parade ground and in the tournament, he was well turned out with beautiful trappings. He and his brother began to bring order to Milan's soldiers; they were good second-rate commanders. Lodovico tried to recruit Francesco Gonzaga, victor of Fornovo, but the marquis preferred the Most Serene Republic's favours. In March 1499 Milan's army fielded 1,500 men-at-arms, 1,100 light horse, and some 5,000 infantry. By the brothers Sanseverino estimate, the Milanese had fewer cavalry than Louis and about half his infantry.

When Lodovico finally recognized that neither Maximilian nor the Turks were about to attack Venice, he began to look for immediate help elsewhere. He expected the Florentines to honour an agreement to send 300 men-at-arms and 2,000 infantry, but the Republic suddenly found reasons why those forces were not available at that time. Federigo authorized Prospero Colonna to take some of the 400 men-at-arms and 2,000 infantry which he had promised to Lodovico, but constant hindrances delayed the force. Ercole d'Este had accepted payment for 200 men-at-arms, but neglected to deliver them. The only Italian state to send help was Lodovico's niece, Caterina Sforza, governor of Imola and Forli for her son. She forwarded 500 infantry.

Not until July did Lodovico became aware that he was in serious trouble and needed to hire mercenaries. Louis had beaten him to the cream of the Swiss market. He could hire Swiss but only as individuals or small groups, not whole units like Louis was getting. Lodovico began sending agents to Germany and the Burgundian lands to recruit cavalry and artillerymen. They were successful regarding numbers, but the quality was another matter. The duke organized an artillery train by stripping his fortresses. The fortresses themselves needed repairs and upgrading, but Lodovico refused permission to start the work, reasoning that the work could be done when the fortress became a target of enemy operations. Work only started when Trivulzio crossed Milan's frontiers on 15 July.

Lodovico was still attempting to bring order and training to his forces when the French invasion began. He ordered a levée-en-masse but found the results disappointing. Lodovico's preference for low born people over the aristocrats, over-taxation and general corruption in the administration made the prince unpopular. Lodovico was feared; he was also hated.

Louis XII's Campaign for Milan

King Louis stayed at Lyons, trusting to his commander, Gian Giacomo Trivulzio to manage the campaign. With his two fellow commanders, Ligny and d'Aubigny, Trivulzio decided the campaign should begin in August. There was no clear chain of command among these nobles, that was not the noble way, but all three were experienced in war and had worked together before. In Italian matters, the head of Milan's Ghibellines, Trivulzio, took the lead. On tactical matters, there was consensus though not compromise.

As companies of mercenaries and retinues of great lords arrived, King Louis did not know how many troops he had on the march in Italy. Records indicate six companies of 100 lances each, those of Ligny, d'Aubigny, his brother d'Auson, Trivulzio, de Framizells and Cesare Borgia (Bayard was in Ligny's company). Along with these French formations, there were 200 lances of the Duke of Savoy and eleven small companies totalling 460 lances. Other mounted troops included the Gentlemen and the Archers of the Royal Guard, along with pensioners and mounted arblasters for a total of another 1,000 men-at-arms. The infantry numbered about 17,000, of whom 5,000 were Swiss and 2,000 from Savoy. With at least 2,260 horse and 17,000 foot, with officers' retinues and accompanying soldiers, a total of some 20,000 troops, the French expeditionary force was ready for a campaign. Including sutlers, camp followers, soldiers' servants and families, the total number of the host was probably close to 40,000.

King Louis had fought in campaigns all his life. He grasped the necessities of war in his time. He ordered Trivulzio to make a quick campaign, to risk battle rather than waste his army in sieges. The king specifically instructed Trivulzio and d'Aubigny to harshly lay waste the first places they had to capture to put fear into the rest. The French planned to advance against Alessandria. Since Trivulzio had launched raids in that direction from the start of the year, he had determined the best route.

Trivulzio and his fellow commanders at the head of the troops, led the French army out from Asti. They quickly captured two ill-defended posts on the Milanese border. To cover their rear, Trivulzio sent his nephew, Zuam Francesco Trivulzio with a detachment of soldiers to take Spigno on the Savona road. Under Milan's influence, Spigno was recently upgraded with redesigned fortifications and was said to be impregnable. The French assault ripped into the walls, seized the site, killed 100 men of the garrison and then dismantled the walls.

Now, the French felt secure in advancing into Milanese territory without surprises from the rear. On 11 August Trivulzio sent a demand for surrender to Rocca d'Arazzo, a fair-sized town with a strong castle on the banks of the Tanaro River about five miles from Asti. The governor of Arazzo, confident in his walls and garrison, replied to Trivulzio's herald with contempt. At eight o'clock the following morning, the French marched on Arazzo, reached the town by noon, and before night, invested Arazzo with cannon in position. On the morning of 13 August the heavy bombardment broke a breach in the walls, and by the evening of the same day the French held the Arazzo, had sacked it, destroyed the castle and killed most of the defenders along with many citizens.

On the other side of the Tanaro, opposite Arazzo was the town and castle of Annone. The fortifications were strong, the castle well-garrisoned. The French crossed the river after accepting the requested surrender of Incisa and encamped in a swamp on 15 August. The castle of Annone was stronger than that of Arazzo. The French took three days to capture it; they plundered the town and put the garrison to the sword. The fall of Annone opened the way to Alessandria. Rather than move directly to Alessandria, the French decided to capture all possible sites where a relief force might find a base. Advancing from Annone, the French occupied Solero and sent a detachment against Voghera, which quickly surrendered on 22 August. Two days later the French appeared before Tortona, which commanded the road to Piacenza. The town's citizens refused to defend against the French. The town of Valenza protected a main crossing of the Po. Lodovico's commander, Count Caiazzo, had sent 1,500 ducal guards to stiffen resistance. Initially, Valenza refused the demand to surrender, but after a short cannonade, they surrendered and the rest of the towns around Alessandria quickly opened their gates for the French.

Lodovico's Defences Collapses

Lodovico awaited the French thinking that he would defeat them. He remembered how easily he thwarted Louis of Orleans in Novara and pushed back King Charles from his frontiers. The fact that the French ran roughshod over Italy to the south only showed how weak and disorganized were those states to his south. He intended to impale the French on two impregnable fortresses: Alessandria and Pavia. These fortresses might even hold up the French into winter. He thought he had the time to strengthen his forces and receive reinforcements from Maximilian. He trusted that his loyal subjects preferred him to the French.

Alessandria was garrisoned by 600 men-at-arms, 400 light horse and 3,500 infantry. The fortress commander withdrew some 2,000 men from nearby garrisons for reinforcements. On 9 August another 2,000 German foot arrived. Lodovico recalled the Count of Caiazzo from the Venetian front and moved him into Alessandria to take over the fortress' defence. Lodovico had great confidence that the fortress would hold. But, in his usual out-of-touch understanding, he did not know that the citizens disliked his governor, Lucio Malvezzi, had utter contempt for Caiazzo and feared the French. Many of the citizens knew Trivulzio and expected him to be generous when greeted with surrender but implacable if met by resistance.

The French had isolated Alessandria. Trivulzio thought to mask the town and march straight toward Milan. Ligny saw the well-garrisoned fortress in their rear as a threat once they turned away. In a discussion, Trivulzio agreed with Ligny: they would assault Alessandria. On 25 August, the French encamped before the town's walls and set up their cannons. The members of the garrison were clear in their resolve to defend their post. The bombardment commenced and continued throughout the 28th.

The garrison struck back with damaging sorties but the commanders in the town lost hope of any victory. The French had cut off all communication with Milan; any reinforcements would have to come from Germany which was too far away; the citizens were adamant against defending the town. During the night of 28–29, Caiazzo pulled out of Alessandria taking with him the members of the ducal administration, principal officers and most of the mounted troops. The remaining garrison was leaderless and confused and the town surrendered. Some of the defending troops remained at their posts and became prisoners.

Caiazzo, fleeing with the elite troops and governmental officials, destroyed the bridge across the Po after they passed. A mass of Milanese troops left Alessandria as the French entered. They followed their commanders on foot and when they got to the Po the bridge was broken and the fleeing soldiers found themselves trapped between the swiftly running river and the savage French. Meanwhile, Caiazzo and his party rode toward Pavia, Lodovico's second line of defence. The command in Pavia, in agreement with leading citizens, closed the town's gates against them. The party continued to Milan.

While the French marched on Milan from the west, the Venetians invaded from the east. Starting in late August, Niccolo Orsini with about 12,000 men, including 1,600 men-at-arms and 600 light horse crossed the Adige. Since most of the Milanese forces went west to face the French, there was no serious opposition. The Venetians easily occupied the lands allocated to Venice under the Treaty of Blois. The main city, Cremona, surrendered on 8 September and its citadel gave in a week later. King Louis XII later commented to the Venetian envoy, 'You Venetians are wise in council and abounding in riches, but you lack spirit and courage in war. When we French go to war, we are resolved that the issue shall be either victory or death.' (Given the long and successful Venetian wars in the east, maybe Louis was purposely missing what Venice was all about.)

Still, the French advance in the west was the greatest concern for the Milanese. The fall of Alessandria sent tremors of terror through their lands, the French advance from Alessandria causing great consternation. From the town, the French marched north to Mortara and accepted the terms of Pavia's surrender. In Milan there was desperation; when Caiazzo entered the city, he found confusion and indecision. Duke Lodovico's authority evaporated the closer the French marched. Soldiers swarmed into Milan's squares demanding their back pay. Trivulzio's supporters patrolled the streets, mobs sacked the houses of ducal councillors and on 30 August killed the detested treasurer Antonio de Landriano. Fearing for his and his family's lives, Lodovico barricaded himself, his trusted troops, guns, munitions and food in the castle.

On 31 August, Lodovico sent his brother, Cardinal Ascanio, with his two young sons and a part of the treasury, to safety in the north. Then he called on the citizens to defend Milan from the French. City leaders told the duke they were preparing to submit to the French. Early in the morning of 2 September, Lodovico with Caiazzo and the Ghibelline leaders left Milan with the ducal regalia and the rest of the treasury. The French pursued them, but Lodovico's party gave them the slip at Como, travelling through the Valtellina to Meran in the Tyrol. Here he sent an appeal to Maximilian.

King Louis becomes Duke of Milan

Later on during the day Lodovico left Milan, the Milanese sent envoys to the French who were within six miles of the city. They invited them into Milan, thinking they would receive confirmation of their privileges from the French. Trivulzio entered at the head of 5,000 Italian horse. With Ligny at his side, he ensured that the coming French understood Milan was not an enemy city; the troops were welcomed with cheers of 'Viva Trivulzio!' He announced a ban on plundering and enforced discipline, executing common soldiers who caused trouble and even a French nobleman. Milan's citizen leaders began the process of submitting to the French. On 5 September they held a mass meeting in which the citizens rejected the claims of the Sforza. Then the committee of leaders drew up a list of conditions to accept Louis as successor to the Visconti. The following day the city formally accepted the rule of Louis XII King of France.

The castle remained with the Sforza banner floating over its towers. Lodovico had ensured the castle could hold out until he returned with Maximilian's help. The fortress was garrisoned by 3,000 experienced soldiers with many guns and held enormous supplies of powder and food. They had worked out secret signals so the garrison could communicate with Lodovico's supporters in the city, who then communicated with Lodovico in Germany. The Sforza supporters wanted the castle to hold out at least a month.

Without this citadel in French possession, Trivulzio could not hand over an uncontested Milan to the new duke. He informed the provisional governors that when the castle surrendered, he would withdraw all French troops from Milan. But if he had to attack the castle, he would need to occupy the city and certainly could not guarantee the troops' behaviour. The castle's commander, Bernardino da Corte, a favourite of Lodovico, committed his honour to hold the castle. He was well known to the provisional governors, who begged him to spare the city from wanton destruction. They told him that if he surrendered the castle, he would win high favour from the new duke. The commander did not reject the offer – he ignored it. The next day, Trivulzio sent a personal envoy to da Corte who told the commander that in the event of his surrender he would receive a significant amount of money, but if the French had to assault the castle, every man in the garrison would die. He had two days to answer.

Two days passed and there was no answer. Trivulzio began to invest in the castle. On 11 September he positioned guns and stationed 10,000 assault troops in place. Two days later, as these forces sat ready, leading citizens made another appeal to da Corte. The commander listened attentively and promised a positive response, but said he needed to consult with others and would respond by evening. At nightfall, an agreement was made. Bernardino da Corte's children were delivered up as hostages. There would be an armistice for twelve days, the commander would send a notice to the Duke of Milan (Lodovico): if there were no signs of a sure relief effort in that time, the commander and his lieutenants would surrender the castle intact. The agreement included handsome monetary rewards to the commander and his lieutenants from the French king. Negotiations continued; on 17 September, da Carte handed the castle over to the French. Some later complained that Bernardino da Corte lost his honour in this transaction, but da Corte was very comfortably situated and the citizens of Milan were saved from a destructive battle in the middle of their city.

As soon as King Louis learned that the castle had fallen, he set out for Milan from Lyons. The royal party entered Pavia on 2 October, where the streets were decorated, bands played and a procession of town leaders and clergy came to greet the new ruler. The townspeople set out tables laden with meats under awnings at which every man might take his fill. Then, to Pavia came representatives from all the Italian powers to congratulate Louis on his success. After all arrived, King Louis started from Pavia in the morning and after lunch at Certosa entered Milan that afternoon. He stopped at a Dominican convent to prepare for the procession into the city.

Milan Becomes French

The royal party waited before the city gates. His Majesty was mounted on a fine bay courser with golden trappings. He was dressed in ducal robes, a mantle of white damask lined with grey fur and with an ermine collar. This partially covered a tunic of cloth of gold. On his head was a biretta that matched his mantle. The mounted lord Trivulzio, accompanied by the leading citizens of Milan, approached King Louis coming through the open gates and with words of welcome presented to the king the keys of the city, two gilt batons of command and a naked sword. King Louis XII grasped the sword which he carried upright. He had passed the batons, one to Marshal de Gie and the other to the lord Trivulzio.

The Grand Chamberlain then marshalled the procession. Through the city gate marched the 500 men of the Royal Guard with pikes and axes, next came 300 men-at-arms, picked men, armed and armoured. Directly in front of his majesty, rode the three commanders, the lords Trivulzio, Ligny and Gie, accompanied by the commanders of the royal companies of horse. The king rode under a golden baldachin, carried by eight city fathers of Milan mounted on horseback. By the side of the king and his canopy, rode sixteen more important citizens of Milan in their finest. Surrounding the king and citizens was the college of doctors, each in scarlet robes with collars and hats trimmed in fur. Behind his majesty rode the Papal Legate, Giovanni Borgia and also Cardinal della Rovere, then His Eminence of Rouen and the Duke of Savoy. Behind them came the other great Italian lords and the ambassadors of the republics. The procession proceeded to the cathedral through sumptuously decorated and crowded streets, but few were the cries of 'France!' or ringing of bells.

The citizens of Milan were not pleased with their new master. They wished to escape French domination, trying to convince Louis to govern as suzerain over a republic which held the duchy as under the Visconti or Sforza. Other cities in the duchy preferred to have their autonomy. Instead, King Louis intended to rule Milan as a monarchy. He and his advisors set up a new administrative structure for the duchy. A senate of seventeen members chosen by the Duke oversaw the civil administration. Most were Italian, but the presiding chancellor was French. A general of finance ran taxes and spending as in a French province. Power was concentrated into the hands of a royal lieutenant, as in a French province. He was also head of the military. The royal appointee for that post was Trivulzio. Louis also confiscated Sforza and their supporters' lands, granting them to his nobles and commanders.

This new regime was upsetting not only because it placed a foreign master on their backs but also gave hard-won lands of the Duchy of Milan to hated enemies. The Venetians were objects of scorn for their short-sightedness. 'You dogs! The king has made his first meal at our expense, but you Venetians will provide his next meal!' Worse was to come. On 29 October, the day representatives of the people of Milan formally swore fidelity to Louis, tax offices burned during rioting. Louis left Milan on 8 November to return to France but the situation still simmered. The French insisted on billeting soldiers in the city whereas both Visconti and Sforza had kept their soldiers in the countryside. The French soldiers were unpleasant and dangerous. Discipline was harsh against offenders, but that was of little satisfaction to the citizenry. Taxes were high because Louis thought they should pay for their liberation from Lodovico.

Adding to the problems of the French in Milan was the fact that the royal Lieutenant, Trivulzio, was unpopular. Many disliked the man since the time he had been a *condottiere*. He stepped on toes. While he was head of the Guelphs, the whole Guelf-Ghibelline faction struggle was involved and complex and he was out of step with many of his faction. Hostility to Trivulzio began to shift into support of the Sforza.

Chapter 11

Lodovico Strikes Back and Fails

L odovico, his brother Cardinal Ascanio and his supporters established themselves in the southern reaches of the empire. With the support of Maximilian and Milan's treasury, the Sforza began planning their return. A new army was collected from the empire, consisting of German Landsknecht, Swiss pikemen, Burgundian men-at-arms and Albanian light horse. The concentration of soldiers to their north did not escape French attention. Trivulzio sent reinforcements to Milan's northern border, commanded by Ligny. Sforza troops advanced south into the Alpine foothills, marching through Chiavenna to Domodossola. At the same time, Cardinal Ascanio pushed forces against Como. Ligny blocked the Sforza advance with artillery.

When news of Lodovico's offensive reached Milan, the city grew restless. Trivulzio knew he could not hold the city by force, so he stationed troops at key points in the city and started negotiations with the Ghibellines, who were busily distributing arms. When the French tried to disarm people they saw as threatening, mobs formed and forced the French to back down. Negotiations with city leaders broke down as each side blamed the other for infractions. Trivulzio recalled Ligny and his troops to Milan and ordered Yves d'Alègre, who was operating with Cesare Borgia in the Romagna, to bring his troops north to protect French bases.

Milanese armed mobs took over the streets on the night of 1 and 2 February 1500. Trivulzio and his troops withdrew into the castle. Later, on 2 February, Ligny arrived and after conferring with Trivulzio, the commanders with the French field army marched out of Milan, leaving a strong garrison in the well-stocked castle. The well trained and battle-tested French soldiers were not bothered by Milan's citizens as they left because the Milanese were happy to see them leave. Together with Ligny's force, Trivulzio marched toward Novara, with difficulty because Sforza light cavalry harassed their flanks and rear. The French dealt with the horsemen by taking harsh reprisals on nearby villages, sacking, burning, and putting their population to the sword.

As soon as Trivulzio and the main body of French troops left Milan, gangs looted French houses and businesses, all the while hunting down any remaining Frenchmen, beating and killing them. The adventures of Zuam Dolce, a Venetian agent, was typical. As the French left, he burned his confidential documents while an armed band started to break into his lodging. He narrowly escaped by climbing over a wall and temporarily found safety in a monastery. Staying in Milan was not safe and he made his way back to Venetian territory.

A troop of arblasters was the first Sforza formation which entered Milan. They came early in that day, 2 February. Later the same day, Cardinal Ascanio arrived accompanied by Hermes Sforza (son of Duke Galeazzo and Maria Sforza and brother of Duke Gian Galeazzo Sforza who died just before Lodovico was made duke), Galeazzo di Sanseverino and 7,000 troops. On the morning of the 5th, Lodovico made a formal entrance at the head of his troops. Along the streets the crowds cried, 'Moro! Moro! Duca! Duca!' The restored Duke of Milan announced his resumption of rule, apologized for any offence he might have made previously and promised restitution. Then he pardoned all of the citizens except members of the Trivulzio family.

In setting up his new administration, Lodovico presented himself as a warrior prince, ready to defend the people of Milan against their rapacious enemies, the frightening French and cunning Venetians. He was now a wise prince, humbled by his experience, ready to consult and take advice. He would fight for his people at the head of their army. His brother, Cardinal Ascanio would administer the duchy. He promised that the Guelf and Ghibellines would agree on Milan's common interests.

The Sforza armed might was impressive. Lodovico reviewed Milan's troops in mid-February: 6,000 German and 4,000 Italian foot supported by 500 men-at-arms. Guns had come from Germany. Some 15,000 Swiss, 1,500 Burgundian and 300 German men-at-arms were on their way. How Lodovico was going to pay for all of this was a question, but he would solve that problem after he defeated the French. His army successfully bombarded Pavia which surrendered on 9 February and Vigevano surrendered while Lodovico's force prepared for the assault a few days later.

The French Duchy of Milan fell as fast as it was conquered. However, the French intended to hold on to both Novara and Alessandria while the Venetians kept Piacenza and Lodi. But when Trivulzio approached Novara on 4 February, he found that the townspeople had declared for Lodovico and closed the gates although the French garrison held the citadel. Using his usual methods of persuasion, Trivulzio regained possession of Novara the next day. Numerous isolated French detachments fought their way to Novara by force and inflicted severe retribution on Lodovico's supporters. French strength began to increase.

Interlude: some Italian adventures of the Good Knight Bayard
A Tournament

The Italian wars caused massive loss and suffering throughout the paths of armed forces and their suppliers. Not only theft and wanton destruction of property, but rape and murder followed the arrival of any body of soldiers. Most people fled, taking what they could, leaving the rest. Some, of course, found opportunity and profit in the disruption. Surely all the thefts, rapes and murders were not done only by soldiers. Some, though, found the wars exciting, enjoying the adventure. These were the aristocratic warriors, masters of their business of fighting and killing. They were the lords of the battlefields and so rulers of men.

After Louis XII had returned to France, he left some garrisons in Lombardy to be the core of any new army that might be needed. The Chevalier Pierre Terrail, seigneur de Bayard, member of the royal company of Louis of Luxembourg, seigneur de Ligny, was now 26 years old. He returned to the court of the Duke of Savoy where he had been a page in his youth. His reputation was well known: an outstanding horseman, valiant warrior in the Battle of Fornovo and victor of many tournaments. He knew his first master's wife, Blanche of Montferrat, the Dowager Duchess of Savoy. Granddaughter of Francesco Sforza, Duke of Milan, she lived in her dower town, Cargnan. She welcomed Bayard and his friends. The duchess still had as lady-in-waiting, Maria Terrebase, now Madame de Fruzasco, wife of the duchess's chamberlain. The young Bayard and Maria had been close when he was a page.

While with the dowager duchess, Bayard expressed his deep appreciation of her beauty and grace, requesting she give him a sleeve of her gown, which she did. Taking the sleeve, the good knight announced a tournament for men-at-arms in full habiliment. There were to be three courses with lance without a barrier and twelve sweeps with the sword. The prize was the noble lady's sleeve, with a ruby worth 100 ducats attached. Fifteen proven knights accepted the challenge. The duchess was very pleased with the honours shown her and ordered a tribune erected and decorated in the tiltyard.

An hour past noon on the appointed day, Bayard with companions in arms rode out onto the field, all armed *càp-a-pie*, ready for action. In the first event Bayard jousted with the Lord de Rouastre. Rouastre charged Bayard, shivering his lance. Bayard's counterstroke hit Rouastre on his helm, breaking his visor, shivering his lance. Rouastre straightened his helm and charged into the second course. His attack was more skilful than the first run, but Bayard's lance struck Rouastre's visor with such force that lance carried away his visor, crest and plumage. Rouastre reeled in the saddle but kept his seat. At the third lance, Rouastre raised his lance while Bayard's shattered, which was welcomed with applause. In the swordplay, Bayard sent Rouastre's flying but his own broke. Following Bayard's contest, other knights took the lance and the sword, two by two while the spectators enjoyed the sport.

That evening, the lord Fruzasco invited all to enjoy dining with the duchess. After the banquet the tournament umpires, the lords Grammont and Fruzasco, collected the votes of all present for the best competitor. Bayard won the vote but refused to accept the honour and returned the sleeve to the Lady Blanche. She gratefully accepted the sleeve, but awarded the ruby to the lord Montdragon, who was voted second. Then the company danced past midnight.

A Mistake

When Lodovico returned, Bayard was part of a garrison some 20 miles from Milan. Hearing that some 300 of Lodovico's Lombard horsemen had come to Binasco, Bayard convinced forty or more men-at-arms to ride out and drive the Lombard men away. At dawn, they rode forth. What Bayard and his companions did not know was that the commander of Binasco was a noble knight, Jean Bernardino Cazache, who had spies in the French camp. He knew all about Bayard's planned attack. Rather than be caught in the nest, Cazache brought his men out of the town, at about two to three bow shots. There, they waited.

Bayard and his troop came upon Cazache and his men. They formed for battle and charged, yelling, 'France! France!' Cazache and his followers formed up and met the French charge, yelling, 'Moro! Moro!' The knights clashed and fought for more than an hour. Then Bayard rallied his side, drew them together into a cohesive formation and charged the Lombards.

Lodovico's men gave ground but still returned blow for blow, retiring four or five miles. Once they were near enough to the gates of Milan, they turned and galloped toward the open gates.

Bayard, at the head of his troop, charged hard, hoping to catch the Lombards before they passed the gates. As the troop charged ahead, Bayard rode pell-mell after the fleeing horsemen. He did not hear the cry, 'Turn! Turn gendarmes!' So, as his troop turned about, abandoning the chase, Bayard rode straight through Milan's gates and into the city. Suddenly, Bayard found himself surrounded by the horsemen he had been chasing. The townspeople who saw his charge into the town yelled, 'Stupid! Stupid!' Seeing his unfortunate position, with his characteristic casual approach, Bayard yielded to Cazache. The commander took Bayard to his quarters and disarmed him. He found him to be a young man of noble character. Lodovico had heard the commotion and asked what it was all about. He was told of the great warrior but also a foolish young man. Lodovico ordered that the young man be brought to him. When the palace lackey told Cazache about Lodovico's order, rather than send the valiant chevalier to Lodovico as a prisoner, Cazache dressed him in one of his robes and accompanied Bayard to Lodovico.

The noble Bayard gave a good account of himself 'By my good faith, my lord, I did not believe myself to come alone but thought my comrades followed me. But they are better acquainted with the usages of warfare than myself.' After a pleasant discussion, Lodovico returned Bayard's horse and equipment, sending him back to the French camp. While the story is amusing, we need to look at it a little closer.

First, there are no casualties mentioned of either the French or the Lombard knights. This should not be surprising. The gentlemen on both sides liked nothing better than an afternoon of whacking and battering at each other, after which they would enjoy a fine dinner and dancing. The engagement of Bayard and Cazache's men was more like a tournament than a real battle. Second, Bayard was a well-known master of the tournament. What was the best use Lodovico could make of his prisoner? Killing him was out of the question. One did not simply kill nobles, that was only for peasants and other commoners. Throw him in the donjon and demand a ransom? That was the usual thing to do, but the money would do little for Lodovico's vast needs, and there remained the question of who earned it. So rather than get involved with these questions, Lodovico decided to grant mercy, hoping to exact mercy in return at some future day, which he did as we shall see.

Lodovico's Regime Collapses

King Louis XII was furious when word came to him that Lodovico had returned and taken Milan. The king swore he would kill Lodovico and lay the land waste. He soon began organizing his response. He sent companies of men-at-arms toward Italy, agents to Switzerland to hire infantry, and appointed La Tremoille, the general who had defeated him during the civil wars early in Charles's reign, as supreme commander along with George d'Amboise as civil administrator for the territory to be reconquered. In the Swiss Confederation, dissension broke out when Emperor Maximilian announced that since Milan was a part of the Empire and that Duke Lodovico was an appointed imperial potentate, subjects of the Swiss confederation should not fight against him. The Swiss Diet of the Cantons took up this question and ruled that the rights of His Majesty of France should have protection, but the cantons ought not to recruit for either side. While this question rattled through the Diet, the Bailli of Dijon arrived in the Swiss lands and began recruiting individuals. Soon, he had thousands on his rolls. A French army arose under the hands of La Tremoille. He organized his forces, disciplined the men and appointed officers. He now counted some 30,000 men. Besides establishing his military might, Tremoille set up an extensive espionage network.

Lodovico knew King Louis. He understood that if the French did solidify their hold on northern Italy, they would surely lever him out and retake Milan. Having carried Pavia and invested Vigevano, Lodovico had promised his Swiss mercenaries that they could loot the town if they carried it by assault. Then he turned around and negotiated with the townspeople, telling them that if they did not agree, his soldiers would loot, burn and kill. They paid Lodovico 15,000 florins to accept their surrender without looting the town. Lodovico and the townspeople were satisfied with the arrangement, but the Swiss felt cheated.

Just as during King Charles's campaign in northern Italy, the key to holding western Lombardy was Novara. The French force under Yves d'Alègre, 100 men-at-arms and more than 1,000 foot had begun marching toward Novara just before Lodovico's offensive started. Trivulzio stayed at Mortara with some 11,000 men. French company commanders were very upset with Trivulzio because he kept his force within fortifications and did not pursue the Milanese soldiers. Trivulzio said that he acted as he did because of a direct order from King Louis. The king was preparing strong forces in France and they were coming to smash Lodovico but, in the meantime, he did not want any unforeseen disasters. King Louis, remembering how his efforts to secure western Lombardy caused difficulties for King Charles a few years before, wanted to ensure such events did not repeat.

Lodovico came to Novara on 3 March 1500. If this campaign to re-establish his rule as master of Milan was to succeed, he had to take Novara quickly before Louis' reinforcements arrived. He did not have siege cannon at hand; they were still coming from Germany. He could not assault the town unless he allowed the Swiss and the rest to plunder and he did not want to lose the wealth or the allegiance of Novara's citizens. Trying to play both ends against the middle, Lodovico announced that if Novara did not surrender by the afternoon of 7 March, he would give the town over to plundering. But his bluff failed. Novara ignored his ultimatum and, worse, a powerful French troop made their way into Novara as reinforcements. Two days later, Lodovico assaulted a section of the walls with his Italian troops, and they gained a foothold in the town, but the Swiss refused to back them up because they did not trust Lodovico to allow them to plunder. The Italian troops had to withdraw.

Finally, on 20 March, the German cannon arrived, were set up and by evening had blown a breach in the town walls. The next day representatives from Novara surrendered the town on terms, paying Lodovico 60,000 ducats. As part of the agreement, the French troops marched out with the honours of war, taking what guns they could manage and leaving the rest in the citadel which was not included in the surrender terms. On the morning of 22 March Lodovico and his soldiers entered the town. He paid his Swiss mercenaries, but they were not happy. Nevertheless, Lodovico had recovered Milan and sufficient territory on the west to hold off any attempt by King Louis to oust him again – or so he thought.

As expected, the French forces began to arrive. In early April, the French commander-in-chief, Louis la Tremoille, came with 500 lances joined by many French noble knights who came to fight for their king. Making a junction with Trivulzio and his force, the French camped near Novara on 6 April. Tremoille sent troops to take Trecate, cutting off supplies to Novara. Not to be ignored, Lodovico's commanders sent out from Novara, bands of light horse to harass the French. Skirmishing continued throughout the next day.

Lodovico's strategy suddenly collapsed. In Switzerland, the arguments about Swiss obligations to the Empire continued. At the Swiss Confederation Diet at Lucerne, the delegates decided on 31 March that because the parties were seeking peace, Swiss soldiers on both sides needed to refrain from combat. The Diet sent orders to all Swiss soldiers, but Lodovico's Swiss received them quickly because Lodovico was at Novara leading his troops. The orders sent to the French had to go through King Louis and so took much longer. Cardinal d'Amboise's spies found out about the decision and ordered Tremoille to attack Novara at once.

Tremoille advanced against Novara on 8 April and deployed his troops to take the convent of Saint Nazaro in the suburb. Lodovico drew his army out of Novara and formed in battle order: Milanese men-at-arms stood on the right, infantry in the centre and light horse on the left. The French advanced, cavalry skirmished and the bodies of infantry clashed. The French infantry pushed hard and the Italian infantry began to waver, but behind the Italian infantry, the Swiss pikemen refused to engage, quickly followed by the Landsknechts. The whole of Lodovico's army disengaged and withdrew in disorder back into Novara.

Lodovico stared at disaster. Here he was, trapped in a small town, with supplies cut off and with an army that would not fight. Novara was not going to hold out very long and he was too well known to slip away. The Duke of Milan took his employee, the commander of the Swiss, to task. He had always paid the Swiss what he owed them, now why were they leaving him in the lurch? The commander told Lodovico that he and his Swiss infantry had to obey the orders of their government; a stipulation in their contract required that they would not act against the orders of the Swiss Confederation.

Lodovico's Swiss began fraternizing with the French-employed Swiss and his German infantry followed. Tremoille began negotiating with Lodovico's Swiss, offering rewards for Lodovico's surrender. They refused to be party to such treachery, but they still would not fight. Lodovico began scrambling for a way out. He sent a Swiss envoy to Ligny asking for terms. Ligny responded that if Lodovico renounced the coronet of Milan, he could have his freedom. But Tremoille refused to agree to those terms. The French anticipated that Lodovico would try to escape Novara and so drew a tight cordon around the city.

At dawn on 10 April the French put guards in front of the town's gates, reinforced by strong men-at-arms ready on their horses. After 6am, the Italian troops came out, thinking that the negotiations that went back and forth yesterday would include them. After the soldiers in their formations came out, the French suddenly attacked, killing and plundering them. Some fled, but the French horsemen pursued and cut down those who were not fast enough. The Albanian light horse rode out, attempting to ride away. The French heavy cavalry turned them and pushed the Albanians into the Ticino River. Lodovico's Swiss and German pikemen stood in battle order but did not move while the French killed the others. Lodovico, dressed as a Swiss mercenary, was part of the Swiss formation.

Even without cavalry support, the massed formations of pikes were formidable. Tremoille and his commanders ordered them to leave Italy. The Germans were to march toward Trent, the Burgundians toward Vercelli and the Swiss toward Domodossola. Before they left, Tremoille ordered, the French would examine each soldier in their ranks to catch Lodovico. The former Milanese mercenaries were to pass under the pikes of the French-employed Swiss. Some 8,000 passed under the eyes of the French inspectors and still, no Lodovico. Tremoille halted the process and told the Swiss officers that if they did not immediately surrender Lodovico, they and all their men were going to die, right then and there. The French loaded their cannon and pushed them into the firing position, the men-at-arms donned helmets, couched lances and assumed battle formation. As this took place, suddenly, behind these troops, the French-employed Swiss snapped into fighting formation. Their officers announced to Tremoille that if the French attacked, these Swiss would strike them in their rear. The French backed down.

All this took some three hours. During that time, Lodovico moved from place to place to avoid the French inspectors. Many Swiss had seen him. One Swiss soldier shifted over near the Bailli of Dijon and asked him how much Lodovico was worth. The Bailli offered 100 crowns. The soldier replied that he wanted 200 and the Bailli readily agreed. Then the soldier took the Bailli to Lodovico. Realizing he was caught, Lodovico resisted, demanding that Ligny take charge of him. Ligny came with a horse for Lodovico who mounted and requested that he not be taken before Trivulzio, whom he hated. No doubt remembering, if not reminded, of the good turn Lodovico had done to Ligny's man Bayard, the French treated Lodovico with respect and dignity. Tremoille received him well and had him escorted to the citadel in Novara. Given rich dress and comfortable quarters, a week later Lodovico was carried by carriage to France. There he was confined, first in an estate; then, after repeated attempts at escape, the French imprisoned him in a tower. He died eight years after his capture.

After Tremoille took Lodovico into custody, the Sforza regime collapsed. In Milan, Cardinal Ascanio bundled up Lodovico's two young sons and sent them north to Maximilian's protection. Then he fled Milan, hoping to find sanctuary but the Venetians seized him. The Guelph partisans took charge of Milan, the Ghibellines evaporated and French flags broke all over Milan. Cardinal d'Amboise entered the city on 12 April with 2,000 men and took up residence in the castle. Three days later Trivulzio arrived. Joining with the cardinal, Trivulzio received a delegation of important citizens of Milan who came to beg forgiveness and swear allegiance. The delegation and people of Milan knelt bareheaded saying that, like Saint Peter, they were consumed by remorse because they had forsaken their master. The cardinal replied that he hoped the resemblance to Saint Peter was only partial because the saint had denied his master not once but thrice. But, he continued, the city would not be given over to looting and there would be a general amnesty for all except the leaders of the revolt. While the French thus received Milan back into their good graces, they charged an indemnity of 800,000 ducats. However, as Milan settled down, the indemnity was reduced, first to 300,000 ducats, payable in instalments and then simply ignored.

As the French swept through the duchy and reoccupied their former lands, Sforza supporters fled. The Venetians apprehended all those they found in their land and turned them over to the French, including Cardinal Ascanio. Unlike Lodovico, King Louis released the cardinal on his pledged word early in 1502. He died of the plague in Rome in 1505. Although Cardinal d'Amboise did not allow general looting of Milan, French soldiers and locals seizing opportunities found many targets for acquiring goods and participating in mayhem. Sforza partisans, those who fled but to a lesser extent even those who stayed, found their houses ripped apart. Often, the looters were not particular in looking up the political background of their targets. Brutal soldiers and locals grabbed women off the streets, stripped them naked and carted them off. Even the convents suffered disgrace; many cried for 'the shame of our poor Italy'.

Cardinal d'Amboise headed the new administration; he followed King Louis' orders having only Frenchmen in the upper administration. The French kept 1,200 lances and 10,000 Swiss in the duchy to suppress any revolt. The cardinal worked repairing the war's damage but found himself constrained by Trivulzio who constantly interfered in administration. The *condottiere* was arrogant, vengeful and worked through unworthy favourites. The Count de Ligny returned to France where he told Louis that both he and the cardinal had lost confidence in Trivulzio and that he had to leave Milan. King Louis recalled the *condottiere* and appointed d'Amboise as sole administrator of the duchy. He did a fine job and Milan quickly recovered.

Chapter 12

Cesare Borgia: The *Impresa* Begins

Cesare Borgia as Military Commander

Jesus of Nazareth did not make personal comments about individual politicians except for one: Jesus refers to Herod Antipas as '…that fox' (Luke 13:31). As a label for a cunning and unscrupulous politician trying to better his position in difficult times, 'fox' is particularly good. Such a label is particularly appropriate for Cesare Borgia, because, as many have suggested, he was the Prince of Foxes. Charming, personable, able to convince sceptics against their better judgment, Cesare fascinated those with whom he dealt. The official secretary and diplomatic envoy of the Republic of Florence, Niccolo Machiavelli, was impressed with Cesare's qualities. The Borgia's facility for accomplishing his objectives by means fair or foul, and his ability to convince people that what he did was for the best, amazed Machiavelli. Brilliance bound together with audacity marked Cesare's passage.

Cesare Borgia, born in 1475, was the son of Giovanozza de Catanei (diminutive Vanozza) by Cardinal Rodrigo Borgia. The cardinal, nephew to Pope Calixtus III, was in the good graces of the House of Aragon. Many of the minor nobles of Aragon found their fortunes in Italy, particularly in the church. Rather than train only in the martial arts, this nobility valued education and the emerging humanist thought. Rodrigo Borgia, entered the Church at the age of six, was well educated, studied law at the University of Bologna and was elevated to cardinal at 25. As he climbed the stairway of power in Rome, Borgia saw to the education of his five children. Cesare was educated in Aragon and was elevated to bishop at the age of 16.

The young man was an alert and precocious student. Cesare studied civil and canon law at Perugia and Pisa. When Rodrigo Borgia became pope in 1492, he elevated Cesare to cardinal at age 18. But Cesare did not want to remain a churchman. His brother, Giovanni was captain general of papal forces and enamoured of Sanchi of Aragon, wife of younger brother Gioffre, and mistress to both Giovanni and Cesare. When Giovanni was murdered in 1497, many blamed Cesare. Still, the path to military glory opened for

Cesare. After the failure of King Charles VIII's expedition, Louis XII began organizing a new expedition. Nothing was more propitious to success than buying Pope Alexander's favour. Cesare Borgia became the first person to resign the cardinalate, which he did in 1497, and went to France to meet with King Louis.

As part of my account of Fearless Knights, Ruthless Princes and the Rise of Gunpowder Armies, Cesare Borgia is a villain. He is the villain not because he was unscrupulous while the Fearless Knight was as honest as he could be, although that was very true, not because Cesare's notorious and skilful seductions, willing and otherwise, of countless women, but because Cesare saw the power of money joined with physical force generated a new and different purpose of war than that seen by all the good knights and their liege lords. Cesare Borgia would not be a liege lord. He was master. Because King Louis needed Pope Alexander's support to recover his predecessors' successes in Italy, he accepted Cesare as one of his allies and gave him the noble title, Duke of Valentinois. If the king was to succeed in gaining and holding Italian lands, he needed to ensure more stability in Italy. As far as northern Italy was concerned, the most difficult area was the Romagna, those lands held in title by the popes but ruled by a motley crowd of competing princelings.

King Louis wanted to keep Milan. Alexander wanted his son to have a powerful principality. Giving Cesare support in his efforts to build a state out of the chaos of the Romagna appeared to Louis the way to solidify his positions in northern Italy and secure his alliance with Pope Alexander. Alexander proposed regularizing the administration of the Romagna by imposing an *impresa*, the removal of local lords and appointment of papal officials. The pope would pay for this, Cesare was to accomplish this and King Louis' soldiers were going to provide any necessary extra force.

The *impresa di Romagna*

The problem of the *Status Ecclesiasticus*, the Papal States, had existed for centuries. Built on the wreckage of the Byzantine Exarchate, Frankish kings as part of their wars with the Lombards recognized papal control over these areas of central and northern Italy. During the wars of popes and emperors, papal control waxed and waned. After the collapse of the Hohenstaufen, the popes solidified their dominion over these states in northern and central Italy: on 30 June 1278 Emperor Rudolf of Hapsburg renounced fealty of lands listed in a schedule of towns with a description of boundaries, thus ceding these places to Pope Nicholas III. These are the same lands which remained under papal suzerainty until the wars of Italian unification. Towns and jurisdictions in the Papal States were self-governing for the most part under a recognized signor. The Roman Curia appointed rectors to ensure justice was done and order maintained. As long as overlords recognized their municipal privileges, it mattered little if some papal vicarious or local lord ran the administration. Of course, there was always tension between the citizen body and the ruling power, hence the usual split between Guelph and Ghibelline.

For the most part, the Papal States functioned fairly well, cardinals and aristocratic families (often the same) carving out choice dominions for their homes and estates. Such family networks extended deep into the social fabric with generations of people, high and low, mutually working together with all the strengths and weakness of familial relations. Since the change of a pope would upset the power structure, social affairs were often chaotic, but the interrelations of families lessened these jolts to everyday life. One area of the Papal States, however, tended to drift out of papal hands. This was the Romagna. In the northernmost of the papal lands, on the east of Romagna, sat the Florentine hinterlands; to the northeast was the duchy of Modena, backed up by ever expansive Milan; to the northwest, there were Ferrara and Mantua, backed up to Venice. Each of these powers fished in the turbulent pond of Romagna. Even worse, the Romagnole themselves were said to be most untrustworthy. They exercised a truly uncouth style of political action.

King Louis and Pope Alexander were not alone in their desire to bring order to this running abscess of a land. Many of the townspeople and small estate owners were eager for the return of papal oversight. They were fed up with the lawlessness and arbitrary extractions they had to endure under their self-appointed rulers. Louis satisfied his agreement with Pope Alexander, but peace and stability in the Romagna also would benefit his Milanese subjects. As part of his alliance with Alexander, Louis appointed Cesare Borgia as *Regius generalis Locum-tenens*, Louis' lieutenant for the projected expedition into the Romagna. Cesare was actually under the direction of Louis' commanders; Yves d'Alègre was in charge of the troops and Cardinal d'Amboise oversaw political results. Only after Milan fell to the French (for the first time) was the expedition organized.

The French released 300 lances of which one company was d'Alègre's command along with 4,000 Swiss and Gascon infantry under the Bailli of Dijon. Louis included in the force a full siege train with heavy guns, field cannon and falconets. Pope Alexander paid the cost of the forces into the French military treasury by borrowing through the *Camera Apostolica* from Milanese lenders. Cesare did lead a force of papal troops who were to provide camp guards and security but, next to the French, they were of minor importance.

The Romagna was a complex quilt of many colours, but Louis and Alexander agreed on where they needed to begin. The one major city, Bologna, was in the firm hands of Giovanni Bentivoglio. He quickly recognized papal authority, made an agreement with Alexander and paid a goodly sum to Louis; he humbled himself to the masters and so preserved his position. After Bologna, the next troublesome land was held by Caterina Sforza.

The lordships of Imola and Forli sat astride the route from Venice to Florence. Pope Sixtus IV della Rovere appointed his nephew, Girolamo Riario, lord of Imola when he married Caterina Sforza, natural daughter of Galeazzo Maria Sforza, Duke of Milan, in 1471. He added the lordship of Forli in 1481. After Sixtus died, Caterina lived an adventurous life; she could use a sword, had her own suit of armour, and understood defence engineering and the artillery trade. She would be a most difficult target to remove, but after her domino fell, more would follow.

The fall of Lodovico signalled to Caterina the threat to her rule and her life. She lived through the murder of two husbands and saw to the demise of a number of her enemies. She had sent an agent to ferret out what terms she might have to make with Louis. Finally, the king granted an audience to discuss Caterina's situation. Attending at the king's service, Gian Trivulzio answered for the king; he was direct: the axe was going to fall. His Majesty of France was not interested in Forli; His Holiness, on the other hand, was her enemy. Louis tried to avoid campaigning in the Romagna, but Alexander insisted because he intended to build a Duchy of Romagna for his son, Cesare. The pope would pay the expenses. Moreover, the Florentines feared that Alexander would give Pisa to the new Duke of Romagna; they would do nothing. The agent continued with the information he had received, 'Everyone is waiting for your undoing and ruin, but most of all Rome whence all this evil comes.'

Caterina received her agent's letter on 31 October 1499. The next day, she began preparing Forli for defence. She ordered all buildings within a quarter of a mile of the town walls razed and trees cut down. All those who lived within three cannon shots of the town had to leave, taking all supplies with them. Caterina bought large supplies of food and gunpowder, storing them in her castle, Ravaldino. She sent her superb horse breeding stock to Mantua where their high quality was appreciated. Officially, Florence had no interest in what happened in Romagna, but Florentines sent weapons and supplies to their friend, Caterina, while the government refused to sell gunpowder to Cesare because, they said, they had none.

Madonna Caterina Sforza (as many referred to her in her time) was well known and connected. Her many exploits surrounded her reputation with a positive glow. Alexander IV Borgia's reputation was never very good, and the fact that it was His Holiness' son who was aiming to eliminate her politically if not, in fact, raised a bad smell. True, Alexander insisted Cesare was conceived before he took his vow of celibacy, but this did little to lessen the stink. Never one to allow a negative image to get in his way, the pope announced that Caterina had just tried to poison him. The story emerged in two versions: two men from Forli came for an audience with the pope to present a letter begging for his support and they had a vial of poison intended for His Holiness' cup or, indeed, the letter itself was sealed in the grave of a plague victim for two days. Clearly such a misguided person should not have power in a just Italy.

On 9 November 1499, Cesar Borgia marched out of the gates of Milan to begin the *Impresa di Romagna*, the return of legitimate government to the lost sheep of the pope. Accompanied by the Marquis of Mantua, the victor of Fornovo, Cesare took the Via Emilia passing by Parma, where the marquis left him. The force arrived at Modena on 15 November where they stayed for a few days waiting for the Bailli of Dijon and the infantry. While at Modena Cesare sent envoys to Bologna to discuss passage and supplies for the army of the papal vicar and lieutenant of the King of France. The sons of Giovanni Bentivoglio, master of Bologna, met Cesare at the bridge over the Reno and escorted him to their father's palace. Cesare did not stay the night in the palace but returned to his camp outside the town's walls.

At the same time, while Cesare dealt with Bologna, commander of papal troops Achille Tiberti marched into Imola with a squadron of men-at-arms. He suggested the citizens open their gates for Cesare and the message was well taken. Cesare and his forces entered Imola on 27 November; the leading citizens saw a better future in papal control and immediately accepted the new regime. But Caterina's castellan, Dionigio di Naldi, refused to surrender the castle to Cesare. Naldi was a well-known *condottiere*. His garrison was made up of hardy mountaineers from the Val Lamone in the Apennines. Bombarding homes of important townsmen was how he greeted Cesare

Borgia. Vitellozzo Vitelli was with the papal forces. He was the brother of Paolo, whom the Florentines had executed because of his alleged failures in the Pisan campaign. Vitellozzo hated anything to do with Florence and saw Caterina as a tool of the Florentines. He also was a friend of Naldi.

If Naldi simply surrendered the castle, he would violate his contract which would look very bad. However, no one demanded he lay down his life for Madonna Caterina. On 28 November Cesare wheeled up his guns and began bombardment of the castle. With slow and deliberate fire, the cannon opened a breach in the castle walls. Naldi sent word, if he were not succoured in three days, he would surrender. Three days passed and Naldi with his garrison marched out of the castle with the honours of war and went their way. Cesare stayed in the town, arranging supplies and organizing the administration.

On 13 December Cardinal Borgia arrived from Milan and received, in the name of the pope, the oath of fidelity offered by the citizens through their representatives. On 17 December Cesare Borgia marched to Faenza where the Venetian resident and the boy lord, Astorre Manfredi, welcomed him. Now Cesare was going to confront Madonna Caterina in Forli. She quickly sent her son and legal lord of Forli, Ottaviano to join her other children and sister in Florence. When Cesare was in Faenza, Achille Tiberti arrived at Forli. He announced the abolition of the existing vicariate by papal decree. The town's spokesman, Luffo Numai, responded with the renunciation of loyalty to Ottaviano. Forli recognized Cesare as representative of their papal overlord. On 19 December Cesare marched into Forli and took formal possession.

Madonna Caterina had already provisioned and prepared her castle; she quickly moved into the building and prepared for a siege. The core of her castle of Ravaldino is still standing although much repaired and restored. The Rock of Ravaldino was first constructed from 1360 to 1371, replacing an older fortress. In 1471 Pino III Ordelaffi contracted with the military architect, Giorgio Marchesi Fiorentino to replace that old structure with a more modern design, protecting the castle from cannon fire and accommodating cannon of its own. After the House of Riario replaced the House of Ordelaffi as masters of Forli, Girolamo, husband of Caterina Sforza, contracted with the same architect in 1481 to add significant improvements to the Rock to handle the latest gunnery advances. The new design strengthened the citadel and added two ravelins, one on either side. In 1496 Caterina oversaw the construction of a third ravelin in the front. With 1,000 practiced soldiers in her garrison, Caterina intended to hold off Cesare as long as possible.

As Cesare was on his way some citizens began demonstrating in the piazza. Caterina sent troops to crush dissatisfaction but, seeing the press of people, her commander decided to withdraw into the castle. Instead, Caterina ordered her guns to hit the houses of important citizens. In the evening of 17 December, Cesare and his troops approached the Gate of St Peter. The senators and council members of Forli awaited him there. Cesare agreed to delay any occupation of the town until both parties signed the capitularies. The next day, they reached an agreement, gave guarantees and set a scale of payments for supplies. Cesare prepared his formal entry into the town for the evening of 19 December. Heavy rain fell, and cannon fire still hit here and there. Infantry – Swiss, German and Gascon 8,000-strong – marched into Forli, followed by 2,000 men-at-arms. Behind the troops, guards carried the Gonfalon of the Church and bringing up the rear were the French commander Yves d'Alègre and Cesare, taking possession of the town in the name of the Church. Cesare rode a white horse, both clad in polished armour and with silk trappings bearing the Duke of Valentinois' coat of arms.

Cesare settled his troops in Forli and celebrated Christmas. With French, papal and mercenary forces which he hired, he commanded about 12,000 men. Most of his troops were disciplined, but the Gascons tended to get out of hand and the camp followers were simply unmanageable. Cesare didn't worry about this problem. His artillery train consisted of five big cannon, seventeen field guns, eleven falconets (three-foot-long anti-personnel weapons) and one great wall buster, the Tiverina, nine feet long, shooting a projectile almost a foot in diameter. Caterina spent Christmas time siting cannons under the direction of her gunnery expert, Bartolomeo Bolognesi. The houses of Cesare's supporters continued to provide targets for practice shots.

Just after the Christmas celebrations, on 26 December, a herald announced that Cesare requested a parley. Caterina assented. Coming to the great door of Ravaldino, the drawbridge up and accompanied by his guards, Cesare rode a white horse. He wore a silver and black cloak over a suit of shining armour without a helmet but a black velvet beret with a long white feather. He removed his hat and spoke to the countess. Looking down on him from above, Caterina had her suit of armour, shaped to her body's form, covered by a cloak of renaissance colours. Cesare asked her to surrender to save the lives and property of her people and to do what was right. She answered, she was of honourable birth, not like the untruthful, duplicitous Borgias and so she would defend her fortress because her brother-in-law, Emperor Maximilian would come. Cesare withdrew. Just a few hours later, word came to Cesare: Caterina reconsidered and would speak to him again. Cesare returned to the great door. The drawbridge was lowered. Caterina was standing, almost alone, on the bridge. She requested Cesare come close so she could speak directly and quietly to him. Cesare began walking toward her as she withdrew a little. Suddenly, the bridge lurched up and began to rise. Cesare managed to scramble off and get back to his guards: she nearly had him!

The Siege of Ravaldino

The siege began in earnest on 28 December. Cesare's cannon, placed by his gunnery master Constantino da Bologna, were dug in and well-aimed. The artillery master constructed two batteries: one was near the Capuccini, holding lighter pieces used in counter battery and anti-personnel work; the other was emplaced in open fields to the southwest of the town which faced the Apennines. Here, in Battery della Montagna, sat the wall smashers. Cesare's cannon shattered residential halls and took down a tower that overlooked Cesare's lines. Caterina's master gunner, Bartolomeo, carefully laid some cannons to fire on the Capuccini, timed the firing just right and killed Cesare's gunner, Constantino. Bartolomeo's cannon caused Cesare grief. It was said, 'Bartolomeo never fails to salute any who pass by.' Cesare offered 1,000 ducats for his death and 2,000 for him alive.

All Italy was following the siege of Ravaldino. Some, who hated the Borgias, saw only virtue in Caterina's defiance of the pope and his son. Others, who hated the ever-continuing wars and constant quest for power, saw Cesare's quest for stability in the Romagna a harbinger of better things for Italy: freedom of foreign domination, unity and peace. In Florence, Ottaviano was welcomed by those who wished to help his mother's cause. Together, they formed a conspiracy to give Caterina aid. One cold January morning, a group of pilgrims came chanting through Forli and Cesare's siege lines. They begged safe passage and alms on their way to celebrate the Holy Year in Rome. They promised to pray for those who let them pass. As the band passed by Ravaldino, the drawbridge dropped and the band hurried into the castle. They were soldiers carrying supplies.

Pope Alexander was most upset. 'The Seed of the Serpent Satan' was holding up Cesare's campaign, costing money and making the Borgias look foolish. Cesare was furious that his guards and soldiers were so gullible. He ordered all local people to wear the white cross of the penitent.

Cesare and the *condottiere* Vitellozzo worked together to improve their artillery's effectiveness. Beginning on 5 January 1500, Cesare's cannon began a concentrated bombardment. The keep was the main target. The fire reduced the top of the keep and the two buttressing towers to ruins. This pulled the teeth of a good part of Caterina's offensive abilities. The artillerymen found a section of wall vulnerable to a sharp bombardment which would create a breach leading into the fortress's heart. Taking two days to dig the trenches, construct the ramparts and emplace the guns, the gunners pledged Cesare that the castle would soon fall. Cesare allowed his troops to celebrate the Feast of the Three Kings and the next day the cannons spoke again. Great damage was done to the wall. The garrison repaired shattered walls at night as Borgia blew them apart during the day. Hard as they worked, the garrison could not stop the growth of a talus pile at the bottom of the moat, filling it up. On 12 January Cesare ordered local farmers and workers to bring logs which he had stockpiled and throw them into the moat; he also had two river barges brought from Ravenna. The coins for his men's pay came; Cesare paid his men in full and gave extra coins to the bold and foolhardy.

When his engineers thought the time had come, the attackers placed their falconets to keep the wall under fire, hindering efforts at wall repair. Some barges were readied for the final assault, emplaced to cross the moat. Cesare bet 300 ducats on Sunday that he would have Caterina as a prisoner by Tuesday. Caterina saw the coming storm and had her men dig a trench to contain the coming assault and mounted her artillery to best advantage facing the breach. The French came in squads of sixteen soldiers each, one after another and rushed into the breach. The garrison surrendered without a shot being fired. Caterina, waiting in the keep to direct fire rushed out with loyal guards and in her armour with sword and shield attacked the French. It was more like a tournament than a real fight, Cesare's men took wounds but gave none in return as one after another they were slowly grinding her down. Cesare rode up on his white horse and called on her to surrender. Taking a moment from the fray, Caterina tried to flay him with words as she was attempting to slay his men. As she was yelling at Cesare, a French soldier came from behind and arrested her.

And so Ravaldino fell. Cesare distributed rewards for achievements and payments for services rendered. Many claimed Caterina's commander was a traitor, but in truth, Caterina was arrogant and demanding; she was certainly respected but not loved. Her garrison did what they could, but the inevitable was going to happen. Cesare and representatives of his allies argued about who would take custody of Caterina and, in the end, Cesare refused to surrender her to anyone. Stories circulated that he raped her but the chance of that is slim. The word for Caterina used at the time was 'virago', a woman with the temperament of a man. The game of power was tough. A person could lose property, titles, even life – that was all part of the game. Whatever one lost, one could always retain honour, but without honour, nothing else mattered. To rape Caterina was to dishonour her. When her husbands were killed, she struck back harshly, so honour was preserved. Now, if Cesare raped her, he needed to thrust her into a deep dungeon or kill her outright, otherwise he would find a stiletto in his kidney or suffer convulsions due to a painful poison. She would certainly take revenge and that when he least expected it.

As it happened, after some time Caterina went to live with her family in Florence. She found a home but no kingdom. Caterina Sforza had eight children; she died aged 46 in 1509.

Chapter 13

Cesare Borgia: The Second *Impresa*

The *Impresa* Comes to a Halt

After he took Forli, Cesare set his sight on Pesaro. Giovanni Sforza, discarded first husband of Cesare's sister Lucrezia, was lord of Pesaro. But before Cesare organized an attack, Lodovico's return caused panic in the French ranks. In early 1500, the French recalled their troops operating with Cesare. Without Louis' troops, Cesare had to end the *impresa*. Given what he had accomplished, while not a decisive success, Cesare's campaign produced significant results and he was now lord of a powerful territory. The problem was that his security and that of his father, Pope Alexander, now rested with the French. The Spanish, busy with many interests, did not seem able to provide a counterbalance to King Louis.

Waiting to see the outcome of Lodovico's return, Cesare installed new administrative machinery to give shape to the Duchy of Romagna. He chose Cesena as his capital; the town was well placed and had a strong citadel. Cesena's main difficulty was the town's unending internal strife. But to the new duke, this condition presented an advantage because all of the townspeople were not going to unite against him. Contention between the Houses of Tiberti and Martinelli enveloped most of the issues and actions in Cesena.

The duke had sent Bishop Jaime Serra, a Borgia cousin, as governor of Cesena in 1499. Working with the civic leaders, the bishop-governor smoothed tensions and prepared the way for the town to invite Cesare to take up the town administration. Polidoro Tiberti convinced the citadel's garrison to acclaim Cesare as lord on 22 April 1500, but many in the town were not happy with having him as their direct ruler. Cesare sent small contingents of soldiers into the town and made sure they behaved well and paid for goods. On 2 August Cesare's *Consiglio* accepted Cesare as lord and so secured the duke's hold on the town.

The disruption caused by Lodovico's return had brought hope to Cesare's enemies in the Romagna. Venice might provide the aid needed to counter Cesare's efforts, particularly if the French found dealing with Lodovico difficult. The lords of Faenza, Rimini and other places appealed to Venice for protection. Many of these lords offered to surrender their sovereignty to Venice. Such an expansion of power and influence into the Romagna and Adriatic coast appealed to the Venetians, but they kept an eye on how well Lodovico was doing. They did not want to face a situation with the French on one side and the never-ending wars with the Turks on the other. Venetian spokesmen during July and August never refused to help the lords of Faenza and Rimini but did not gave clear promises either. Beyond any direct help, however, the Venetians reaffirmed the rights of asylum to all refugees.

Cesare Builds his Army

During the spring and summer of 1500, Cesare stayed in Rome enjoying the delights of the papal court. Despite the time spent in the affairs of the court, Cesare attended to his business of war-making. He negotiated a *condotta* with the artillery expert, Vitellozzo Vitelli now lord of Citta di Castello, and another with Gian Paolo Baglioni, the lord of Perugia and his trained infantry formations. Paolo Orsini, head of his noble Roman house signed with Cesare for himself and his family to support the Borgia cause. Cesare hired individuals and groups of men-at-arms; he brought young men of good families onto his staff and he hired Spanish sword and buckler infantry.

The Duke of Valentinois understood the two powers most important to his plans were the Venetian Republic and the Kingdom of France. The Venetians were sceptical of the Borgias, fearing Cesare's interests in the Romagna might run counter to theirs. And King Louis with his advisors knew they could trust Pope Alexander only as far as any proposition remained profitable for the Borgia. But Cesare was another matter; his charm, charisma and spirit appealed to Louis. With his experience as an adventurer and rebel, Louis saw Cesare as a kindred spirit. Further, the commotion of Cesare's campaigns in the Romagna provided Louis with at least some cover for his assault against the Kingdom of Naples.

The new *impresa* took form on 8 August 1500, when Pope Alexander excommunicated the lords of Faenza, Rimini and Pesaro because they failed to fulfil the obligations of their vicariate. Alexander also pressured the Venetians to concede that Venice had transferred her protections to Cesare and to issue a blanket refusal for any of the lords of Romagna to raise forces in her lands.

All over Italy, commentators discussed with their principals what was the significance of these shifts. All became clear on 24 August when His Holiness received King Louis' commissioners and confirmed the terms of the *impresa*. The agreement assented to the establishment of a signory in Romagna for Cesare Borgia. What Alexander paid for this concession from King Louis is not known. But as soon as the news of this agreement seeped through northern Italy, envoys from Cesena and Bertinoro came and offered Cesare the lordship of these two towns followed by the same offer from Arcangelo, a town between Cesena and Rimini.

The Borgias knew that French agreement and support of the *impresa* pivoted on their support of French ambitions regarding Naples. They understood the necessity of swallowing their support for the Neapolitan House of Aragon. The main hindrance was the marriage of sister Lucretia to a prominent member of the Neapolitan dynasty. This problem disappeared surprisingly and violently when street thugs murdered her husband. Usually, this is blamed on Cesare, his capacity for such actions being well noted, but the French were not above solving political difficulties with such means.

Cesare's military preparations cost a lot of money so he and his father looked for more sources of income. In September, His Holiness informed the College of Cardinals that the church needed twelve more cardinals. That such an increase in the number of cardinals might appear to devalue the status of existing cardinals was obvious. The task of smoothing over such difficulties fell to Cesare. He did not hide the fact that money was a part of the plan. At the Consistory of 28 September the pope elevated twelve new cardinals. The creation of twelve cardinals at one time was unusual; the sum raised, 120,000 ducats, was unprecedented. Cesare had secured the cost of the *impresa*.

Cesare Begins the Second *Impresa*

Cesare reviewed his Spanish men-at-arms and infantry on 30 September in front of the entrance gate of St Peter's with Pope Alexander looking on from the loggia over the gate. Ceremonies completed, on 2 October the Duke and his army marched out of Rome on the Via Flaminia. As he marched north, misinformation, disinformation and wild speculation spread across Italy. No one knew what plans were actually at work, just the way the Borgias and French liked it.

Cesare has left a record of the size of his forces on 13 October. Baglioni and Paolo Orsini commanded 4,000 infantry, including the Spanish sword

Right: Chevalier Bayard.

Below left: Lodovico the Moor.

Below right: Cesare Borgia.

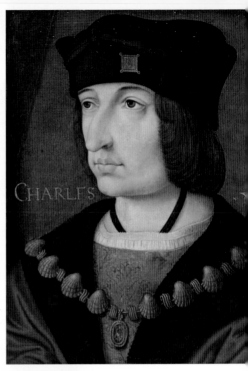

Above left:
Pope Alexander VI.

Above right:
King Charles VIII.

Left: King Louis XII.

Above left: Francesco
Gonzaga, Marquis
of Mantua.

Above right:
Vitellozzo Vitelli.

Right: Spanish and
Italian armour.

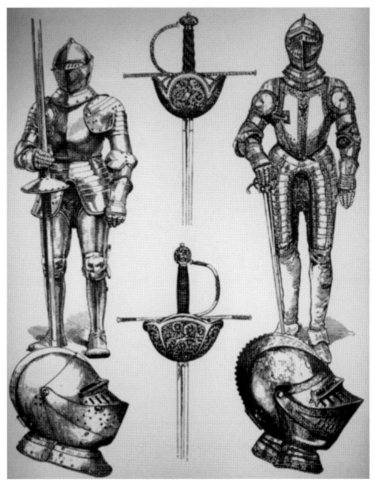

Above left: The Chevalier, an ideal.

Above right: Armoured foot.

Left: Bayard as he was in Southern Italy.

King Charles's cannon on the march in Italy.

King Charles enters Florence.

Battle of Fornovo, contemporary image.

Right: Bayard in battle.

Below: Bayard defending
the bridge at Garigliano.

The New Castle at Naples.

Left: The Egg Castle at Naples.

Below: Milan, contemporary image.

and buckler men. Vitellozzo, artillery master, oversaw sixteen cannons of which six were wall-smashers, nine were sakers (medium cannon fired at formed units of soldiers) and one colubrine (anti-personnel gun). The Duke's guard were some 700 men-at-arms. Waiting for Cesare, Ercole Bentivoglio, lord of Bologna, brought 175 men-at-arms and five large cannons.

Following Cesare's army were many camp followers, smiths, foragers, sutlers and their families. The Spanish infantry formed the fighting core of his army, ruthless and implacable, with an eye to plunder and rapine. While most of his fighting men were professional soldiers, many noble young men joined for the adventure.

The immediate objective of this campaign was Faenza, although should opportunity offer, a further advance toward Bologna would please the duke. The fortified towns of Forli, Imola and Cesare held plentiful supplies. Cesare's army marched up the Via Flaminia in long columns; his headquarters stayed with the artillery. Autumn rains made the road slow and passage difficult, but the army trudged onward. Sometimes a single cannon needed twenty oxen to plough through the wet and the mud. The army reached Orte on 13 October; by the 20th, Cesare's forces under his immediate command were moving through Deuta, Torgiano, and Bettona. The *condottieri* pushed further east, Baglioni advanced toward Montefalco and the Orsini moved through Trevi and toward Foligno. As the Borgia forces passed, news spread of many bitter complaints concerning depredations, especially regarding the Spanish soldiers.

When Cesare reached Foligno, he split his forces; Vitellozzo took the artillery along better but less direct roads through Gubbio to Scheggia escorted by two companies of infantry, one Spanish, the other French. They pushed through Umbrian lands at about 17 miles a day moving toward Fano. Cesare made it known that Umbria and San Marino were under his protection and any depredation was worth the perpetuator's life. By the time the artillery train reached Umbria, it had held two long colubrines, six great cannon, one of which was very large, sixteen sakers, and falconets with thirty carts of ammunition. The baggage train stopped at Cagli, allowing the 200 oxen and 300 pack horses to rest and recover.

The main body of troops, under the duke's direct hands, marched along the Val Topino toward Fossato. This town stands at the Apennines' foot and dominated Cesare's intended route. The people of Fossato closed their gates to him. His forces stormed the citadel, and the Spanish troops sacked the town. From devastated Fossato, Cesare pushed over the hills to Fabriano, then descended the Essino River reaching Fano on 22 October. There, he waited for Vitellozzo and his artillery.

Ten days after Cesare left Rome, leading citizens of Pesaro marched through the streets loudly chanting, 'Duca! Duca!' (meaning: we want the duke Cesare to rule). The former husband of Cesare's sister Lucretia, Giovanni Sforza withdrew into the citadel to consider his options. He attempted to garner support, but it was not to be had and he fled. In a few days, one of Cesare's commanders rode into Pesaro with forty men and received the town. On 18 October Cesare's representative, Olivieri Bishop of Isernia, assumed the town's administration. The commander of the citadel refused to surrender until he made sure that Giovanni Sforza was not returning and then he opened the gates on 23 October. Giovanni moved to neutral territory.

Cesare reached Fano, at the mouth of the Metaurus. This town in the centre of Cesare's projected Duchy of Romagna was an excellent site around which to organize operations. Staying for five days, the duke set up a permanent camp and supply base. Soon, Vitellozzo brought the artillery train and placed them in the camp for maintenance and training. Cesare took formal possession of Pesaro on 27 October, granting internal autonomy under his direction.

He went to Rimini on 30 October, granting terms similar to Pesaro which were popular and appreciated. Once Venice had withdrawn her protection, the citizens of Rimini saw their inevitable inclusion in the new duchy. On 4 November he received Forli in the same way. Using Forli as a base, he began organizing the siege of Faenza. Vitellozzo and the cannon met Cesare there, the *condottieri* with his own company of men-at-arms and supporting infantry, all in fine white uniforms. The guns and troops impressed locals who had never seen the like.

The duke was at Forli with his forces of 500 men-at-arms and a strong body of infantry. His army was arriving piecemeal, spread out from Imola to Forli so the number of men would not overwhelm any single spot. In the first week of November 1500, Cesare called his commanders together for a conference in the citadel of Forli. He and his first lieutenant, his cousin Bishop of Elna and now Cardinal Saint Vitale, outlined instructions of the coming campaign. They also made it very clear to the commanders regarding the high level of order and discipline expected from the soldiers. Cesare meant what he said about discipline; on 7 December he hanged two of his soldiers from the windows of his quarters in Forli.

Since spring, there had been no secret about Faenza being Cesare's target in the *impresa*. The lord of Faenza, Astorre Manfredi was popular in his town, but he had no allies or even support. Venice stood aside and His Holiness excommunicated the town and Astorre personally. When, on 30 October, as Cesare approached Forli, the people of Faenza sent a desperate appeal to Venice, the answer was no.

Nevertheless, most of the people of Faenza rallied to Astorre Manfredi; the garrison and people were united in their commitment to keeping their independence. They sent valuables to Ravenna and Ferrara while they renewed fortifications and drilled. At the same time, a group of unsatisfied citizens left the town and joined the Borgias.

The duke ordered his forces from Forli to invest Faenza on 10 November. As the Borgia forces approached, important people in Faenza sent reports to their friends in Ravenna expressing confidence in their ability to defeat Cesare. By the 17th, Cesare himself arrived in his camp to oversee the siege. His camp was set in a suburb just outside the southwestern gate. Next to the gate stood Faenza's citadel, a newer bastioned structure typical of the Romagna. Vitellozzo had emplaced his wall-smashing cannon opposite the main bastion of the citadel. With the duke present, he ordered the bombardment to begin. The shot broke apart the bastion's facing, providing a talus pile which soon reached toward the bastion's top. The rubble looked climbable and a strong infantry force attempted to scramble up the incline. But the defenders on top kept up a steady rain of missiles and stones, the footing of the attacking soldiers was treacherous and the attackers found themselves sliding down the pile as fast as they could climb up. Just as soon as impetus was lost, the duke ordered the men recalled. Even so, the loss was heavy. The repulse of Cesare's attack heartened Faenza's defenders and gladdened Cesare's enemies. Then came the winter.

First came cold and rain, then frost and snow. Supplies ran short because of muddy and flooded roads and shelters became damp or wet. The large force of soldiers and even larger mass of camp followers were very uncomfortable: Italian armies did not readily suffer winter's privations. One after another, the *condottieri* and their formations withdrew to more comfortable quarters. Cesare sent another summons to surrender but, on 3 December spokesmen from Faenza announced their general assembly's resolution: the people of Faenza was going to defend their town and their lord to the end! Cesare transferred his headquarters to Forli on 5 December 5, leaving detachments in the suburbs and along the roads near Faenza, maintaining a blockade to stop any major reinforcements reaching the town. Cesare's spies reported that supplies were coming into Faenza by way of Ravenna and Venice was sending the material to Ravenna. He persuaded Pope Alexander to convince the Venetians that sending supplies into the Romagna was not a good idea.

Cesare returned to Forli on 5 December. He sent a message to Cesena to prepare for his arrival and provide winter quarters for his troops. The Christmas court was brilliant, ornamented by men of letters and young noble officers. Cesare enjoyed the bull fights but was not much interested in the tournaments. Most of Romagna enjoyed a prosperous and peaceful winter. Cesare was particularly adept at administration. He managed finances with a sure hand and allowed full autonomy to the towns. More important to the Italians than independence, he suppressed local feuding and brought peace to Romagna.

Due to the winter, Cesare's army was dispersed which allowed his units to remain in supply. Giuilio Orsini moved to Cesena, Paolo Orsini to Imola, Conti to Bertinoro, and Vitellozzo moved into the Val Lamone above Faenza. To consolidate his position, Vitellozzo took Brisighella with its two citadels. The duke now controlled the whole coast region of Romagna and the lands from Fano to the borders of Bolognese except for the holdings of Faenza. The Venetians were attentive to his actions but not threatening. The *condottieri* remained satisfied and did not quarrel with each other.

Cesare Borgia's position was exceptionally powerful; although Faenza had not fallen, he had good reason to have confidence in the future. His west flank was open, but the Duke of Urbino remained peaceful and the French kept Florence quiet. The duke had a touch for good government. His policies were popular and effective. He retained or gained the goodwill of his holdings and in those places where he replaced the regimes. His greatest weakness and primary objective were the security of his power if Pope Alexander died.

January 1501 was a time for Cesare to prepare for the elimination of Faenza. Quick trips to the port of Cesenatico and Forli shaped up supply lines for the spring. Reinforcements began arriving giving Cesare a total of 1,200 men-at-arms and 4,000 Gascon foot. In Cesena, the duke conferred with the Orsini and Vitellozzo to plan the coming campaign. Vitellozzo went to Faenza where he commanded and tightened the blockade. On 21 January the defenders of Faenza launched a major sortie which Vitellozzo repulsed. But the people of the town maintained their defiance, renewing their defences from winter's ravages. Supplies increased despite the blockade and on 4 February the citizens renewed their oaths of fidelity in the Duomo. Through February, French reinforcements continued to arrive in Cesare's camps. The duke's forces took Rossi and Solarolo, neither place particularly strong, but in his hands they provided useful bases to strangle Faenza's supply lines further back to Ravenna. Pope Alexander, with King Louis' permission, pressured Bologna to provide provisions and lodgings for the French reinforcements travelling to Cesare after the lord of Bologna refused to surrender the Castel Bologna.

His Holiness had become very concerned. He complained to the Venetian ambassador that he was spending 35,000 ducats a month. Faenza was the problem. The campaign should have concluded by the New Year, at least. Now funds to pay the many troops were becoming harder to come by. Cesare fell under great pressure to end the campaign as soon as possible. While managing the mass of unruly men and the demands of divergent allies, Cesare faced many difficulties, but the worse incident erupted regarding the duke and a woman. The affair of Dorotea Malatesta Caracciola exploded at the time and has rumbled down the centuries ever since. She was a young and beautiful high noblewoman who was to be married to a much older noble commander of infantry in the service of Venice and stationed on the Turkish frontier in the Balkans. She was travelling across northern Italy under armed escort after a proxy marriage. A band of armed men ambushed the escort and took her away. The Venetians blamed Cesare and made a huge cry of outrage. The duke denied having anything to do with the affair, blaming it on one of his Spanish officers who conspired with Dorotea Malatesta. No matter, the furore did not die down.

The Fall of Faenza

By the beginning of April, all the French reinforcements had joined the duke's Italian forces before Faenza. Cesare requested and received permission from Duke Ercole d'Este to base his supply trains at Lugo. Under Cesare's command, the siege recommenced. During the winter, Faenza's defenders had extended their fortifications by including as an outpost the Monastery of Osservanza, beyond the town walls. What would have done well in 1480 now became wasted effort. On 12 April Cesare's cannon under Vitellozzo trundled up, took aim and opened fire, quickly shattering the new fortifications and forcing the small garrison to surrender. Then sappers dug into the ruined walls and built a masked battery.

Cesare sent invitations to Duke Ercole's sons, Alfonzo and his brother, Cardinal Ippolito to watch his taking of Faenza. On 12 April Cesare set about taking the citadel. Starting in the morning, the cannon bombarded the citadel's wall for three hours. Once the walls had shattered sufficiently, storming parties brought up climbing gear to get over the talus piles. From the ruined tops, the defenders threw down stones, burning tar, shooting bolts and arrows at the ascending soldiers. The storming troops finally reached upper walkways and soldiers from both sides fought with swords, while others used falconets to shoot down leaders. Many of Cesare's officers died that day from small cannon shot. The defenders repulsed the storm.

The next day, Cesare's determination only increased because he saw that the citadel was badly damaged and if he had lost a goodly number of brave men, so had the defenders. And, while he could easily replace his lost forces, the defenders could not. Vitellozzo moved his cannon to within a few hundred yards of the citadel and began another bombardment. They fired as often as they could. The great cannon exploded, killing Achille Tiberti and the gun crew, but the bombardment continued. Suddenly some deserters came to Cesare from Faenza and told him food and munitions were short. Cesare, ever chivalrous, announced to his court how greatly he respected those who fought against impossible odds and hanged the deserters in the sight of all.

For the next ten days, Cesare tightened the blockade of Faenza and set up assault points so his army could attack from many different directions. The expense was heavy, but sometimes a little patience pays well. On 25 April the town's leaders called a general meeting. What everyone saw was clear: the duke was going to carry Faenza. The assembly authorized representatives to go to Cesare's camp to negotiate terms. Cesare readily accepted their essential conditions: he guaranteed life, liberty and property to the lord Astorre Manfredi, his family and all his subjects. The town's leaders gave the terms to the people of Faenza on the afternoon of 25 April and the next morning the representatives returned to Cesare's camp and took the oath of loyalty. The young and handsome Astorre Manfredi came to Cesare who made it clear he was free to go as he pleased. Instead, Manfredi joined Cesare's forces as a young officer. Afterwards both parties observed the agreement. On the 27th Cesare went to Imola. He appointed a well-respected citizen as temporary governor of Faenza with a Spanish garrison of 500 men. In May Giovanni Vera, Cardinal of Salerno, came as governor and he respected the full civic autonomy of the town (a year or so later, Manfredi was found drowned in the Tiber; there were rumours of imprisonment).

Chapter 14

King Louis XII in Italy

K ing Louis XII was a more insightful and conscientious ruler than the careless and juvenile Charles VIII. After Louis' first campaign had removed Lodovico from Milan and established French power in the area, the king returned to France to plan and prepare for his expedition to the Kingdom of Naples. Lodovico's hopeless efforts at regaining his duchy slowed down Louis' timetable but afforded the king opportunity to strengthen his military might in northern Italy. When he was once again ruler of Milan, Louis carefully fashioned a robust administration dominating not only Milan but Lombardy, managing the communication and trade nexus of the many smaller powers in northern and central Italy.

Control of the many small squabbling states surrounding Milan had long eluded Italian powers since the collapse of the Hohenstaufens 250 years before. Louis intended to bring order into this chaos, not so much by physical conquest as by the threat of force supported by the promise of peace. Genoa submitted to the French on 6 September 1499. King Louis claimed dominion by right because Genoa was at one time subject to the French crown. As Duke of Milan, Louis demanded the same authority as Lodovico exercised. But rather than order his demands, Louis had extended negotiations balancing Genoese autonomy with direct French rule. The agreement emerged: the French recognized Genoa's involvement with European trade. When France was at war, they could use Genoa's port as they wished and Genoa would supply ships to the French, but Genoa was excused from active hostilities with England, Spain and Flanders. The Genoese were pleased with the protection offered by the French crown and when Lodovico returned in early 1500, Genoa remained loyal to King Louis.

Venice was a bastion of stability in northern Italy. Venetian interests were to the east, in the Adriatic and beyond. As long as their *terra firma* was secure, they were not a problem to Louis. While he could let Venice go its way, Louis' difficulties involved the many small north Italian states. These states had rallied to Lodovico when he returned and were disappointed with his quick defeat. King Louis claimed they forfeited any consideration because of former friendship and alliances. With powerful forces mobile and ready, Louis acted as if he was about to launch an offensive to subdue many of the small states. Of course, which states were his targets was a matter of guesswork. Among the rulers concerned for their holdings and safety were the Marquis of Mantua, the Duke of Ferrara, Giovanni Bentivoglio of Bologna and the Republic of Lucca. They all had heard about the deal King Louis was trying to make with the Venetians: the French and Venetians would partition all the smaller states between themselves. What they didn't hear was that the Venetians thought they already held too much *terra firma* and were not at all interested. Nor was Louis interested in trying to rule a squabbling mob of Italians. In the end, Louis gained what he wanted – substantial sums of money to recognize the small states' security.

Dealing with the Florentines was always a problem. The republic could change policy direction without warning; civil upheavals were always a possibility. But King Louis had no intention of being pulled into the never-ending morass of Florentine politics. Pisa was a problem and, as far as Louis was concerned, the problem could remain a problem because no solution was possible. The Florentine nobles, some 400 lances, rode with the French, backed up by some 3,000 infantry. Beyond that, Louis demanded payment of any money owed to Lodovico. Establishing Cesare Borgia's new state in Romagna was King Louis' answer to north Italian chaos.

The Lord de Ligny Comes to a Settlement with his Subjects

When the French took Milan, King Louis awarded some towns, including Tortona and Voghera, to Lord de Ligny. When Lodovico returned, these towns immediately recognized the Sforza restoration. After Lodovico's defeat, Ligny returned and threatened to sack all of his towns because they joined with Lodovico. Here, we will see a display of medieval theatre. Lord de Ligny could not say 'welcome back'. He really could not trust these subjects and they would not respect him. To re-establish a firm lord-subject relationship based on mutual respect, the parties decided to ritualize a new affiliation.

The Lord de Ligny came to Alessandria, accompanied by his captain, d'Ars and his retinue including the Chevalier Bayard, called Picquet (spur). Ligny's towns joined together and sent a delegation of twenty worthies to pay their respects and beg to be readmitted to his lordship's good graces. The Lord Ligny passed them by without acknowledgment. The delegation returned to their towns and gave their report. His lordship was most upset with them. The town leaders sought the help of Captain d'Ars, requesting he arrange an audience with the Lord de Ligny. Usually, such arrangements were accompanied by a gratuity which we may assume d'Ars accepted because he agreed to arrange the meeting.

The next day, after the early afternoon main meal, fifty of the most important citizens went to the hotel where Ligny resided. When he came out, the fifty took off their hats, fell to their knees and begged for mercy. Besides heartfelt entreaties, the citizens presented Ligny with a silver dinner service of many silver cups and vessels, worth 300 marks which he should accept as a token of forgiveness. (This was not an extravagant gift. A mark was worth about as much as a French crown, so 300 marks was a nice sum for an individual, but a drop in the bucket as far as a great lord was concerned. On the other hand, if they gave a lot, the Lord de Ligny might think that there was a good source of income.) The Lord de Ligny refused the gift and condemned the townspeople as ungrateful and treasonous.

Then Captain d'Ars fell to his knees and offered surety for the towns-people, expressing his faith in their gratitude and loyalty. The citizens joined as a chorus, begging Ligny to accept d'Ars request. The Lord de Ligny, with tears in his eyes, cried that they truly erred, but for the sake of Captain d'Ars, who was loyal and always gave good service, he would grant them pardon. As for the gift, he would not touch it. Rather, he turned and told Picquet, 'Take these vessels.' But the good knight replied, 'My lord, I thank you for your consideration, but for the sake of God, please do not make me take into my house that which belongs to these wretched people because it would bring misfortune.' Then Bayard took the vessels, one by one to each one present although at that time he had not ten crowns.

Later, the Lord de Ligny remarked to his court, how the goodness of the world is portrayed in Picquet. He sent to the good knight, a crimson velvet robe lined with satin, a goodly charger and a purse with 300 crowns. Bayard shared the money out with his companions.

Trouble with the Swiss

After King Louis recalled Trivulzio, the city of Milan and the duchy settled down and accepted French rule without many problems. But a new difficulty suddenly blew up. When Lodovico had resurfaced, Louis' agents worked quickly to hire and bring Swiss infantry into the fight. Perhaps they overstepped their instructions; perhaps the king merely wanted the soldiers quickly and decided he would handle the consequences later. Then, added to the questions about the base contract, came the Treason of Novara, in which Lodovico's Swiss mercenaries ended up turning him over to the French and imprisonment. The Swiss were upset when they had to violate their contract with Lodovico, then nearly came to blows with Louis' Swiss troops, something which was very much against the Swiss way of doing business. They saw themselves dishonoured and cheated.

The trouble erupted when Louis' agents started to dismiss the Swiss companies. The Swiss spokesmen told Louis their invoice was for two months' pay and a gratuity of a third month for surrendering Lodovico; added to that was the requirement of the train of sumpter animals to carry their booty over the mountains. King Louis, who was business minded and knew the value of money, counted that the actual time the Swiss were under contract was four weeks and said the invoiced charges were excessive. The Swiss spokesmen replied, if they were not paid what they were owed they would seize some towns and collect on their own. The Bailli of Dijon had negotiated the original contracts and was the point man for the pay-off. When the Swiss found they were not convincing King Louis, they seized the Bailli as security.

After some negotiating push and pull, the Swiss freed the Bailli while the question went to King Louis. Louis agreed to their demands and set the payment place at Vercelli. Coming up with that amount of hard currency to pay everyone at once was a problem, so the French staggered the pay-outs. As the Swiss companies collected at Vercelli, they demanded that payments speed up. The Bailli, who was overseeing the operation, hurried off to collect more cash and had just returned. While the Bailli was gone, the civilian commissioner, Doucet, refused to pay the gratuity to the Gascon mercenaries. A Gascon mercenary company led by their two commanders went to the commissary to teach Doucet a lesson in manners. On the stairs before the commissary, a Swiss captain and some of his company were waiting for their payment. They had no intention of letting the Gascon scum go ahead of them.

The commotion attracted more unsatisfied mercenaries and a full riot broke out. The rioters organized an attempt to break down the commissary's door. In the office, Doucet, the Bailli of Dijon, and the Swiss captain, who was still trying to collect his company's payment, barricaded the door. The rioters smashed the door and forced their way into the chamber. There, the Swiss captain and the Bailli tried to calm them. Doucet had taken the uniform of a Swiss soldier and was not recognized. The mob refrained from attacking the Swiss, so they soundly beat the Bailli.

The trouble with the mercenaries was a clash of French pride and Swiss greed. The solution was money. Much more difficult were the claims of the Forest Cantons to parts of the Duchy of Milan. During the first conquest of Milan in 1499 the French accepted the surrender of Bellinzona. When Lodovico returned in 1500, Bellinzona welcomed him. Then the French returned and made the town pay. The following March, Swiss companies entered Bellinzona on their way to join la Tremoille. The people of the town begged the Swiss to accept their submission in the name of the Canton of Uri. During the wars between the emperors and the popes, Bellinzona supported the imperialists. The Dukes of Milan, supporters of the papacy, had pushed up the Alpine valleys and annexed a number of imperialist mountain towns by 1350. Under the Visconti and Sforza the towns were prosperous. The coming of the French threatened both peace and prosperity. The citizens liked the Swiss, accepted the Italians, but despised the French.

The citizens convinced the Swiss companies to stay and support their efforts to join the Swiss Confederation. In April 1501 representatives of Uri, Schwyz, and Unterwalden accepted Bellinzona's act of homage and allegiance. The town's citizens delivered keys of the town gates to the representatives. The canton's representatives maintained they were fulfilling the agreement they had made with King Louis when he so desperately needed aid when Lodovico returned. They claimed that not only had he ceded Bellinzona, but also Locarno and Lugano.

King Louis denied any such claim. He demanded the evacuation of Bellinzona or he would withdraw all commercial privileges held by the Swiss in the Duchy of Milan. The king's official letter to the federal Swiss Diet expressed his astonishment at the attempted land-grab and the hope that the Diet would put this right. The Diet members became upset with the cantons of Uri, Schwyz and Unterwalden because all the cantons would suffer the consequences of these cantons' actions. The Diet representatives suggested inviting the Forest Cantons to accept restitution of their claims with a sum of money and the restoration of commercial privileges as they were under the Sforza. Unterwalden accepted these conditions, but Uri and Schwyz increased their complaints against the French and officially requested the confederation's assistance in asserting their rights. Even worse, angry mercenaries demanded the confederation attack the current government in Milan and so started a war with the French.

The issue of Bellinzona became a major distraction to King Louis. The Diet tried to avoid the problem by sending messages to Louis about means of satisfying the mercenaries' demands. This ended in August 1501, when the mercenaries occupying Bellinzona invaded Lombardy, attacked Lugano and plundered the countryside, while calling for reinforcement from their fellows in the Forest Cantons to join them. In Milan the Cardinal d'Amboise collected 4,000 infantry and some men-at-arms from nearby garrisons. He sent orders for reinforcements to come from Lyons, calling for men-at-arms and archers.

French forces marched toward Lugano, relieving a post on 26 August which had held out against the mercenaries for over a week. The Swiss at Lugano found themselves facing converging French forces with only paths up the mountains open for retreat. Pulling out of Lugano, the mercenaries trekked up the mountains, reaching Bellinzona with their booty on 12 September. The French forces followed. The mercenaries' spokesmen claimed they were victims of contract violations and not rebels; they were merely collecting what they were owed.

The French commanders discussed their options. Rather than just let the Swiss go, and so reward bad actions, the French prepared to attack the mercenaries who withdrew into Bellinzona but opened negotiations. King Louis was concerned about the squabble because he needed Swiss mercenaries for his coming campaign to recover Naples. While French forces dealt with the mercenaries at Bellinzona, Swiss envoys negotiated with Cardinal d'Amboise. They settled on 14 September: Louis sent the money claimed, the Swiss would send legal experts to the French royal court to hammer out legalities. Meanwhile the people of Bellinzona received full commercial privileges without regard to their ultimate allegiance, and none of the parties involved would provide support for the Sforza exiles.

The men of the Confederate Diet saw reason in Louis' offer, but the Canton of Uri refused to accept the settlement. After much discussion on the Swiss side, in August 1502 the Diet sent envoys to the French court with revised demands. Many members of the Diet had had about enough of the issue but, because of the constitution of the confederation, they could not just bury it. King Louis received them graciously but would not move away from his claim on Bellinzona. The Diet members should have expected no less but implored Uri to refrain from hostilities. King Louis' problem was the large numbers of Swiss mercenaries he was employing for the campaign in Naples. He could not expect adherence to contract if he went to war against the Swiss Confederation.

The men of Uri were aware of Louis' problems. They told the Diet how the French in Milan injured them and how justice required Bellinzona be part of their community. If this did not happen soon, they would take up arms. The French negotiators replied that if the Diet maintained the peace, they would submit to arbitration. The Diet principals pressed this solution but the Forest Canton, the core of the confederation, refused the offer. In February 1503, a Swiss formation accompanied by Milanese exiles crossed into the Duchy of Milan and plundered. The other Swiss cantons joined in the outrage of the Forest Cantons and raised 14,000 soldiers. In Milan, the French had only some 500 lances, 8,000 foot, and 50 cannons. The Swiss were superior in all things military, and the only probable outcome was ignoble French defeat. Louis, fighting in Naples saw the best solution; he ceded Bellinzona.

King Louis and King Ferdinand Partition
the Kingdom of Naples

While he was settling his conquests in Northern Italy, Louis prepared for the expedition to recover Naples. His preparations were, as usual with him, carefully made and thorough. The main force that had pushed Charles VIII out of Naples was under the orders of King Ferdinand the Catholic, King of Aragon, one of the sovereigns of the United Kingdom of Spain. Ferdinand had wealth, fleets and powerful armies in his hands. Beginning a major war with Ferdinand would cost far more than any possible gain. When the Spanish commander, the great Captain de Córdoba, pushed the French out of Naples, Ferdinand accepted Federigo of Naples, uncle of the previous king, as King of Naples. Ferdinand, as King of Sicily, might have taken Naples but decided against the move because that might have united too many of his enemies together.

This situation appeared to King Louis to offer an opening for an easy conquest of Naples. By accepting half a loaf rather than the whole thing, he sought to disarm King Ferdinand. Louis knew, as did everyone at the time interested in such matters, about Ferdinand's reputation for trickery, cunning, artful mendacity and downright dishonesty. But, by proposing a bargain structured so Ferdinand could pick up rich lands without expense while at the same time facing him with the consequences of a major war, Louis hoped to take Naples without much trouble. Louis' and Ferdinand's envoys discussed the agreement. They wrote a treaty, which the French signed at Chambord on 10 October, and at Granada on 11 November 1500.

Louis would become King of Naples and have Naples, Terra di Lavoro and the Abruzzi in the kingdom's northwest; Ferdinand was to be Duke of Calabria and Apulia in the south. The two provinces, Capitanta and Basilicate were a buffer zone dominated by neither party. Revenue was shared between the king and the duke. The treaty was secret; no one outside of a close circle had any idea about the agreement. The parties did approach Pope Alexander who approved the partition and granted the royal title to Louis and the ducal title to Ferdinand in the papal role as overlord of the Kingdom of Naples.

In early summer 1501, the French expeditionary force mustered in Milan. In June the army marched south in two sections: one through Pontremoli, Lucca and Cascina; the other went through Bologna, Imola, Faenza and the Sieve Valley. The sections joined together at Siena and marched to Rome. Altogether, under d'Aubigny's command, there were 1,000 lances, 4,000 Swiss, 6,000 Gascon and French foot, 36 cannon of which 12 were large and 100 supply wagons. The march was without disturbance to the civilian population and the army paid for needed goods. When the army approached Rome, the French and Spanish ambassadors requested to meet His Holiness in Consistory. There, they officially informed the pope of the secret treaty and requested formal investiture of their respective masters of the kingdom. On 25 June the pope granted the request with a papal bull. His Holiness received the French commander with great respect, causing d'Aubigny to sit by his side. When the army marched south from Rome, Pope Alexander was present and bestowed apostolic blessings upon the departing host.

The news of the secret compact spread out from Rome throughout Italy. Guicciardini tells there was general astonishment: on the one hand, King Louis gives up half of a kingdom and by doing so invites another power into Italy, and on the other King Ferdinand conspires against a king of his blood with a centuries-old enemy and after he promised to give help to that king. Before the parties revealed their secret treaty, King Federigo was preparing to meet the French; he thought the coming Spanish fleet was protecting his interests, so he opened Calabria to Gonzalo's return to Italy. Federigo also sent his young son, Ferdinand, to Taranto in case the French prevailed, but to avoid that the king contracted with the brothers Colonna for armed support. The king marshalled his army and marched to San Germano to await the French.

Chapter 15

Cesare Borgia: The Third *Impresa*

Cesare and King Louis

The most important factor involved in Cesare's efforts to build the new Duchy of Romagna was the correlation of ambitions between Pope Alexander Borgia and King Louis. The French king's ambitions in Italy centred on accomplishing what his predecessor tried to achieve but failed: securing the coronet of Milan and the crown of Naples. For Louis to succeed in Naples, he needed Pope Alexander's support and goodwill and so he had to back Cesare Borgia's ambitions in Romagna. Equally important, the French King found Cesare a bold, imaginative person and was drawn to him as a fellow adventurer. So, he had created Cesare Duke of Valentinois and supported the *impresa*.

The problems in Italy which Louis faced were more complex than just Naples. What Louis had to do to secure Naples often ran against what was needed to secure Milan. The powers he needed to worry about in southern Italy were King Ferdinand of Spain and the Venetian Republic; in the north of Italy, he had to consider the Duke of Savoy, the Florentine Republic, a mass of minor but powerful princelings and the Venetians (whose interests in the north were not quite her interests in the south). The efforts to build a Duchy of Romagna was going to cause trouble to all the northern Italian powers.

Louis had signed the Treaty of Granada with Ferdinand on 11 November 1500, but the fact remained secret. This was why, when Florence's envoy to Louis, Machiavelli, insistently pointed out the danger to Florence of Cesare's *impresa*, Louis seemed unimpressed. Bologna, under her lord Giovanni Bentivoglio, was under Pope Alexander's protection and trusted to His Holiness. Venice was tied to King Louis after she had taken Cremona as part of her agreement with France in the war against Lodovico. Without hinderance from Florence, Bologna, or Venice, the Duke of Valentinois was free to build his Duchy of Romagna and Louis was free to take Naples.

The Second *Impresa* Concludes

In the First *Impresa* (1499–1500), the Duke of Valentinois employed French troops at critical times. Now, Cesare planned using *condottieri* troops. He came to depend on Vitellozzo who demonstrated the greatest skill and expended exceptional energy in accomplishing Cesare's objectives. Vitellozzo was an artillery expert and son-in-law of Paolo Orsini who managed infantry. Together the two *condottieri* worked well in artillery-infantry co-ordination. Cesare set his plans directed against Bologna in motion on 27 April 1501. His forces marched out of Imola under Vitellozzo, pushed eight miles and took over Castel San Pietro on the Bologna Road. The Duke's idea was to move faster than French awareness of his actions. His actual target was the Castel Bologna. Cesare's lands surrounded the Castel Bologna; by taking it, he would remove a threat to the integrity of his territories. Ravenna, to the east, was under Venetian suzerainty, to attempt to take it was dangerous and, at this time, King Louis had no intention of allowing Bologna to fall to Cesare. Cesare knew how far he could go and so he went no further.

While Vitellozzo proceeded on his assignments, Cesare sent a commissioner to Bologna to demand the surrender of Castel Bologna. The government of Giovanni Bentivoglio told the duke's representative that Bolognese envoys were on their way to investigate the matter at Imola. They did not know Vitellozzo had already arrested these envoys so they could not report Cesare's men and already held some strategic sites guarding access to Castel Bologna. When the situation became clear, Giovanni Bentivoglio agreed to the cession of Castel Bologna to Cesare with conditions. On 30 April Cesare accepted the conditions and occupied the castle and town. His northern borders now secured; Cesare looked to the west. Here was Tuscany and so the Florentine Republic. In early May 1501, the Florentines saw the threat.

The duke understood Florence was under King Louis' protection and the Florentines wanted him away from their lands. The independent town of Piombino, on the sea in the north of Tuscany, however, was there for the picking and would allow Cesare to pressure Florence without violating Louis' demand. Instead, Cesare marched through Florence's territory toward Piombino. He established camp nearby on 4 June and called on Vitellozzo to bring artillery. Basing his supplies on Siena, Cesare brought papal galleys to blockade the seaways and sat down to starve the town into surrender. Vitellozzo conducted the siege until Piombino gave in on 2 September 1501.

The Third *Impresa* 1502

During April and May 1502, Cesare began organizing the third *impresa*. He announced the target: Camerino. As usual, complaints about the Lord of Camerino, Giulio Cesare Varano, rang out in the camera. The lord Varano did not properly respond so the camera revoked his right to rule. Military measures moved along quickly. Between 7 and 23 of May, Cesare received almost 55,000 ducats and further payments of 4,200 ducats went to Francesco Orsini for artillery. Another payment of 6,000 ducats was spent to acquire 'engines of war' from Ischia. Between 10 May and 12 July, the camera paid some 3,300 ducats for 83,000 pounds of gunpowder (about 25 ducats per ton at 2,000 pounds a ton).

Florence was very concerned about Cesare organizing a campaign against a town near their borders and approached King Louis about obtaining firm protection against hostilities. In return for France's protection, Florence agreed to pay France 40,000 ducats every year for three years. In return, King Louis sent a force of 2,400 cavalry for their defence. The Florentines were not wrong. Vitellozzo and Baglioni induced communities in the upper Tiber and the Val of Chiana to remove themselves from Florentine allegiance on 25 May. French officials caught up with Cesare, demanding an explanation but he said he knew nothing about such actions.

Cesare marched out of Rome on the Via Flaminia on 10 June. He halted at Spoleto on the 15th to establish his operational base. After sending off a vanguard under Francesco Orsini of young and able men-at-arms toward Camerino, he marched his main body of troops along the main road by Nocera and Fossato. As this was occurring, Cesare's commissary general, the Bishop of Elna was stationed at Perugia and ensured supplies for Vitellozzo and Baglioni on the upper Arno (and so, opposing the Florentines). Pope Alexander then ordered the commissary general to contract with the Duke of Urbino for oxen to pull artillery and supplies for 1,500 men to pass through his lands. The Duke, Guidobaldo, had endeavoured to keep Urbino out of the turmoil engulfing central Italy and out of the Borgia's clutches. He immediately sent an envoy to Spoleto to offer passage, his goodwill and obedience. Cesare sent the envoy back, requiring Guidobaldo to supply Vitellozzo with 1,000 infantry at Arezzo.

Cesare's order put the Duke of Urbino in a difficult position. He was strongly attached to Florence and, more important, he hoped for King Louis' protection, but that was at risk if his troops appeared to threaten Florence. Stationed at Arezzo, that is just what they would do. But Cesare and his army were nearby and to expect the Duke of Romagna to forgive a slight was not likely. On 20 June the Duke of Urbino replied to Cesare, that he had to have a written order from the Captain-General of the Church Lands to deliver the formation. Regardless, Vitellozzo's agents were welcome to recruit 1,000 men from Urbino lands. His reply came to Cesare accompanied by a handsome charger.

In fact Cesare's intentions were very different from what Guidobaldo imagined, but were what he feared. Cesare called up troops, collecting them at garrison towns in Romagna. Each household had to supply one soldier. Concentrated at Fano and Forli, they then marched to the borders of Urbino. One force of more than 1,000 troops with artillery moved into the hills and built bases commanding the routes between Urbino and Singaglia. Another force worked through the mountains upon which stands San Marino, threatening Urbino from the north. By 20 June word reached Urbino of the approaching troops. By then Cesare was in the heart of Urbino with a powerful army.

From the passing of the old year and dawn of 1502, Cesare's objective was Urbino, Camerino was but a mask behind which to hide. Cesare had pushed forward joining his forces descending on Urbino on 20 June. He had covered forty miles in a day. On the afternoon of the 21st, after storming their way across the landscape, Cesare entered Urbino at the head of his vanguard. He immediately established order and discipline in the town, appointed administrators, keeping the existing civil officials in place.

During mid June, Duke Guidobaldo was waiting for news of the peaceful transit of Cesare's troops through Urbino toward Camerino. Only on 20 June did the realization dawn that his lordship was under attack and he was unprepared. Late in the evening of the 20th, his guards told him that only the western passes were open. At midnight, Guidobaldo fled Urbino with a few mounted archers, three men-at-arms and his nephew. The party rode across the countryside on the road to San Leo. At daybreak word came that Borgia's men were headed to San Leo. Turning west by southwest, he reached a small village tired and dishevelled, high in the mountain ridges near the headwaters of the Tiber and Savio. He thought to continue through the high country to Florence or Bologna.

Guidobaldo was surprised by the warm welcome and friendly assistance given by the local peasantry. He trusted to their help. Reversing course, he followed behind Cesare's Forli column, crossed the Romagna and on 23 June reached Venetian Ravenna. On the eighth day, he arrived at Mantua where his wife was visiting Isabella Gonzaga and they joyfully reunited. He and his nephew had split up, and the young man travelled through

Tuscany and joined another of his uncles, the Cardinal San Pietro in Vincoli, who took him to France.

From the Mantuan Court, Guidobaldo addressed the cardinal in a letter dated 28 June relating his account of what he called the Great Betrayal. He was, Guidobaldo said, a loyal and supportive ally of Pope Alexander and Cesare. Despite that, he was suddenly and without warning removed from power and just barely escaped with his life. Cesare, understanding his seizure of Urbino needed explanation, sent a detailed defence of his actions. He claimed and had supporting evidence that Guidobaldo was secretly giving aid to Camerino, collecting money, supplies and troops. Of course, given the policy of hedging bets at that time, some of what Cesare alleged was probably true enough: but everyone did it. Whatever the rights and wrongs, Cesare's bold and quick moves amazed all Italy. His exercises in strategy, quickness and luck demonstrated an amazing virtuosity.

Having taken Urbino, Cesare still had the men and resources to continue the *impresa*. He set up Camerino to cover his move against Urbino; now he would take Camerino. The lord of Camerino, Giulio Cesare Varano was 70 years old. He had no mercenary troops nor support from the local nobility but trusted to his castle. The campaign started when Oliverotto da Fermo marched eastward from Foligno into the hills with 200 light horse and 1,000 foot. Supporting him, came armed peasants from Spoleto who raided the countryside. Francesco Orsini with 100 men-at-arms, 100 light horse, and two large companies of Spanish foot and the same of Romagna foot marched on Camerino from the north, following the easy road up the Esino valley. In summer the grain crops were still in the fields and the Spanish troops, particularly, ravaged and burned the land. Refugees swarmed to the towns.

The citizens of Camerino were in turmoil. They were not going to defend against Cesare's *condottieri*, but the question was, how to avoid it? Lord Varano opened negotiations with Orsini on 19 July. The talks dragged on into the 21st, with Cesare's troops more and more threatening. The town guard simply opened the gates, Varano surrendered the castle and he and two of his sons became prisoners. Two other sons were in Venice. Varano was thrown into the dungeon of Urbino. On 7 October the old man died and the other captives were executed.

Cesare and King Louis

King Louis was preparing his expedition to recover Naples. He expected Pope Alexander and Cesare to clear the road. But he also needed Florence and Florence's influence to provide and protect French supply lines to Naples. On 7 July the king reached Asti from Grenoble. The incursion and occupation of Florentine lands by Cesare's *condottieri* concerned Louis and his advisors. Nor was Louis pleased with the Borgia's plans to bring Bologna into the Duchy of Romagna. Before he arrived at Asti, King Louis had sent an order to the Duke of Romagna demanding that he must not annoy the Florentines and sent a detachment forward to Arezzo. In fact Cesare's spies at Louis' court kept him informed about the various policies discussed by his majesty and his counsellors. By 15 July Cesare had sent orders to Vitellozzo to withdraw from the valley of the Arno but Vitellozzo began to equivocate. Cesare, not happy, threatened to annex Vitellozzo's Citta di Castello and add it to Romagna. This irritated Vitellozzo who, with Baglioni, evacuated Arezzo on 29 July. By the end of August all Florentine lands were restored.

The Duke of Romagna was aware of his precarious political position. King Louis was not satisfied with Cesare's explanation about self-willed *condottieri*; his support for Florence was unwavering. He wanted Cesare to punish Vitellozzo and Baglioni. Cesare knew that to inflict punishment on loyal servants who commanded their own armies was to cut off his right hand. The temper of the French court in Milan changed. Those who found themselves deceived, cheated and dispossessed found welcome in Milan, including Guidobaldo of Urbino, various members of the Varano family, the Marquis of Mantua and certain Orsini.

Cesare was aware that he needed to appease King Louis. On 25 July Cesare, accompanied by only four officers, left Urbino early. In a few days, dressed as a Knight of St John, he came to the French royal court in Milan. Cesare's charm and initiative again won King Louis' admiration. Indeed, after he heard of Cesare's approach, the king rode out of Milan to greet the champion. Louis embraced Cesare, welcoming him with the words, 'my cousin and dear kinsman'. The lords who had joined together in opposition to Cesare in Milan melted away.

Louis and Cesare made a *capitoli*, but it has remained secret ever since. Basic understandings, however, are obvious. Florence was not in the Borgia sphere of influence. Bologna was Cesare's, if he could take it. Cesare would get rid of the *condottieri*, Vitellozzo, Baglioni, the Orsini and the rest. In return, King Louis would supply armed forces for Cesare. Machiavelli questioned this agreement saying, why would the French king reject traditional allies in favour of powers which usually supported Spain? But Louis saw in Cesare a strong individual who would see Spanish pressure as more threatening than French. The convention of August 1502 of King Louis and Cesare Borgia opened the road to Naples. King Louis' vision was certain: with Milan in his control and then Naples, the French would control Italy from end to end. Whatever Borgia did then could not shake French control.

Cesare had other ideas. With French aid and support, his new state could build a strong military, overawe the rest of the smaller northern Italian princedoms and eventually absorb Florence, Rome and even Savoy. Cesare thought big. The place to begin now was Bologna, which would make an admirable capital for a time. The problem with Bologna was the ruler, Giovanni Bentivoglio. He was a wily man, well versed in the habits and desires of successful *condottieri*. That he was allied with some, or all, of Cesare's *condottieri*, was obvious. The *impresa* of Bologna would probably involve a rupture with his captains. He wanted French forces to replace the *condottieri*. He would become a vassal of King Louis, but he would be master of his own state. While he depended on the French, Cesare wanted to raise a force loyal directly to him and to his state.

The core of Cesare's own force was the body of Spanish infantry and his companies of men-at-arms. He organized new units using some of his loyal officers, recruiting and drilling men of Romagna. During September conscription proceeded under the direction of Don Michele; the principle of the draft was '*un uomo per casa*': one able-bodied man from each household. The peasantry was happy to comply; the money was good and their duke was a true leader of men. Cesare's new foot soldiers had leather or cloth protection with metal arm guards and carried a pike and a sword. Their uniforms featured the Borgia colours – a jacket and breeches striped in yellow and vermilion. Companies were 500 strong, drilled and trained under strict discipline.

Cesare needed more than foot. He had some 650 men-at-arms loyal to him personally. He hired companies of more men-at-arms by contracting with individuals rather than dealing with *condottieri*. Through his father's influence, Cesare brought companies of Spanish cavalry from Rome, including *schioppettieri*, horsemen with matchlock carbines. Cesare's cannon came from a variety of sources. Large cannons needed eighteen horses to move and eight for smaller cannons. Cesare adopted the French practice of constructing carriages for the guns from which they fired. Using designs by his military engineer, Leonardo da Vinci, he continued producing new cannon and carriages. Machiavelli said that Cesare's artillery was as strong as all the rest of Italy put together. Further, Cesare's army building process impressed Machiavelli; he saw the type of force as the start of the army of the future.

To pay for all of this, Pope Alexander sent 1,000 ducats a week. Cesare garrisoned all his fortified towns along the highways of Romagna, and this took up a large number of his soldiers. He still had to employ Vitellozzo and Orsini to hold Urbino and its hinterland. Cesare organized his duchy along his line of communication, providing mobile forces to face any threat. Ramiro de Lorqua was commander of the men-at-arms, quartered at Rimini near the centre, and Don Michele stayed at Imola, drawing in new soldiers, training, disciplining them and sending them out. Fano, on the other end of the chain, provided for its defence. Cesare had Leonardo da Vinci prepare reports on civic improvements as Cesare reformed and improved the administration.

Chapter 16

King Louis and his Campaign for Naples

The French March to Naples

On 17 June 1501 Cesare took a ship back to Rome in preparation for joining King Louis' campaign to take Naples. Cesare joined with his father, Pope Alexander. In welcoming his son, Alexander issued a number of bulls investing Cesare as Duke of Romagna with territories he had taken. The French came to Rome; d'Aubigny arrived with Louis' vanguard which included the company of French lancers accorded to Cesare by Louis in 1499. Once in Rome, the French required the Borgias to release Caterina Sforza to Florence. The main French army entered Rome on 28 June. Pope Alexander and Cesare reviewed the troops as they passed over the Ponte Saint Angelo on their way through Rome. The 2,000 finely equipped horse, 12,000 foot and 36 cannon, accompanied by continuous martial music, impressed the Romans. Cesare with his commanders, Vitellozzo and Baglioni and some of their troops marched with the French in the Naples expedition.

When Federigo received confirmation of the French-Spanish agreement, he gave up the idea of defending his kingdom's frontiers and fell back to Capua. There, the brothers Colonna joined him. King Federigo left Fabrizio Colonna in charge of Capua with 300 men-at-arms and 3,000 foot. He sent Prospero Colonna to hold Naples while he went with strong forces to Aversa.

After he left Rome, d'Aubigny occupied Marino which the Colonna had quickly abandoned. The French plundered then burned the town. From Marino, they marched by way of Velletri to Rocca Secca near San Germano. None of these towns offered any opposition. Here, Cesare Borgia joined the expedition with his elite force of men-at-arms and together the French and Borgia forces crossed the kingdom's frontiers and reached Tiano on 8 July 1501. They marched on to Capua where Fabrizio Colonna waited for them with his powerful garrison backed up with strong artillery, including some captured from the French when King Charles lost Naples.

The French held the further bank of the Volturno River and cleared the neighbourhood of Federigo's supporters. They sent a demand that

Capua surrender. Fabrizio Colonna refused and prepared to defend the town with Neapolitans and his own troops. The French began the siege, setting their cannons in position and bombarding Capua's outworks. Fabrizio's cannon returned fire. The French artillery kept firing and after four days the bombardment had shattered the outworks. The French foot charged, carrying the bastions and killing the defenders. The French then moved the cannon and took the town wall under fire. The cannons blasted a breach in the walls. The imposing destruction of what appeared to be fine fortifications disheartened the townspeople and refugees from the countryside who clamoured for surrender.

Envoys came from the town to negotiate terms, but the French refused to grant the Capuans' main demand: that the French army not enter the town. Finally, they reached an agreement but somehow the 40,000 ducats the town agreed to pay the French went missing for a while. So, while the defenders thought the deal made and relaxed, the French forced their way into the town which they proceeded to plunder and ravish on 24 July.

The horror inflicted on Capua caused consternation throughout Italy. The official French history comments: 'Entered with tumultuous noise, slaughter, and bloodshed.' The foot, who entered first, killed all the men they found in the streets or hidden in houses. They raped all the women they found and herded the best looking back to Rome for the slave market. Many French and Swiss soldiers took enough plunder to be rich for life. The French captured many officers of Federigo's army, including Fabrizio Colonna who had to pay a heavy ransom.

A large number of high-born women found refuge in a tower. The first wave of violence past them by. Eventually, they had to surrender to the French. The French herded them to the Roman slave markets after raping them all except for forty of the best looking, who fell to Cesare Borgias' personal attention.

Just after the sack, Federigo's envoys came to arrange ransom for certain prisoners. Then d'Aubigny took the envoy on a tour of the ravaged city and told him, 'Go! Tell them in Naples that tomorrow I shall be there and will do worse!' He did not need to say more. The French advance continued. Gaeta immediately surrendered when the French appeared. Federigo abandoned Aversa and retreated to Naples. When the French came to Aversa, the gates opened. For two days, the French army rested, making necessary repairs to equipment, cleaning soiled trappings and repacking supplies.

The French, arms resplendent, appeared just outside Naples' gates on 25 July. Heralds presented themselves to the city. Next day, the city council sent a delegation to d'Aubigny's camp, begging the French commander to accept their homage to the Kingdom of France. Naples paid 6,000 ducats to avoid a sack. On 2 August 1501 the garrison of the New Castle surrendered and two days later d'Aubigny made a formal entry into Naples. He extended French control from Naples into the Terra di Lavoro and then sent detachments to occupy the Abruzzi. The key to d'Aubigny ability to take Naples was his agreement with Federigo. The French commander agreed to allow King Federigo to leave the New Castle in Naples and take his court to Ischia. His rationale was that King Federigo could deal with King Louis to make a settlement. The agreement included the provision that if they did not settle in six months, Federigo could reassert his rights.

Just how realistic was the agreement made between d'Aubigny and Federigo remained to be seen. Later, the French fleet under Philip de Ravenstein came to Naples and found Federigo still in control of Ischia. Ravenstein said d'Aubigny's efforts at peacemaking were ridiculous. The French denounced the agreement and told Federigo he was going to France. Once in France, he found life comfortable in a chateau with 50,000 crowns a year. Federigo died in 1504.

King Louis respected d'Aubigny's abilities as a military commander, but as a civil administrator the king had his doubts. On 12 October Louis d'Armagnac, Duke of Nemours, arrived in Naples; the young nobleman was royal viceroy. He came with the king's appointment as chancellor of the Kingdom of Naples, along with Jean Nicolay an experienced administrator with his staff. Cesare Borgia received Louis' thanks for his assistance and invited him to go home. Ravenstein sailed away to join the Venetians in the never-ending Turkish wars. The wheels of administration began to turn, disposing of opponents, rewarding supporters, and proclaiming, 'Good order, justice and upholding the law.' Profits for the French and their supporters rolled into their hands.

The Agreement between the Kings Ferdinand and Louis Collapses

While d'Aubigny and the French marched south toward Naples, the Great Captain Gonzalo de Córdoba landed in Calabria on 5 July 1501 and was received as a deliverer. He brought 190 men-at-arms, 300 light horse, and 4,000 infantry, along with a full set of instructions written in code in a series of letters from King Ferdinand. Gonzalo marched to Taranto because Federigo's eldest son, Prince Ferdinand was there, protected by the most loyal Neapolitan troops. The Spanish army blockaded the town while Gonzalo extended Spanish administration through Calabria and Apulia. Ferdinand's instructions ordered Gonzalo to avoid any hostile actions with the French while he swept up any loose pieces that he happened to find. Taranto finally surrendered on 2 March 1502. Gonzalo gave his word that Prince Ferdinand would go free before the surrender, but once in Spanish hands he was sent to Spain to live in gilded captivity. Once Taranto was in Gonzalo's power, Fabrizio and Prospero Colonna joined him.

The partition of the kingdom between the French and the Spanish aroused grave political tensions. The Angevin noble houses supported the French and the Aragonese houses gravitated toward Ferdinand, but the problem was that both groups of noble houses owned property in both sections of the kingdom. Worse, the soldiers of both sides found the lawlessness profitable. Complicating the political split was the question of who controlled the buffer provinces which were not assigned to either France or Spain. The three districts were the Capitanate, between Apulia and the Abruzzi, the Basilicate, between Apulia and Calabria and the Principate, between Basilicate and Terra di Lavoro. Spain claimed the Basilicate and the Principate belonged to Calabria, and, using King Ferrante's fiscal organization as proof, claimed the Capitanate was part of Apulia. The French disputed those claims. The most important territory was the Capitanate since there, a land of pastures, the collection of *dogana delle pecore*, a tax on flocks and herds, provided a primary revenue source for the crown. Both Gonzalo and Nemours tried to work out a method of dealing with this revenue until their rulers made up their minds, but this accomplished little.

Because Gonzalo was occupied in the siege of Taranto, French forces entered the disputed lands occupying strongholds. They installed an administration and court in Avellino. Once he settled with Taranto, Gonzalo marched north to rectify the situation. Local barons had no desire to see fighting break out in their lands; they convinced the two sides to come to a conference to find a solution to their disagreement. At the meeting on 1 April 1502 there was no agreement except to refer the problems back to their respective monarchs.

Feelings between the French and Spanish ran hot. When a French formation marched through Rome, an ugly riot broke out in the streets because some Spaniards ridiculed King Louis' claim to Naples. The French viceroy, Nemours, knew his army was larger and he believed better than the Spanish army. He looked for an excuse to attack the Spanish forces. On his initiative, he ordered Gonzalo to evacuate the Capitanate, threatening to push him out if they didn't leave. Receiving no answer, Nemours attacked the Spanish-occupied Troja.

Gonzalo was still under orders to avoid fighting with the French, but skirmishes broke out here and there developing into a low-level sequence of raids and counter raids. Soon, new instructions arrived from Ferdinand in his coded letters: the Kingdom of Spain was at war with the Kingdom of France; Gonzalo, with far fewer troops than the French, needed to hold key places and keep open a path to the sea because the Spanish fleet was coming with reinforcements and supplies. Gonzalo had received no reinforcements nor supplies or money since he initially landed in Calabria. But, well aware of his position, by the end of June Gonzalo withdrew his mobile forces into Barletta, a sea town on the Apulian coast where Spanish or Venetian ships could supply him if necessary, or by which he could withdraw by sea. The rest of his troops he placed in garrisons, including Andria, Canosa and Bari.

The French Offensive

A month after Gonzalo withdrew into Barletta, the French advanced, laying siege to Canosa in mid-August. Canosa was defended by a force of 700 men commanded by Pedro Navarro, an experienced infantry captain and renowned military engineer. In July Nemours invested the stronghold, battering at the walls with his cannon. The walls crumbled but Navarro's soldiers repulsed the French assaults. Gonzalo wrote to Navarro, telling him to surrender rather than face destruction and the negotiations began. The French, relieved of the need for further hard fighting, received the town and gave Navarro and his soldiers the Honours of War, allowing them to march out under arms with their property to join with Gonzalo's army in Barletta.

Reinforcements of more than 2,000 Swiss reached Nemours by ship from Genoa. Then, Nemours marched his main force to Barletta where his men–at–arms and infantry demonstrated in front of the gates, challenging Gonzalo to battle. But the Spanish refused the temptation. The French withdrew, thinking the Spanish were going to ignore them. Gonzalo led out his whole cavalry, backed up by strong infantry units and hit the withdrawing French. The French men-at-arms turned and charged the Spanish horse. As the French heavy horse drew near, the Spanish cavalry turned and fled, drawing the French after them into an ambush by their infantry. A hard hit, indeed. Then the Spanish withdrew into Barletta.

The French invested Barletta and spread out through Apulia, bringing the province under French control and collecting plunder. They blocked all the sources of supply to Barletta. The French saw ships sailing in and out of Barletta and traced them to Venetian bases along the coast. Nemours formally complained to the Venetians that they were supplying the Spanish but officially, they denied this.

The French held a council of war to decide on the best path forward. They could pick off all the outlying positions, slowly constricting Gonzalo's holding to Barletta or they could simply attack Barletta, thus eliminating Gonzalo's main base. The attack against Barletta was made easier by the fact that the fortifications were obsolete. They were built in the years before the coming of newer types of cannon. Without a single bastion, the fortress would crumble. But even if the French swept the walls of Barletta away Gonzalo and his best forces would evacuate by sea and go elsewhere. The situation would remain. Nemours decided that rather than attack Barletta or pick off Gonzalo's outlying garrisons, he would block any sortie from Barletta and consolidate French control of the areas which Gonzalo had abandoned.

At the time, there was much said about the clash of personalities between d'Aubigny, the military commander and Nemours, the viceroy. The rumour explained Nemours' decisions as efforts to keep d'Aubigny from gaining credit for any victories. True, d'Aubigny disliked the young court aristocrat, and no doubt had some harsh words about him, but Nemours had to consider the objectives of his royal master. King Louis saw a larger picture than simply squabbling in southern Italy. He thought about finances and conserving of forces. Great victories were expensive, great defeats were very expensive. By avoiding one, he thought to avoid the other. Unfortunately, in southern Italy, the king miscalculated.

Nemours decided to let Barletta sit and die on the vine. He sent d'Aubigny through Calabria, consolidating French rule. The lord d'Aubigny was popular with the inhabitants and without much fighting, reached the Gulf of Messina. The French estimate that Gonzalo was not going to accomplish much was only too true. His men were not being paid, food was short and Gonzalo personally paid for weapons he bought from a Venetian ship. But his men trusted him and he pledged that better times would come.

The French in Southern Italy: The Adventures of Bayard

The striking power of the army of the King of France was the gendarme, the man-at-arms. Landed aristocrats, lords of the kingdom, they were an independent, violent and impulsive fraternity of strong young men. We can see how these warrior-soldiers managed their tasks in the stories of Bayard. Yes, the details as they have come to us are worthy of scepticism, but the nature of these forces is clearly shown. The lord d'Aubigny assigned Lord de Ligny's companies as garrisons in the kingdom. Bayard and his company held the town of Minervino under the overall command of Louis d'Ars. They faced the Spanish holdings. The Good Chevalier and his companions found their peaceful existence annoying. Said he, 'Either we shall become effeminate or our enemies will think we fear them.' He suggested they ride out toward the Spanish garrisons at Andria or Barletto and see if any Spanish men-at-arms might like a bit of sport; later that day, they all prepared their horses and armour. Early next morning, some thirty men-at-arms rode out following the Good Chevalier. The same day coming from Andria, Don Alonzo de Sotomaire led some forty Spanish men-at-arms riding out, looking for sport with the French.

The two bands rode through the countryside but did not see each other in the hilly ground. Suddenly, the two groups came upon each other. The Spanish wore red crosses on their cassocks and the French had white crosses. When they saw one another, both sides raised their war cry. 'France! France!' was met by 'Espagne! Saint Iago!' Both sides lowered lances and charged. The bands clashed in a massive melee lasting a half an hour. Many on both sides found themselves unhorsed. Bayard led the final assault, pushing the Spanish back. The Spanish left seven dead and some prisoners in French hands when they fled the field. Bayard pursued, catching up with the Spanish men-at-arms. Don Alonzo and some of his companions turned and faced the Good Chevalier, allowing the rest of their compatriots to reach safety. Don Alonzo fought with Bayard, both mounted, with swords until Don Alonzo's horse broke down and would not move. Don Alonzo stood, facing the French who surrounded him. 'To whom do I surrender? he asked. 'To the Captain Bayard.' Came the answer. At this, Don Alonzo surrendered his sword to the Good Chevalier.

The company returned to Minervino with Don Alonzo in tow. They had lost no one although five or six were wounded and two horses killed; but no matter, they had picked up some horses from the Spanish. Their Spanish prisoner gave his word not to escape and the French gave him clothes and pleasant quarters, setting his ransom at 1,000 crowns (ecu, gold coin, so valued by weight). A messenger was sent to the Spanish, but weeks passed without an answer. Don Alonzo made a friend of an Albanian. Together, Alonzo and the Albanian took horses and rode away to the Spanish camp.

When Bayard found his prisoner had gone, he was angry. Organizing a band of his followers, Bayard gave chase. Don Alonzo fled as fast as he could, but his saddle strap loosened and he fell, unable to remount and the French recovered their prisoner. After he was returned to the French quarters, Bayard confined Don Alonzo in a tower cell. He was fed well and not mistreated. After fifteen days, a trumpeter came to request safe passage for the ransom payment to come. The sides exchanged hostages, the ransom came and Bayard immediately released Don Alonzo.

The Spanish in Andria received Signor Don Alonzo with rejoicing. Once he returned, Alonzo praised the Good Chevalier but made complaint of his treatment by the French. When Bayard heard of Don Alonzo's charge of mistreatment, he was angry. He wrote to Alonzo saying, if the Don thought so little of his treatment, the Good Chevalier would gladly render him satisfaction. Soon, a noble trumpeter came to Minervino with an answer for Bayard. Signor Don Alonzo accepted the challenge.

On the day set for the contest, Bayard came ready for fighting followed by some 200 of his supporters. Bayard's companions proclaimed that the Good Chevalier was ready. Don Alonzo's companion announced that choice of weapons and methods was his and he chose to fight on foot. Bayard replied that he would accept any conditions. The Field of Honour marked off, Bayard's second was Bellabre and his Keeper of the Ground was the Lord de La Palisse. Don Alonzo's second was Don Diego de Quinonez and Don Francesco d'Altamesa his Keeper of the Ground. Alonzo offered as weapons, either long rapiers or daggers. Bayard chose the rapiers.

Taking the rapier in hand, Bayard approached the Field of Honour and fell upon his knees, made supplication of the Lord and Saviour, stretched on the ground, kissed the earth and rose with the sign of the cross. He then walked onto the field toward Don Alonzo. His opponent said, 'Senor de Bayardo, *que me queries*.' Bayard replied, 'I will defend my honour.'

They approached each other and began thrusting with the long swords. Bayard nicked Alonzo's face. Swiftly, Alonzo stepped aside and quickly thrust at Bayard. Seeing that Alonzo was avoiding exposing his face to his rapier, Bayard allowed his opponent to make repeated efforts without strongly replying. Alonzo kept making upward thrusts. Waiting until he tried again, Bayard moved as if to also thrust upward but held back from completing his effort. When Alonzo's thrust reached its extent, Bayard made a powerful sweep across Alonzo's throat, breaking Alonzo's gorget and deeply cutting Alonzo's throat. Bayard's sword was stuck in Alonzo and Bayard had to release it as Alonzo lunged toward him in a grapple.

Both fell onto the ground. Bayard drew his dagger, sticking it into Alonzo's nose, saying 'Yield or die!' Don Alonzo's second cried out, '*Senior Bayardo ya es muerto; vencido habeis!*' Bayard gave the body to the Spaniards rather than hold it for ransom as was the custom.

Duel of the Thirteen

Soon after the duel, the French and Spanish command made a truce for two months. Both French and Spanish men-at-arms went out for rides looking for adventure. They often ran into each other but could not fight, so they amused themselves by saying nasty things to each other, in elegant language. One day, a band of thirteen Spanish men-at-arms, well mounted, rode near Minervino, where Bayard happened to be. At that time, Bayard and the Lord of Oroze with a few companions were riding nearby taking the air. They came upon the Spanish thirteen and the two groups intermingled to lightly discuss arms and men. One of the Spaniards, Diego de Bisegna, a well-known knight and firm companion of Don Alonzo, announced how very bored he was with the inaction caused by the truce. He suggested that they might meet together, a group of Spanish and a group of French, in a contest of arms. Those who lose will be prisoners of those who win.

The Lord of Oroze asked Bayard what he thought of this. Bayard stated, 'Let's have thirteen men for each side and come to an appointed place at an appointed time. Let he who has a good heart will show it!' The Spaniards replied, 'We so wish it!' On the appointed time, at the appointed place, Bayard, the Lord of Oroze with their select champions arrived and found the Spanish who likewise came. Many were the spectators of many nations. The contestants fixed the field and discussed conditions: any who left the field were losers to the other side and disqualified to fight further. Any who were unhorsed were losers and disqualified. If at nightfall, one side had not vanquished other, the last man on horse wins. All men held as prisoners on his side become free to go.

Then the Spanish men-at-arms ranged on the field along one side and the French on the other. They sat, lances at rest, until the signal. At that, they spurred forward, but the Spanish champions lowered their lances to strike horses rather than the riders. They overthrew eleven French horsemen. However, the Lord of Oroze and the Good Knight remained mounted. The Spanish attempted to charge them, but their horses would not move over bodies of dead and thrashing wounded horses. The Lord of Oroze and Bayard then rode out from behind the bloody mass and charged the Spanish and when the Spanish attempted a counter charge, the two French champions withdrew behind the dead horses as behind a rampart. Thirteen Spanish knights could not defeat the two French knights. For four hours they battled and the two remained in the field. As the sun began to set, the thirteen Spanish knights agreed that the French earned the combat honours.

Bayard Captures a Treasure and Gives it away.

A month after the Duel of the Thirteen, the truce was over. The good knight's spies brought word about a delivery of 15,000 Venetian gold ducats to Naples. The great Captain, Gonzalo de Córdoba needed the money to pay his soldiers. The treasurer was going to take the money from Naples to Barletta. He would pass close to Bayard's garrison at Minervino. The good chevalier wanted to seize this money, promising to distribute it among his soldiers. So, rising two hours before dawn, he and twenty of his fellows went and lay in ambush between two small hills. Accompanying Bayard was a squad of twenty-five Albanians who rode around the hills to head off any move to avoid the ambush. About the seventh hour in the morning, a scout reported the arrival of the pack train carrying the money.

The French, hiding behind two large rocks, saw the Spanish guards and, in their centre was the treasurer and his servant carrying money bags behind them. Just when the train passed, the French men-at-arms raised the cry, 'France! France! A mort! A mort!' and charged out. The Spanish, seeing far more soldiers than were actually there, fled toward Barletta. Bayard and his squadron gave chase for a short time but turned back because the treasurer, his servant and the money bags were waiting for them. He could not escape and did not intend to try. The squadron accompanied the treasurer and his charges back to Minervino. Bayard and his men took the money bags and started to count the amount of money, but the treasurer told him not to bother. There were 15,000 ducats in the bags. Bayard received charge of the moneys and gave it all away.

Chapter 17

The *Condottieri* Conspire

T he *condottieri* were under no illusions about the emerging threat Cesare's new policies presented to their occupation and positions. The duke's strong connection to the King of France was one problem and that both of them were in league with Pope Alexander's projected powerful Italian state was another. But the worse threat was the growing antagonisms of the duke, the king and the pope to specific noble Italian families, particularly the Orsini. The *condottieri* were themselves masters of the fine art of treachery; they began to fear a masterly *tradimento* similar to that sprung on Guidobaldo and Urbino. Fear grew into suspicion and became alarm.

In the last week of September 1502, Pope Alexander demanded Giulio Orsini prepare for the *impresa* of Bologna. Giovanni Bentivoglio, Lord of Bologna, was closely tied to the Orsini in many ways and it did not take a fortune teller to see that the target after Bologna was going to be Umbria, the core of Orsini power. The family Orsini secretly called for a conference of interested parties. The conference convened on 26 September at Todi where the Orsini had a strong garrison.

There, the Orsini decided the situation was dire enough to widen the scope of participants. They called for a larger conference at la Magione near Trasimene which belonged to Cardinal Orsini. They invited Bentivoglio of Bologna and Petrucci, Lord of Siena, to send commissioners. In the last days of the month, assembled in their Umbrian stronghold were Cardinal Orsini, along with Paolo who was the vain and unstable head of House Orsini, nephew Francisco, another nephew Franciotto and the famed Cavaliere Orsini. They waited for their fellow *condottieri*. These men came. Vitellozzo, crippled by *il mal Franzese* (the French Pox), was carried in a litter. Baglioni followed. Oliverotto, Lord of Fermo was there. Soon, Ermete Bentivoglio, son of the Lord of Bologna arrived. From the House of Urbino came a nephew. Petrucci of Siena sent his confidant, Antonio da Venafro.

They met together and agreed that their days were numbered unless somehow, they upset Borgia's plans. Bologna, Citta di Castello and Perugia were already in Cesare's line of attack. If they were to survive, they had to strike before the French lances reached Romagna. Together the conspirators began to hammer out a compact to destroy the enemy of the 'liberties and peace of Italy'. But as soon as the compact formed, Cardinal Orsini not so secretly reached an accord with Alexander in Rome; Paolo Orsini secretly offered to help the Borgia cause. In short, as soon as the *condottieri* made their pact, many ran to Cesare to cut a deal with him. Cesare later called the conference 'the assembly of bankrupt politicians'.

Still, the compatriots continued to negotiate. On 8 October they reached a final agreement. By the next day, the agreement was recorded in a *capitoli* and signed. The terms: the Orsini, on account of their wealth and their connections with the French king would handle negotiations with other powers; included in the pact as principal members were Bentivoglio of Bologna, Petrucci of Siena, Vitellozzo and Baglioni; they would have the most say. Other members were included but they would follow the principals' directions. In reality, Pandolfo Petrucci, Lord of Siena, was the brains and director of the organization. The objective of the alliance was to support each other in defence and offence. Any member who lost his state was to be reinstated by the efforts of the rest.

The *condottieri* commanded some 700 men-at-arms, 100 light horse, and 9,000 infantry and they easily could call up more. This was a large and experienced force, very threatening to Cesare. At the beginning of October, the fortress of San Leo, while being rebuilt, was carried by a handful of armed peasants who rushed the gate and killed the small Borgia garrison. Soon the cries of 'Marco' and 'Montefeltro' rang out in district villages. On 8 October men from the countryside crowded into Urbino, with the news that some places had rebelled. The mob seized Cesare's officials, turned the cannon against the fortress and received its surrender. Certainly, if not directed by the *Condottieri* Alliance, these upheavals were part of the same reaction against Cesare's state-building efforts.

The War with the *Condottieri*

Cesare heard about the fall of San Leo on 7 October. He understood that local loyalties around Urbino were very strong and the rough countryside allowed a widespread resistance not easily put down. Rather than immediately swinging into action opposing the rebels, Cesare organized his forces to solidify defences of the line Fano to Imola. The northern section, Forli-Imola, was secure unless Cesare moved his forces south, then the area was open to attack from Bologna. Also, Cesare was aware that Venice might move against him. His force at hand consisted of some 2,500 infantry, 250 lances, 750 horsemen along with his excellent and numerous artillery.

Cesare's commander-in-chief, Ramiro de Lorqua, withdrew all field troops and garrisons from Urbino back to Rimini and Pesaro. Don Michele marched to Fano, where local forces were pressing the town to join Urbino. As he passed, he inspected the forces and readiness for defence of each military governor. Further, commanders ordered the well-trained corps of 800 infantry in Faenza to strengthen the defence of the towns on the coast. Cesare sent agents to Lombardy to hire 500 Gascon infantry and 1,500 Swiss. The French at Milan, as per the agreement, mobilized two detachments, each of 300 lances, sending them to Cesare's service. Cesare concentrated his troops, expecting that his enemies would not be able to respond to quick and powerful manoeuvres.

The rebel alliance had formed their final agreement on 8 October. The next day, Baglioni advanced from Perugia into a nearby section of Romagna. By the 11th Vitellozzo had sent cavalry to occupy Urbino and Baglioni reached Cagli with his infantry on the 12th. Then, news came that Pergola and Fossombrone, having risen in rebellion in response to the rebel success at Urbino, were suddenly attacked and mercilessly plundered and ravaged by Cesare's Spanish men-at-arms under Don Michele. The Spanish troops saw their enemies as simply crude peasants; they did not expect to meet trained soldiers. On 15 October the Orsini occupied Urbino with their 600 highly trained infantry and from Urbino, the troops attacked the Spanish men-at-arms in the rough country, smashing the unwieldy, heavy cavalry at Calmazzo. They took some officers prisoners and pushed the rest of the Borgia force down the Via Flaminia to Fano.

The *Condottieri* alliance had strong forces at hand, but their core flaw was fatal: final victory was beyond their grasp because while they all opposed Cesare, they did not trust each other, and each looked only to his own advantage. They handled their troops and tactics well, but none had operated as a strategist. Not one of them ever ran an operation designed to achieve a decisive victory. Cesare Borgia, on the other hand, understood the concept of strategic manoeuvre and had achieved it. Each *condottieri* fought his own battles well, but Cesare was able to manoeuvre between them, so he exploited their weakness.

Rather than get into knock-down fights with the *condottieri*, Cesare ignored their major operations and allowed them to take what they could without sacrificing his lines of communications and significant bases.

Soon, some more perceptive of the rebel allies were ready to come to favourable terms with Cesare at the expense of their fellow rebels. On 22 October Cesare received word that Bentivoglio, Lord of Bologna, would abandon the Orsini for the right price, perhaps a Borgia marriage with the lord of Bologna's son. While the Duke of Romagna considered this, another message came through unofficial sources: Pandolfo Petrucci, Lord of Siena and chief of the military alliance sent a representative to Imola to seek a basis for reconciliation. Seeing the lay of the land, Paolo Orsini, head of his house, in response to a feeler Cesare had sent, went to Imola in disguise to see Cesare Borgia on 25 October. The official Florentine representative to Cesare, the secretary Machiavelli, was at Cesare's court during these events. He reported about Paolo Orsini: 'He has come to explain late events, to learn the attitude of the Duke regarding them, and to report them to his friends.' He carried a statement of the alliance's common views. But what was said, what was agreed, if anything, Machiavelli could not learn.

On 29 October Varano partisans took back Camerino from the Borgia. But Cesare ignored the loss. More important, strong French forces were passing by Bologna with a five-company vanguard which reached Faenza on 31 October, followed by 600 infantry from Ferrara. Alexander continued to send 1,000 ducats a week. The fall of Camerino and continued raids sent out by Vitellozzo from Urbino seemed to imperil reconciliation between the Orsini and the Borgia. At this time, Cesare told Machiavelli that he had no terms to offer Florence. The suspicion in Florence was they would pay the price of accommodation between Cesare and the Orsini. But perhaps Cesare simply wished the Florentines understood that his military was necessary to them and they needed to pay for it.

On the first day of November the rebel alliance joined their forces together, moving down the valley of the Foglia from their base at Urbino. Their forces had 800 men-at-arms with 10,000 infantry. Giulio Orsini, Baglioni, Vitellozzo and Guidobaldo were with the army. They planned attacks on Pesaro and then Fano in the south and Rimini in the north. Baglioni drove an exploratory raid within sight of Pesaro, but that was as much as the rebel alliance could accomplish. The *condottieri* had no common trust. They all knew about Bentivoglio in Bologna dealing with Borgia's interests and Paolo Orsini's concerns about his family's northern holdings. Vitellozzo and Guidobaldo were physically unable to lead forces in the field because of infirmities. Even worse, none of the captains were willing to follow anyone else as supreme commander, not that any of them was capable of developing a serious strategic campaign.

Cesare had nothing but contempt for the rebel alliances' pretention or, indeed, abilities. He played at negotiations, willing to concede any point as long as nothing happened. Paolo Orsini came with offers from the alliance, some of which the Borgia accepted. His men called Paolo Orsini, 'Madonna Paolo' because of his vanities. He was fodder for Cesare's charm and flattery. On 14 November they reached an agreement and Paolo went to Urbino to gain the alliance's assent. The agreement was complex and involved, with enough pieces to satisfy everyone but too many pieces to be practical. Any disagreements were going to arbitration by Cardinal Orsini, Cesare Borgia and Pandolfo Petrucci. And, for security, each signatory was allowed one of his lawful sons to reside with Cesare. Cesare commented to Machiavelli that they had no choice but to accept his offer.

The *condottieri* came together at a Church of Santa Maria isolated on a knoll. Cesare's representative, Gorvalan, stayed before the closed doors of the church, ignoring the jeers of the *condottiere*'s guards standing around the church entrance. Inside, the confederates argued back and forth. In the end, only Baglioni voiced strong objections to the whole idea, denouncing Paolo Orsini as a fool taken in by the Prince of Foxes. But the Orsini had already prevailed. Only the lord of Perugia refused to agree; as he walked out of the conference, he announced that if Cesare wanted him, let him come to Perugia in arms. Gorvalan returned to Imola with the signed agreement. Paolo Orsini and Vitellozzo, representing the signers, both wrote letters explaining away their rebellion. Machiavelli reported to Florence on how Cesare's party received these letters: here are men who stabbed us in the back and then hoped to heal the wound with words.

Machiavelli noted that no one knew what Cesare Borgia was going to do until he started doing it. The Orsini and their allies went about their business in serene complacency during the rest of November into December as if everything had returned to normal. What the allies were unaware of were the efforts of Cesare to solidify his position. On 23 November he reached agreement upon the basics of a settlement with the Lord of Bologna, Bentivoglio. Since Bologna was not part of the settlement with the rebel alliance, Cesare thought it expedient to grant them highly satisfactory terms. The *capitoli* were signed at Imola on 2 December. Cesare received money and troops.

Now Cesare was ready to balance his books of debts and assets. First, he reorganized the administration of his duchy of Romagna and by 10 December he was prepared. He broke up his headquarters at Imola and took a large army south. No one knew where he was going except him. Supplies were stockpiled in the towns along the coast south to Fano which meant he could call to as many places as necessary to keep supplied. On the first day he reached Oriolo Secco; on the 12th he reached Cesena, an administration centre where he spent fifteen days. Cesare paid a great deal of attention to civil administration matters. His troops were well disciplined and were severely punished if they bothered civilians. He placed camps for troops some distance from towns. Cesare's rule was widely appreciated.

Within call, Cesare had 12,000 crack troops. There were 3,000 French horsemen with a solid core of men-at-arms. Cesare had some 3,000 light horse and 7,000 infantry, Spanish, Swiss and Gascon backed up by his local militia. His artillery amounted to 20 guns from large siege cannon to long serpentines. Moreover, there were strong garrisons in the line from Imola to Fano. All these troops were loyal to the Borgia, either through their fidelity to the King of France or personally to Cesare.

'Bellissimo Inganno' (Magnificent Deceit) of Sinigaglia

Just what Cesare planned was unknown but as Machiavelli observed then: '... an adventurous Prince will often frame his action according to the openings which fortune offers to him; since in affairs it is only after taking the first steps that one can rightly discern the path ahead.' However, it was here in Cesena that Cesare generated the plot, 'Bellissimo inganno' (magnificent deceit) of Sinigaglia. The duke had presented to the condottieri his projected seizure of Sinigaglia. This town sat on the Adriatic coast and provided egress to Romagna's hinterland leading to Urbino. Sinigaglia was now a vicariate of the Holy See but held in defiance of the pope by the Prefettessa, widow of Giovanni Della Rovere, sister of Guidobaldo and sister-in-law of Cardinal San Pietro in Vincoli. Her younger son and heir, Francesco Maria, was that nephew whom Guidobaldo had saved from Cesare's seizure of Urbino in June. He was now safe in France. Cesare concentrated his condottieri forces.

On 20 December Cesare ordered the French contingent to leave him and return to Lombardy. Of all the French forces which had joined Cesare, only two companies of 50 lances each remained. Cesare had now decided that the most effective battle force of the modern army was composed of disciplined infantry backed up by artillery. The spectacular and expensive armoured horsemen were powerful and represented high status, but massed infantry backed up by gunpowder weapons were a cheaper, more reliable tool of organized violence.

Cesare also used the dismissal of the French to convince the former rebel alliance that all was well. The plot proceeded. On the day French troops left his command, Cesare took a further step; Ramiro de Lorqua, Cesare's close lieutenant and supreme army commander found himself suddenly under arrest and thrown into a dungeon. Paolo Orsini had told Cesare that Lorqua's severity was part of the cause of the *condottieri*'s rebellion. Vitellozzo took Lorqua's downfall as a sign of Cesare's goodwill.

By 22 December the Duke had calculated his decisive moves. Only Don Michele was aware of his master's will. That day the court issued specific charges against Lorqua of a fiscal and administrative nature, but most knew the deeper reason was some treachery Cesare had unearthed. Of course, any judicial investigation would not help Cesare's objectives; on Christmas morning Lorqua's headless body lay on a mat in the main plaza of Cesena. On the 30th, Cesare informed the seven closest members of his entourage of their roles in an upcoming action, the whole of which was not made plain. Even Pope Alexander did not know what Cesare was going to do, but on the last day of the year, Cesare told his father what was afoot. His Holiness was more than pleased.

On 26 December 1502 Oliverotto Euffreducci, in Cesare's name, entered Sinigaglia. The citizens surrendered the town but the commander of the citadel, Andrea Doria, the Genoese admiral, declared that he would surrender the citadel but only to Cesare Borgia in person. Oliverotto was a *condottiere* who, sometime previously, had seized Fermo from his uncle and the important citizens at a banquet. After the food and entertainment concluded, Oliverotto praised Borgia accomplishments. When his uncle and others protested, Oliverotto said such matters needed a more private place to clarify matters. They all went into a chamber, and when assembled, soldiers suddenly emerged and killed them. Oliverotto then challenged the governing council who, in fear, surrendered to him. Such was the man who Cesare had sent to Sinigaglia. Once the town surrendered, and Doria made it clear he would hold in place, Oliverotto withdrew his troops from the town and set up camp in the Borgo outside the south gate.

On the 27th Cesare marched toward Fano, which he reached on the 29th. By the evening of the 30th, Cesare's entire field army, marching by parallel roads, were encamped in and around the town. That night, Cesare assembled his eight closest commanders and issued secret instructions.

At daybreak Cesare moved out from Fano at the head of his strong field army. He heard early in the morning that Vitellozzo had reached his formation of men-at-arms in the valley of the Misa, a short distance from

Sinigaglia. Cesare sent instructions through Paolo Orsini ordering Vitellozzo to deploy his troops across the lower hills and flat plain along the Misa, to prepare for an advance toward Ancona. Paolo Orsini assured Vitellozzo that Baglioni, who refused to leave Perugia, was wrong about Cesare's bad faith. With their forces organized for an offensive, the *condottieri* had about 2,000 foot and 300 light horse in support at Sinigaglia.

Cesare reached Sinigaglia in the late afternoon. Paolo Orsini, his brother, the Cavaliere Orsini, Vitellozzo and Oliverotto, each man having a small escort, rode a mile and a half out of Sinigaglia to receive Cesare. It is said that Vitellozzo was most reluctant to come. He was ill and rode a mule instead of a warhorse. When Cesare and his staff came up, Paolo Orsini rode out from the group to greet him. Cesare asked about his little brother, Vitellozzo, who reluctantly came forward. Cesare stooped down from his charger, threw his arm round Vitellozzo's neck and kissed him on the cheek. Then, in a most friendly way, he greeted the rest.

Cesare's troops were a short distance away. The two groups, Cesare and his commanders and the *condottieri* and their escorts, remained mounted in friendly conversation. The word to advance given, the *condottieri* companies wheeled about and preceded Cesare and his staff. Skirting the town, they slowly rode toward the bridge that led into the Borgo. As they moved forward each of Cesare's officers attached themselves to one of the companies of *condottieri* as if this was a mark of respect, following Cesare's secret orders.

Opposite the citadel stood a palace. Here, Don Michele established Cesare's quarters. Accompanied by the five *condottieri*, Cesare and his guards rode through Sinigaglia to the palace. In their rear, guards quietly secured the town gates. Except for the one company of Oliverotto's men, the only soldiers in the town were those of Cesare. When Cesare's party reached the palace, the five *condottieri* began to take their leave but, saying they needed to discuss important business, Cesare convinced them to come into the palace. The *condottieri* walked up the stairs to the audience hall, where they found seats. Cesare, once the men were settled, took what he said was a brief leave. Suddenly many armed men surrounded the *condottieri* and bound them as prisoners.

Paolo cried out for Cesare, but he had already exited out the back. The duke went up to Oliverotto's company of men-at-arms and told their officer to withdraw his men. On their way to leave Sinigaglia, Borgia's troops cut them down. By this time Oliverotto's main forces in the Borgo faced a much larger body of troops coming down the Fano road. The *condottieri*'s troops laid down their arms. Vitellozzo's troops were across the Misa creek when Borgia's troops came to disperse them. They quickly split up and went their ways.

The Borgia troops then plundered the town unhindered. All of those suspected of being a partisan of della Rovere or the *condottieri* were killed. At 2am on 1 January 1503, Don Michele oversaw the killing of Vitellozzo and Oliverotto by a rope with a twisting stick. That way, not only were they strangled, but their neck vertebrae were broken: a quick and sure death. There were stories of reproaches between Vitellozzo and Oliverotto, the grave Vitellozzo bitter because of his stupidity for trusting the rest and the terrified Oliverotto begging for life. The *cavaliere* Orsini disappeared but he was eventually released. Cesare carried along Paolo Orsini and his brother in his train. After certain news reached him from Rome a month later, he ordered both Orsini strangled. Once the deed was done and some dust settled the Borgias put out the story of a desperate last-minute effort to save Cesare from sudden treachery. Pope Alexander told the tale that on the eve of his execution, Ramiro de Lorqua confessed to being involved in a plot centred on the Orsini and had planned for Vitellozzo and Oliverotto to kill Cesare. Further, he added, Vitellozzo confessed the night of his arrest.

Chapter 18

The Borgia Collapse

The Borgia Ascendancy

The Duke of Romagna looked at many corpses of his enemies; he held many more of them in his dungeons. After years of struggle he was near to achieving his goals. When he was born, he had little except his father's drive toward power. Now he was about to put the finishing touches on the new powerful state he had constructed. Threats to his and his state's survival were many, but he was ready to deal with them. Newly acquired lands, Urbino and Camerino, seethed with hostility; careful administration would settle them down. Venice, Florence and the minor principalities were unhappy with their new neighbour and looked for cracks in the body politic to exploit; a strong army, made up of citizens of the new state would fix any dangerous cracks. To make his state stronger and make it the premier Italian state, Cesare needed more. If he could add Perugia, the upper Tiber and even Siena to the Romagna, the state would form a core around which all Italy would revolve.

Before noon on New Year's Day 1503, Cesare marched out of Sinigaglia. The fortress was his and the town was quiet. He and his entourage followed the valley of the Misa; they came to Corinaldo before nightfall. There, he sent out dispatches explaining the problem of the *condottieri*. For two nights he stayed at Corinaldo, organizing his forces for the march on Perugia. Now, he insisted, his actions were as Gonfalonier of the Holy See not Duke of Romagna. His lands were the Romagna, Urbino and the near reaches of the March down to the Misa River. As Protector of the Church, he projected a campaign starting at the Sienese frontier through Tuscany to restore all the lands of the Orsini to the Holy See. As payment for the lands granted from the Holy See to Romagna, he would liberate the Holy See from the power of the Roman barons. His Holiness welcomed Cesare's aid.

A messenger had brought the news of Cesare's coup to Pope Alexander about 8pm on the night of 2 January. News of the coup spread in Rome the next day during the carnival. Pope Alexander was pleased; he sent information to Cardinal Orsini telling him that Sinigaglia had surrendered.

The following morning, Orsini rode to the Vatican to offer congratulations. On the way, he was approached by the governor of Rome as if by chance. As soon as the cardinal entered the papal palace, he was surrounded by armed men. He turned pale; they imprisoned him in the Borgia tower.

Along with Cardinal Orsini, they arrested Rinaldo Orsini, Archbishop of Florence, Jacob Santa Croce and others. The governor and his retainers rode to the Orsini residence palace of Monte Giorgano which they sacked. The mother of the cardinal, 80 years old, tottered through the streets of Rome like a maniac because no one offered her shelter. The cardinal was imprisoned in Saint Angelo; his treasures graced the Vatican. Pope Alexander was in excellent humour.

The Borgia power grab continued: on 5 January Don Jofre and his troops seized the nearby Orsini strongholds. When all the cardinals went to His Holiness to sue for grace for their fellow cardinal, the pope was implacable. Every day important men disappeared into Castel Saint Angelo. On the same day, Cesare reached Gualdo Tadino on the Via Flaminia where he received word that the former holdings of the *condottieri* were all recognizing his rule. The next day, a delegation of citizens from Perugia recognized the Duke as Gonfalonier and overlord, followed by delegates from Assisi. On the day after, Cesare informed the commissioners from Siena of his intention of driving their lord, Pandolfo Petrucci, from his dominions. Within the first ten days of January, Cesare had swept up the detritus from the *condottieri*.

Machiavelli had an interview with Cesare on 10 January. The duke outlined for Machiavelli his objectives in Tuscany. He told the Florentine that his and Florence's enemies were either dead, or fugitives, or doomed. He had Pandolfo Petrucci marked for removal in Siena. Cesare went on: at the moment, Pope Alexander was plying Petrucci with pleasant talk while Cesare's army was advancing toward Siena. Machiavelli's understanding was that Cesare intended making himself lord of Tuscany south of Siena thus binding both Florence and Siena to Cesare's policies. On 13 January the Florentine Signory informed Machiavelli that he was to be replaced by a more eminent representative, Jacopo Salviati.

Cesare advanced against Siena by marching south to cross the long stretch of marshy ground which divides Umbria from Tuscany. On 18 January he was at Sarteano where he gave orders for the execution of Paolo Orsini and the young duke of Gravina. The Cavaliere Orsini, Cesare allowed to go free (he was killed in a private quarrel in 1504). When complaints came to Alexander, he said that he did not know what Cesare was doing. Alexander certainly desired the enterprise of Siena but feared the French reaction. In public, the pope criticized his son, saying that he did everything only for his advantage and wished to embroil the pope with the whole of Italy.

Meanwhile, Cesare had sacked some fortresses in Sienese lands and sent threatening letters to the town, demanding Petrucci's removal. On 28 January Petrucci announced he was leaving Siena for the good of his native land and the same day went to Lucca. Following his agreed obligation to the French, Cesare left Sienese lands and surrendered his spoils.

Despite the Borgia successes, the battle with the Orsini was not over. In late January many of the barons of the patrimony rose in rebellion, considering that their destruction must surely follow that of the Orsini. The Neapolitans supported John Jordan, Lord of Bracciano, and the Venetians supported Nicholas Count of Pitigliano. Joined with these supporters of the Orsini were the Savelli and some of the Colonna. The rising was widespread.

On 23 January the barons approached Rome's Ponte Nomentano causing a great commotion in Rome. The pope mobilized troops to defend the Vatican and the barons had to retire. The duke marched into the patrimony in early February, his troops having looted and pillaged the towns they marched through. The barons, particularly those connected to the Orsini, fled. The Savelli quickly submitted. John Jordan and his town, Bracciano now under French protection, refused to submit. Alexander sent artillery to take the place but Cesare, afraid of the French, countermanded the pope. Alexander, in open consistory, complained about his son.

During this February Cardinal Orsini's imprisonment became harsher. His mother, now somewhat restored and in a better position, brought food so the cardinal did not starve, but soon this became forbidden. She then sent the cardinal's mistress with a valuable pearl which Alexander coveted. He took the pearl and allowed the delivery of food, but those who knew understood: the cardinal had drunk from a cup mixed by the pope's command. Alexander had a message for the cardinal: he should have courage and take care of his health. The pope declared to the cardinals in consistory that he ordered physicians to take care of the prisoner. On 15 February reports came that the prisoner was ill; by 22 February he was dead. The pope commanded forty torchbearers to accompany the procession of the cardinal's body to Saint Salvatore.

The Approach to Spain

Cesare arrived in Rome at the end of February and his arrival filled the city with terror. Apprehension was worse because he did not appear in public. All Orsini fortresses were in his hands except for Bracciano, Caere and Vicovaro. Pope Alexander looked forward to the capture of these places but the King of France still protected John Jordan and the Orsini interests. Cesare's lieutenants kept Caere under blockade but did not press the siege. Working through intermediaries, the Duke of Romagna eventually brokered an understanding with King Louis. Cesare left Rome on 6 April and received the Orsini defenders in a friendly manner. The King of France pressured John Jordan to accept Pope Alexander's offer of the principality of Squillace or other compensation in the March of Ancona. On 8 April 1503 John Jordon signed the treaty set up by the French ambassador and received a safe passage document to France.

The Duke of Romagna was never more powerful than in April 1503. On 10 April Cardinal Giovanni Michael (nephew of Paul II) was imprisoned as part of the Orsini faction in Saint Angelo. He died suddenly and everyone suspected Cesare because just after he died some 150,000 ducats disappeared from the cardinal's palace. The Borgias shattered the different factions of Roman nobility, removed all independent lords from the States of the Church, dominated the administration of the city of Rome, made the College of Cardinals an obedient senate and turned the Curia into a handy instrument of personal power. Pope Alexander thought of raising Cesare to be King of Romagna with the papacy as an office of state. Uniting the political with secular authority, the pope would remain the centre of the new state and Christianity was going to be the source of finance.

However, the Borgia holdings were part of the States of the Church. Their security remained compromised by Bologna and Ferrara. Tuscany was independent, but Pisa had offered Cesare their lordship. Hearing of this, King Louis had negotiated a league between Florence, Siena, Lucca, Bologna and France for defending their independence while also supporting French interests in Naples. This allowed Pandolfo Petrucci to return to Siena on 29 March. Still, there were divisions in the league and King Ferdinand of Spain saw an opening to weaken Louis' efforts by negotiating with Cesare. If he is siding with Spain, Cesare thought, he could extort concessions in Tuscany from King Louis.

All this coincided with Gonzalo's campaign in Apulia in April 1503. The French found their decisive defeat surprising. Gonzalo entered Naples on 14 May and King Louis found himself in an unusually weak position. Never one to give up, the French king raised a new army under la Tremouille and planned to march through Tuscany. The king demanded free passage through church lands and the use of Cesare's troops. In return, the Borgia demanded a free hand in Tuscany and the surrender of Bracciano. Louis refused any such quid pro quo. Nor could the Borgia afford to break with the French while the massive French armed force marched through Roman lands, so they announced neutrality and allowed free passage.

While the French marched south to do battle with Gonzalo, the Borgia began secret negotiations with Ferdinand of Spain and Pope Alexander which allowed Gonzalo to raise mercenaries in Rome. Troche, Alexander's favourite, let the French know about the Borgia's Spanish dealings. Troche fled the Vatican on 18 May only to be captured near Corsica by Alexander's pursuers and was returned to Rome. On 8 June Michelotto Coreglia, governor of Rome, strangled Troche while Cesare looked on from behind a screen. At the same time, the Borgia executed Jacopo Santa Croce whose body remained on the bridge of Saint Angelo until nightfall. His property went to the Borgias.

Borgia's project required more money. Their minions seized rich people and squeezed. The Jews were threatened into making payments. On 31 May Pope Alexander elevated eleven new cardinals at better than the going rate. Cesare Borgia was present at the consistory in which the new candidates were elevated. This is the first time he had appeared publicly since his return in late winter. His appearance signalled the emergence of new plans. All the lands of the Orsini, Savelli and Colonna would return to the church. The sacred college would readjust church lands, so the March became part of the Romagna. Cesare went to Romagna at the end of June to improve the administration and the courts of law. He did not like what he found. One morning, he had his friend and confidant Vicar-General Romiro brought out to the piazza of Cesena. There Romiro was beheaded and quartered. When the job was done, they left the bloody executioner's axe beside the remains to the horror of onlookers.

In August 1503 the Borgia enterprise was reaching completion. This was clear to King Louis. As a way to find common ground, Louis offered to cede to His Holiness the whole of Naples in return for Bologna and the Romagna, to safeguard French interests in northern Italy. But, at the same time, Pope Alexander secretly made overtures to Emperor Maximilian to gain the investiture of Pisa, Siena and Lucca for Cesare. Alexander was keeping an eye over his shoulder because, in this August of 1503, La Tremouille was leading the French army toward Rome.

Balancing between France and Spain, threatening Florence and blocking Venice, secure in the Romagna, the March and the Patrimony, the Borgia quest for power caused their rivals great fear. Their enemies, however, while they continued to fear, now hated. Not only were sons, brothers and fathers killed for their not being in the Borgia scheme of things and mothers, wives and daughters dishonoured for Borgia amusement, but worse, family holdings for generations disappeared into the Borgia coffers. The hatred seeped through the great and not so great, through lord, peasant and lacky: the more intellectually inclined discussed institution, law, and ethics; the rest thought of murder.

Poison was said to be the Borgia weapon of choice. Their specific tool was a compound called Cantarella. This was an arsenic–based powder mixed with materials that masked its initial effects but allowed the victim to ingest the arsenic. The reaction started in a day or so and then got progressively worse.

The tale runs thus: on 6 August, His Holiness and Cesare had a festive outdoor dinner with Cardinal Adriano Castellesi, a new elevation to the Sacred College and confidant of Alexander. Within a few days, all three were sick. The cardinal recovered without great difficulty but Cesare was taken seriously ill and His Holiness was gravely ill and getting worse. The symptoms of Cantarella simulate in some ways, the symptoms of ague (malaria), many commentators in the nineteenth and early twentieth century discount the stories of poison, but contemporaries at the time were unanimous: the pope's death and Cesare's sickness were poison. After an extended illness and most uncomfortable experience, Pope Alexander VI died on 18 August. Cesare did not die, but never fully recovered. He was unable to function for weeks and afterwards he was never able to recover momentum.

The Tragedy of Borgia

The death of Pope Alexander VI Borgia opened a vast vacuum. Since he ascended to the Triple Tiara in 1492, he had filled Rome and Italy with turmoil and disruption. Highly controversial, absolutely ruthless, distrusted and hated, he and his family had made Italy dance to their music. In the eleven years of his reign he was instrumental in pulling the French, Germans and Spanish into Italy. Although there were other factors, the House of Borgia was disruptive of the Peace of Lorenzo. So, when Pope Alexander died, many expectations and plans immediately evaporated. Even more important, other hopes and desires were now possible, if carefully plotted.

The collected ambassadors in Rome demanded Cesare leave the city in order to allow an open conclave. On 22 September 1503 the conclave announced the new pope: Cardinal Piccolomini, who took the name Pius III. A nephew of Pius II Aeneas Silvius, Pius III was a long-time administrator in ill health. He was a compromise candidate, neither pro Borgia nor anti Borgia. Not a priest, Pius was ordained and consecrated on 30 September. He announced many reforms but died on 13 October. Rumour said he was poisoned by order of Pandolfo Petrucci of Siena, but it might have been tetanus.

Cardinal della Rovere was disappointed in the election of Pius III. His ambition to be pope burned. Even during Pius III's reign, della Rovere campaigned for the next conclave. He met with Cesare Borgia and the Spanish cardinals. Looking for support from all sides, he pledged to keep Cesare as Gonfalonier. He also made promises to the French about positions and placements along with promises to other cardinals to reform the church. The conclave elected Cardinal della Rovere on 1 November 1503, in the shortest conclave in history. The cardinal took the name Julius II. His approach to the Borgias was made clear in his statement:

> 'I will not live in the same rooms as the Borgias lived. He [Alexander VI] desecrated the Holy Church as none before. He usurped the papal power by the devil's aid, and I forbid under the pain of excommunication anyone to speak or think of Borgia again. His name and memory must be forgotten. It must be crossed out of every document and memorial. His reign must be obliterated. All paintings made of the Borgias or for them must be covered over with black crepe. All the tombs of the Borgias must be opened and their bodies sent back to where they belong – to Spain.'
>
> (Gregorovius, vol. VII, p. 293)

Chapter 19

War in Southern Italy

Gonzalo Prepares to Attack

In late 1502 King Ferdinand judged that King Louis was sufficiently overextended in northern Italy with his involvements with Venice and Cesare Borgia's *impresa*, that the time had come to push the French hard and see if they broke. The Spanish fleet brought strong reinforcements to Gonzalo; first, 200 men-at-arms, 300 light horse and 2,000 foot; just a little later came another 200 men-at-arms followed by 299 light horse and then came 10,000 Spanish foot. Along with the troops came great quantities of grain, flour, meat, salt, wine and goods.

During December 1502 the tide of war began turning. The Spanish troops did well; they gained fortresses in Calabria while French troops suffered shortages and desertions. When Viceroy Nemours required Naples to come up with 5,000 ducats, the city rioted. The governor of Monopoli commented in January 1503, 'It used to be thought that the French would win, but now the opposite seems the case. This is because the Spanish hold most strongholds and reinforcements keep coming. Ships carrying troops are continuing to pass this place on their way to Barletta. We expect this spring the Great Captain will take the field.'

At the same time, the administration of the kingdom collapsed and was made worse by wet and stormy weather. No business, scarcity, looting and upheaval were constant. The steady stream of ships carrying reinforcements and supplies to the Spanish forces opened opportunities for French corsairs. Their fleet, four galleys, a sailing scout and a caravel supply ship was sailing along the Adriatic coast, plundering Spanish ships. Needing supplies, on 10 February, the fleet put into Otranto, a Venetian port. The Venetian governor allowed the fleet sanctuary in the port. A powerful Spanish fleet blockaded the port, threatening to attack the port to destroy the French fleet. The French fleet commander moved the ship's guns and valuables into the town and scuttled the fleet, with the result that while the fleet was gone, the Spanish still could not get redress. Still, the corsairs were gone and merchantmen were safe. The price of commodities fell by half.

The incident at Otranto pointed directly at Venetian policy or rather lack of it in southern Italy. Venice was allied to both France and Spain. Here, the threat was that her interests were going to be lost because she was in the middle of a fight she did not want. The Venetian Senate rang with complaints from the Great Captain and the King of France. In truth, the Venetians were unhappy with the French. French fleets used Venetian ports as bases to attack the Spanish and this disrupted trade.

Moreover, in northern Italy, France's ally, Cesare Borgia was building a powerful state with French support and that state was close to undermining Venetian holdings in her *terra firma*. Nor was the Great Captain much better. The Venetian governor of Trani, just one of a number, complained how the Spanish drove off livestock, took grain shipments and battled the French in his territory. Then Gonzalo himself complained about the Venetian's governor's behaviour and attitude.

The problem in southern Italy as 1502 turned to 1503 was that the French were just as happy to keep things as they were. There was no greater expense and they thought the Spanish were of a like mind. French men-at-arms and their supporting fellow soldiers saw the area as their playground. While Bayard and boys were thoroughly enjoying themselves, as had their ancestors for generations, the locals, who paid for knightly fun were less than happy. As a good example, the town of Castellaneta, between Bari and Taranto found their French garrison following the traditional role of Chivalry: casual lootings, pretty women abducted and raped, and the usual arrogant and demanding ways. The citizens of the town had had enough. They rose in rebellion, overcame the garrison and received reinforcements from the Spanish garrison of Taranto. This caused upset at Nemours' headquarters. The French would retake the town and teach the citizens a lesson in manners. The French withdrew a strong force from the garrisons surrounding Barletta. Nothing could please the Great Captain more. Waiting until the French were a good day's march away, in the dead of night on 22 February, Gonzalo marched away from Barletta with a strong force of horse, foot and artillery. The Spanish marched toward Ruvo, garrisoned by M. de la Palice with his own company and the company of the Duke of Savoy.

At dawn on 23 February, Gonzalo reached Ruvo and surrounded the town. The French kept no watch and did not know the Spanish were just outside. Ruvo fortifications showed the neglect of years with moats clogged and walls crumbling. The French made an effort at repairing the worse parts of the walls, but they were neither new nor strong. Despite surprise and weak defences, la Palice's force beat back two attacks, but in the third attack, Palice was wounded and captured. The French resistance collapsed, and Gonzalo received the commander of the Duke of Savoy's company, 150 French prisoners, 400 cavalry horses, sumpter mules, and all the plunder, jewels, money, and clothing the French had amassed. After levelling Ruvo's defences, Gonzalo withdrew. Now, with food from Sicily, money from Spain, reinforcements at hand, Gonzalo waited for campaign weather.

King Louis Proposes Peace

King Louis found his hands full in northern Italy with threats from neighbours against the northern parts of France. Just like Charles VIII, Louis easily took Naples but now found himself involved in a desultory struggle that demanded a lot of money with very little return. He thought the agreement made with King Ferdinand would allow his forces time to consolidate their hold and he was prepared to compromise with the Spanish, but Ferdinand had taken him for a fool and intended to swallow the whole kingdom of Naples. This rankled. Louis spent much time figuring out a way to beat Ferdinand at his own game while not losing face or money. He looked to a northern neighbour, Archduke Philip the Handsome, Duke of Burgundy, for a solution. Philip was the son of Emperor Maximilian and Mary of Burgundy, daughter of Charles the Bold. The archduke was married to Joanne of Castile, daughter of King Ferdinand and Queen Isabella of Spain. Joanne was the heir of her mother as Queen of Castile and probably she or her son by Philip, Charles, was heir to King Ferdinand.

Archduke Philip was educated, cultured and saw no need for incessant war. He thought that reasonable people should solve problems like the Kingdom of Naples without war. King Louis and Archduke Philip had already agreed to the engagement of Princess Claude, Louis' infant daughter to Prince Charles, son of Philip and Joanne. Consequently, Louis and Philip agreed that the children assume the title of king and queen of Naples and duke and duchess of Calabria. Until the marriage was consummated, Louis or his appointment would administer the kingdom and Philip, or some other appointment of Ferdinand would administer the duchy. Hostilities would cease; a general amnesty issued for all and peace restored.

With the documents written and signed, the French court celebrated the coming peace. Louis and Philip sent accounts of the agreement to foreign courts. In Venice, representatives of France and Spain who had not been speaking now met and shook hands. King Louis sent instructions to Nemours to stand down and withheld scheduled reinforcements. Archduke Philip sent similar instructions to Gonzalo.

But the threatened outbreak of peace was quickly stifled. King Ferdinand was not going to allow Louis to outmanoeuvre him. But he had to tread carefully as he did not want to antagonize the Castilians and certainly needed to take care with his heirs presumptive. Ferdinand communicated with Gonzalo by secret coded letters; his instructions now would place blame on Gonzalo. When the Great Captain received Archduke Philip's instructions, he responded with the statement that he knew of no authority but that of his sovereigns and felt bound to prosecute the war until he received their commands to the contrary. Somehow such instructions never came.

Gonzalo's Offensive

Gonzalo readied his troops for the coming offensive to decisively weaken the French forces in southern Italy. In April 1503 more reinforcements came to him. Don Ferrando de Andrada landed at Reggio with 300 men-at-arms, 400 light horse and 4,000 Spanish foot. He marched into Terranova. French scouts told d'Aubigny about Don Ferrando's arrival and advance to Terranova. The French commander concentrated his men-at-arms to attack the Spanish and recover Terranova. Unexpectedly, he encountered the Spanish army near Seminara. His scouts made it clear that the Spanish outnumbered him, but ever the brave paladin, d'Aubigny prepared to attack.

The French drew up for battle. The Swiss infantry faced the Spanish foot, three bodies of men-at-arms faced the Spanish horse. The lords d'Aubigny commanded one section of the heavy horse, the Seigneur d'Humbercourt, another and the third were under the command of the Lord Sanseverino. Troops ordered and ready, the Swiss quick-marched against the Spanish line while d'Humbercourt launched against the enemy horse. The clash was loud: the Spanish foot stopped the Swiss dead in their tracks; d'Humbercourt, furiously charging the Spanish men-at-arms smashed their lines and broke through. Commander d'Aubigny, seeing the rout of the enemy horse, ordered Jean Stuart to support d'Humbercourt but Stuart, seeing the Swiss in disarray, charged the Spanish infantry.

Initially not visible to the French, a strong body of Spanish men-at-arms struck d'Humbercourt's formation while their charge disrupted them trying to reform. The French formation broke and fled. The Spanish body then turned and hit Stuart's formation which also broke. Meanwhile, the Swiss were floundering. As usual, they had formed up in their triple unit structure and surged forward, expecting to roll over their opponents. But the Spanish infantry was unlike those of the northern Europeans. Spanish foot carried large spiked shields, short swords and stood in an open formation. They ducked under the pikemen's long spears and struck them with their swords. Collapsing the front ranks of the Swiss, they broke the vaunted squares apart and slaughtered most of the men. His infantry broken, his cavalry dispersed, d'Aubigny's force had to flee the field, his officers taking d'Aubigny with them.

The Great Captain Gonzalo had begun campaigning in Italy in 1495. Usually with a dearth of troops and supplies, he experimented with different ways of fighting, using the many different types of soldiers from his experiences in the wars for Granada. He understood how to use 'small war' tactics against larger and better armies. He tried one set of formations after another. He understood that the French in particular had a winning combination; however, their soldiers had invested heavily in the material and status of the noble class and were not likely to try anything new. As 1503 began reinforcements and money strengthened Gonzalo's hand and he structured new formations to beat the French. These were the *coronelias*, some companies of different types of soldiers under their commanders, organized under a higher commander who controlled the whole formation and directed it in battle. Before the *coronelias*, companies of a few hundred foot soldiers formed the main tactical manoeuvre unit, cobbled together under a commander of foot. Under the *coronelias*, the tactical manoeuvre unit became much larger and so more powerful, taking advantage of different types of weapons. They had pikes, arquebuses and swords. Eventually, the *coronelias* (high royal officers, 'of the crown') formations became the *tercios*, the standard Spanish battle formation.

Battle of Cerignola

Seven days after the fight at Seminara, on 28 April Gonzalo marched out of Barletta to seek battle with the French. His forces threatened a small French holding, Cerignola, some twenty miles away from Barletta. If Nemours was to recover the prestige the French lost in the previous battle, he needed to march from Canosa and rescue Cerignola. The Spanish forces had been held up many months in Barletta; many men and horses were out of shape but, if his manoeuvre was going to be successful, Gonzalo had to move quickly. The sun beat down and the land was dry. When the army crossed the Ofanto River, each man drew as much water as possible, but they could not carry enough for the forced march. The soldiers marched in the simmering heat and suffered. The pace was punishing and Gonzalo rode through the ranks, encouraging his men. Finally, Gonzalo ordered each of his horsemen to pick up a foot soldier on his horse. Gonzalo picked up a German standard-bearer on his horse.

The Spanish reached Cerignola in the early afternoon. The small town stood on a summit of a minor eminence covered with vineyards and encircled at the foot by a ditch. Gonzalo divided all his soldiers into sections and assigned a part of the ditch to each section. Many dug, improving the ditch and throwing the spoil as a rampart on the inner side. At the same time, others cut wood and made sharpened spikes which they drove into the finished parts of the ditch. Scouts reported the French were approaching in the distance. When Gonzalo judged the French were close enough, he had his men stop digging and set them in battle order. Then Gonzalo mounted thirteen guns on the rampart and placed his infantry behind the rampart. The Landsknechts with their pikes were in the centre and on each side of the pikes were swordsmen. Gonzalo separated the close-ordered units by wide avenues which would allow the horse to pass through. Across the infantry's front, arquebusiers stood just beyond the rampart. Gonzalo held his heavy cavalry in reserve back up the hill and sent his light cavalry out into the field to harass the French.

The French army came within striking distance of the Spanish army in the late afternoon. The commanders collected together to discuss their best course of action. Sunset was at hand: both Nemours and Louis d'Ars suggested waiting until the morning to attack. Two commanders, Francois d'Urfe and Gaspard de Coligny agreed with them. Coligny pointed out that he knew the ground around Cerignola, saying it was very difficult. Yves d'Alègre unexpectedly disagreed; the land nearby was dry, and if they didn't water the horses by morning, they wouldn't be fit for battle. Moreover, he added, the Spanish might launch a night attack. He concluded by saying that French fury would push the Spanish off the hill and then they could destroy them. The leader of the Swiss, Seigneur de Chandieu, stepped forward and announced that the Swiss soldiers needed to attack now and if they did not attack this day, the Swiss would go home. Louis d'Ars countered, insisting there were Spanish advantages and French weakness which night would set right. The discussion waxed hot. D'Alègre and d'Ars exchanged unpleasantries. In the heat of the moment, d'Alègre accused Nemours of lacking sufficient courage. That ended the discussion: now, they would fight!

The two armies were not large and their combat worthiness was about equal. All agreed that the French had superior cavalry and the Spanish had better foot. The French commanders decided to overwhelm the Spanish with their heavy cavalry backed up by Swiss infantry. The French formed up in three sections in echelon: forward on the right, Nemours and d'Ars rode at the head of the heavy cavalry; in the centre, slightly to the rear, came the whole of the foot; on the left and more to the rear, came Yves d'Alègre and the light horse. On his great charger in front of the French troops, Nemours signalled for the charge to begin.

The French heavy cavalry launched forward — trotting, then galloping toward the Spanish front, followed by the infantry and light horse. The heavy horse outpaced the infantry while the Spanish light horse dashed hither and thither. As the French drew nearer, Spanish cannon threw heavy shot through the ranks, but the cavalry ignored the shot and smoke. When the horse neared the Spanish front, a couple of Spanish ammunition wagons exploded. Huge clouds of black smoke swathed the field. The charging horse suddenly found the ditch right in front; some horses tumbled, most recoiled. Then the Spanish arquebusiers fired a heavy volley, striking down many, killing Nemours and wounding d'Ars, killing his horse. The men-at-arms milling around tried to work their way to the right, to go around the ditch but crossbow and arquebus fire shattered the heavy horse.

To the left of the heavy cavalry, the Swiss surged forward. Also surprised by the ditch, the Swiss scrambled down and backed up, disordering their ranks and files. Then crossbow and arquebus fire disrupted them and they withdrew, opening the Swiss formation to the attack of the German pikes. Seeing the Swiss in difficulty, the Gascon infantry jumped into the fray. Chandieu, high commander of the Swiss, fell while trying to rally his men. Crossbowmen and arquebusiers kept up fire from the flank, and Spanish horse hit the other flank. Gonzalo, with a view high on the hill, ordered his entire force into the general attack. The whole mass of the Spanish forces launched forward, heavy horse striking into what remained of the French right and the Spanish foot breaking French centre. The French fled the field.

In gathering darkness, Louis d'Ars found a horse, rallied the surviving men-at-arms and escaped the field. The commander of the light horse, Yves d'Alègre, saw the disaster enveloping the other two sections of the French army, he withheld the light horse from the battle and withdrew to Melfi.

The French foot, both Swiss and Gascon, pulled back and found themselves surrounded by mounted arquebusiers. The Swiss reformed and managed to pull off the field but the Gascons did not escape and died. The French lost half their men dead, all their guns, baggage, colours and stores, providing the Great Captain's troops with rich plunder.

Gonzalo Conquers Naples

At dawn, Gonzalo sent his cavalry to pursue and mop up the French. Louis d'Ars made his escape to Venosa. Yves d'Alègre with the light horse rested the night at Melfi and then rode on to Capua. Finding the Spanish coming on behind him and hearing the news about disturbances in Naples, d'Alègre pushed at speed for Gaeta. Once the French withdrew north of Naples, Gonzalo sent out forces to consolidate his victory. Canosa, Aversa, and Capua surrendered as soon as Spanish horse appeared before their gates. Once the Neapolitans heard about the Spanish victory, they sent their submission. On 14 May 1503 Gonzalo formally entered Naples. Still, the French held both major castles.

What a few years ago had presented a serious problem was now an annoyance quickly handled. The renowned military engineer, Pedro Navarro came to reduce the castles. Directing operations near the New Castle, Navarro oversaw the driving of a mine under a strong part of the castle's walls. When the mine exploded, Spanish soldiers easily entered the castle and rounded up the dazed defenders. The Spanish soon had the Egg Castle in their hands. Guicciardini said of the gunpowder mines which were overthrowing great castles: '(Pedro Navarro) greatly increased his reputation, and caused no small alarm among mankind at large, for it was supposed that no walls or fortifications could any longer withstand his mines; but new offensive processes always cause the greater alarm, because the appropriate means of defence have not yet been thought out.'

When Gonzalo marched north, Prospero Colonna invaded the Abruzzi, reducing all the French strongholds. Now, the only remaining French holdings in the Kingdom of Naples were Venosa under Louis d'Ars, a few castles held by die-hard Angevin lords, and Gaeta under Yves d'Alègre who had some 300 men-at-arms and 2,000 foot remained. The French sent a fleet later that spring out of Genoa with reinforcements and supplies for Naples, but the fleet commander found no safe haven and sailed toward Gaeta.

Gonzalo rushed an attack against Gaeta, thinking to defeat the disrupted French forces before they were ready. He assaulted a commanding eminence – Monte d'Orlando defended by the French. Twice his troops pushed up the eminence, but the French repulsed them. Rather than try again, Gonzalo bombarded the town walls waiting to see if the town would fold. Soon the French fleet came from the Bay of Naples, sailed inshore and turned the galleys, bombarding the Spanish camp. The supplies and reinforcements encouraged the French. The French morale recovered and Gonzalo withdrew.

Louis Reacts to Loss of his Kingdom of Naples

King Louis became very angry when he heard the news about French disasters in southern Italy. At first he blamed Philip the Handsome for putting him in a position where Ferdinand made a fool of him, but then he reconsidered: Philip was naïve, surely, but Louis knew that the fault was his own because he let his desires overcome facts he well knew: Ferdinand was crafty, clever and dishonest, everyone knew it. The only way to get satisfaction was to wound Ferdinand by the sword, to force him to give up the gains his duplicity brought to him. King Louis decided he would attack Ferdinand in both Spain and Italy.

The long border with Ferdinand's kingdom offered numerous points where Ferdinand seemed vulnerable. King Louis and his advisors chose three points: the French would march toward Fontarabia under the command of d'Albert, toward Roussillon under Marshal de Rieux and the Marseilles fleet would ravage the Mediterranean coasts. He needed more troops for Italy. The king recalled his old opponent before he was king, la Tremoille, from retirement because he was the best Louis had seen. The Bailli of Dijon returned to the Alps to hire the indispensable Swiss. The old commander was to lead a new expeditionary force of 1,800 lances and 10,000 infantry. Louis had always been very careful with money, but now he wanted two million ducats a year to maintain these efforts. He took loans, raised taxes and begged for contributions.

The Spanish campaigns were disappointing. The army of d'Albert failed to provide itself with sufficient supplies before even reaching Fontarabia and dispersed. Or was this treason by d'Albert? Spanish ships pushed the French fleet back to Marseilles without any damage to Spanish coasts. The army of de Rieux, 20,000 strong and well led, entered Roussillon and ran into the castle at Salses, recently re-fortified by Pedro Navarro. Here Ferdinand had thrown in a garrison of 1,000 picked men. The French reached Salses on 16 September and took a strong position between the lagoon and the hills. There, they opened a bombardment of the castle. While the bombardment was continuous, Navarro's design rendered their impact impotent. Ferdinand sent 6,000 light horse and foot under the Duke of Alva who cut Rieux's supply lines. Repeated raids by the light troops kept the French camp in upheaval. The fortress artillery played against the French, causing heavy casualties including the captain of the Swiss. Ferdinand concentrated a large force of some 40,000 men. He reached Perpignan on 19 October, joining with Alva. Rieux saw that he was not going to carry Salses and, if he did not soon withdraw, the Spanish would entrap his army. On the night of 20 October the French broke camp and marched back to Narbonne, his rearguard pushing back Ferdinand's pursuit. King Louis was most disappointed in his commanders. He could only cut a deal with the faithless Ferdinand, but both sides had had enough of fighting in the Pyrenees. They made a truce for five months later extended to three years. Italy was not included, and so the truce remained in force.

King Louis was determined to protect 'our honour and repute' by recapturing Naples and pushing the Spanish out of Italy. The king sent orders in May 1503 to d'Alègre telling the commander to stay in the kingdom and take Capua; he was to wait there for La Tremoille who, said the king, was coming with 6,000 Swiss, 4,000 crossbowmen, some 1,000 men-at-arms and a large artillery train. A fleet of grain ships and galleys arrived in Gaeta, on 11 June with 1,200 crossbowmen, carrying Ludovico Marquis of Saluzzo. The king appointed him to fill the office of viceroy now that Nemours was dead. Saluzzo organized the French at Gaeta into a formidable force and oversaw the strengthening of the fortifications. In early August 4,000 more French infantry arrived by sea.

The Second French March on Naples

La Tremoille arrived in Milan lands with some troops in June and some French formations in Milan joined him. The problem for the French commander remained the fact that many French and Italian commanders thought the Naples campaign was a waste of time. Most soldiers and commanders were very aware of the difficulties of war in southern Italy. If they had no personal experience, they certainly knew people who had. More problems emerged. The Swiss did not want to fight any offensive wars; they would only defend France or Milan and made it clear they did not want to fight in Naples in any circumstances. The result was that the French could only recruit inexperienced or second-rate men who were willing to defy their government. La Tremoille stayed near Parma while his officers trained the unskilled Swiss.

When La Tremoille started to march south, he found his progress toward the Kingdom of Naples arrested by the problems with Cesare Borgia's *impresa*. The French Cardinal d'Amboise, who had long supported Cesare, now complained that Cesare was possessed of a devil. King Louis, to keep his road clear, had promised Cesare assistance in taking Bologna and in punishing his renegade *condottieri*. Here is when the affair of Sinigaglia began. But when the news came that Egg Castle in Naples had finally fallen to the Spanish, La Tremoille began to march, but immediately fell ill. The army stalled again and it was not until early August that it began to move south again. La Tremoille was too sick to continue and Louis replaced him with Francesco Gonzaga, Marquis of Mantua, victor of Fornovo, who was expected to work with Saluzzo as an equal. Ferrara, Bologna and Florence provided units to the French. When the army entered Rome, a Venetian agent counted 940 lances, 1,500 light horse, and less than 4,000 foot.

The forces did not leave Rome until late September because of the complicated situation which grew out of Pope Alexander's demise on 18 August and the crumbling of Borgia dominance. King Louis' friend and advisor, Cardinal d'Amboise hurried to Rome, hoping for his election as pope, but no, Francesco Piccolomini, a compromise candidate became Pius III. Cesare Borgia, still suffering from his serious indisposition, needed protection. He made the best terms he could with the French and promised to send his troops to help in the recovery of Naples.

Chapter 20

Battle on the Garigliano

The French and Spanish Armies on the Garigliano

The Great Captain was unable to carry Gaeta and knew that powerful French reinforcements were coming. He withdrew his force to Castellone four or five miles inland. The French moved slowly; Gonzalo had plenty of time to set up a proper reception. The Spanish withdrew behind the Garigliano, the river just south of Gaeta. To gain more time as winter was coming, Gonzalo decided that his men should defend the fortresses on the inland road and so make the French take the easier coast road. Also, he set up a land blockade to keep Gaeta isolated. That way, he avoided being trapped between Gaeta and the coming French forces. The papal difficulties in Rome had already cost the French a month of good weather. The autumn rains would begin in October.

The Marquis of Mantua marched down the Via Latina and descended into the upper valley of the Garigliano. As he approached, Gonzalo moved his camp south from his position on the Appian Way where he had held Gaeta under a close blockade. On 6 October he marched inland and set up camp at San Germano with the Castle of Secca in his front. After Gonzalo left Gaeta, the Marquis of Saluzzo marched out with 4,000 men and occupied defensible positions. He sent out light horsemen across the hills and came into contact with outriders from the main French forces coming down the valley of the Garigliano. When the armies drew closer, Saluzzo went with a large escort to meet with Mantua, unifying the French forces.

The Marquis of Mantua marched to the castle of Secca. He sent an envoy who announced that the castle must surrender immediately or the whole garrison would be killed when they took the castle. The castle commander, Villalba promptly had the envoy seized and hanged. Mantua quickly brought up artillery and blew a breach in the walls, but the castle's garrison repelled two assaults. At the same time, Gonzalo sent out a force which threatened Mantua's camp. Stymied at Secca and threatened on his flank by the Spanish force, Mantua moved off. His men had stripped the countryside of provisions and his supply lines were overextended.

At the end of October, Mantua camped at Ponte Corvo and sent out foragers throughout the upper valley of the Garigliano. Gonzalo kept up the harassing of Mantua's supply lines and rear.

Mantua stayed for seven days at Ponte Corvo. He decided that he was not going to force his way by the inland route to Naples' plain. The area was foraged out; the weather was abominable, constant rain made the roads nothing but mud. Wagons and artillery were often stuck, cavalry hardly moved. Many in the infantry were dying of dysentery and cold. Mantua decided to take a short cut to the south and gain the Appian Way. There he would have Gaeta at his back and the large garrison could send out forces to repel Gonzalo's raiders. Gaeta had large stockpiles of supplies and in the port there sat a French fleet.

Battle of the Garigliano

Mantua moved swiftly so when Gonzalo's scouts investigated Ponte Corvo they found it empty. Gonzalo guessed the French had moved south and sent his cavalry to watch the passages of the lower Garigliano. He moved his infantry and cannon by a difficult crossroad across the Auruncan mountains parallel to the French, then he crossed to the east side of the Garigliano. By 1 November 1503 the two armies faced each other near the sea with the swollen Garigliano between them. The river overflowed its banks into the low-lying ground. Mantua needed a pontoon bridge to cross the river and he was prepared to build one, but before he started construction a problem needed attention. Near the best point to place the bridge was the location for a ferry, there was a small fort which overlooked the site. This was the Torre de Garigliano with a small Spanish garrison. Rather than face French artillery, the commander surrendered the fort and was allowed to march out. Unfortunately, when the garrison marched into the Spanish camp, Gonzalo's men mobbed and killed most of them. Gonzalo disapproved but did nothing about it except to remark that 'other garrisons would take warning from it'.

The lower Garigliano has a meandering riverbed and the river's estuary flows through a bog into the sea. Upriver from the bog, there is higher ground on the west side, which is where the French were. Gonzalo saw that the point on which sat the Torre de Garigliano was the obvious place for a bridge. He ordered his men to dig a long trench in meadows facing the Torre but beyond cannon shot from the western side. Well placed as it was, the fieldwork kept any force coming across the bridge from advancing inland. With the continuing rains, water filled the excavation but by using the spoil to build up a rampart behind the trench and strengthening the mounds of mud with fascines, the Spanish built a strong position.

As the Spanish excavated their trench and rampart, the French approached the ferry site on the river. Bringing beams, barrels and small boats, they began constructing a pontoon bridge. They placed large cannon on the solid ground behind the ferry site to protect the bridge builders. The Spanish replied with arquebus fire but were repelled by the cannon. The Spanish could not bring up their cannon because the ground was so wet. On 6 November the French completed a broad bridge and launched their attack across it. About 1,000 men had passed and pushed forward when just then Gonzalo ordered his soldiers, who had collected behind his rampart, to attack the French as they deployed from the bridge. The Spanish infantry collided with the French, clogging up those still coming forward on the bridge. Fierce hand-to-hand fighting stopped the French advance. The French cannon could not support their attack lest they hit their men.

After a gruelling battle, the head of the French assault column recoiled back onto the bridge, losing many who fell into the river. To save what they could the French cannon opened fire on the Spanish massed around the bridge's far end, forcing the Spanish back and damaging the bridge. Mantua sent back to Gaeta for his crews to bring large ships' boats up the river and emplaced them as a new bridge in the same ferry crossing. The crews tied the beams and boats together with cables while the cannon kept the Spanish away. Again, troops pushed across but, instead of attacking the Spanish rampart, they also dug in, erecting a palisaded rampart to fortify their bridgehead. Through 10 November they launched attacks against the Spanish lines but could not prevail.

Mid-November had even worse weather, constant rain alternating a few times with snow. Even if he was able to break through the Spanish lines in front of his bridgehead, the whole countryside was swamped, hindering any cavalry movements and severely hindering artillery transport. He decided to wait for better weather. For six weeks the two armies blocked each other. Both armies dug strongpoints along the lower course of the Garigliano. The sentries were up to their knees in mud and had to use pathways made of wooden fragments or tree boughs laid end to end. The soldiers constructed hovels of wattles above the high-water table. Reliefs were difficult and supplies took a long time to come. The officers implored Gonzalo to withdraw four or five miles and establish headquarters in Sessa, the town behind the position. Gonzalo refused, saying that once they allowed the French to cross the Garigliano, their superior numbers would prevail. To demonstrate to his men the importance of their position, Gonzalo visited his front-line units every day, and he and his officers lived in hovels similar to his men's. The great captain held his army together, waiting on events.

What Gonzalo saw was good news for him. If his men suffered, so did the French. His men had faith in him but the French were not happy with Mantua. While the French were more comfortably placed, their ill-kept outposts and evident signs of indiscipline showed their bad morale. Further, Spanish spies in the French camp reported that the whole French army was on the point of mutiny. Desertion was high and the officers were plotting to remove their commander. The officers openly insulted Mantua, accusing him not only of inability but of treason. Mantua finally had enough; he claimed he was ill and went home. The next in command, the Marquis of Saluzzo, took over.

The change in the high command helped the French, but the main problems remained: this was not a way the French liked to fight. Saluzzo had an adequate track record, fighting for both kings, Charles VIII and Louis XII, but the army was disintegrating. Commanders left their troops in order to find comfortable lodgings or went to Gaeta. Many soldiers left because they wanted to find better employers or better jobs. The horses were not doing well, commanders sent whole squadrons to distant pastures and towns, often ten miles, away. The outpost line was very thinly held. But, given that it was mid-winter, they remained far stronger than the Spanish and the French expected the Spanish were no better off than themselves. In December, the Spanish made a few efforts to destroy the French bridge, at one time floating heavy timbers down the river, at another, sending a fire boat down the Garigliano. The bridge watch fended off the timber with adroit use of poles and the fireboat exploded before it reached the bridge.

The Great Captain Shifts to the Offensive

With the collapse of the Borgia power, the Orsini had revitalized themselves and turned to the Spanish as allies. The new head of the Orsini faction, Bartolomeo de Alviano, joined Gonzalo with 400 lances, 1,000 light horse and 4,000 Italian foot, reorganized Borgia veteran troops. This raised Gonzalo's numbers significantly. Since the stalemate began, Gonzalo had collected materials to prefabricate a bridge. Carpenters shaped beams and planks to exact measurements — the Spanish stockpiled lengths of rope, pitch and connectors. Because the state of the roads precluded using wheeled vehicles, equipment moved in trains of mules and horses to the castle of Mondragone, fifteen miles behind the front.

Gonzalo let Christmas Day and the day after be a time of religious observation and relaxation. The French found out and equally enjoyed the holiday, but on the 27th, while the French continued to enjoy the respite, Gonzalo mobilized his troops, slowly concentrating them in the north opposite the northern end of the French lines. Here, the French occupied the village of Sujo five miles above their bridge. The land in this area was less wet than lower down the river, and the west bank was no higher than the east bank. Here the Great Captain would attack.

Alviano and Gonzalo worked together planning the coming offensive. Alviano commanded the train of bridge parts and the Spanish light cavalry vanguard. The main body, under Gonzalo's command, the infantry and men-at-arms, were prepared to follow. Left in the trenches opposite the French were the rearguard under Fernando Andrada. Commanding a formation of German pikemen and light horse, he was to attack if the northern offensive appeared successful or to block any French counter-attack from their bridge.

Parts and pieces of the bridge were transported, delivered to the site opposite Sujo, and laid down without difficulty at dawn on 29 December. The pieces fell together easily, all measurements being within nominal tolerance. The Norman French troops opposite the bridge were taken by surprise as they were not under arms when the bridging was completed. Their officers and many troopers were gone. Alviano's light horse charged them and swept them away. The Normans fled down the river, through the French lines, spreading panic and disruption. The Spanish light horse closely followed, driving the panic-stricken mob before them. The Swiss and German pike were unable to form because the first they heard of the disaster was when it was on top of them. Castelforte, San Cosmo and other villages fell to the attackers, one after another.

The French heavy cavalry was far into the rear. Saluzzo could initially collect only a small number of men-at-arms. Led by Yves d'Alègre, they charged the Spanish light horse vanguard but were too few and scattered. The French collapse was so sudden that Saluzzo failed in making a stand at Trajetto and saw the French position as hopeless. He ordered a general retreat to the defile between the sea and the hills at Formia. He ordered his bridge destroyed and his artillery pulled out, but too late! The Spanish rearguard, in the line along the river, had begun the attack before the French were ready.

The French had started to dismantle their bridge by cutting its moorings and using the boats and barges which formed the bridge to embark the cannon and send them down the river. All fell into confusion. The Spanish pushed through what remained of the French bridge, seized boats and materials. They jury-rigged the bridge back together and crossed onto the French bank. At this point, Piero de Medici, son of Lorenzo the Magnificent, former boss of Florence, was a minor officer in the French army. He managed a crew who manhandled a cannon into one of the larger boats and was trying to move off downstream when routed soldiers scrambled onto the stern of the boat and capsized it. Piero, in heavy armour, went to the bottom with the cannon. Andrada's troops passed the river on the patched together bridge, seized most of the French artillery and broke into the main French camp with rich spoils.

At the same time, there was a ten-mile pursuit. Pushing through brought the Spanish past Trajetto and Scauli to the narrow seaside defile of Formia, the Molo de Gaeta. Here, a large body of fresh French troops horse and foot, with Saluzzo commanding, stood ready to receive the Spanish onslaught. The French men-at-arms rallied around d'Alègre, Bayard, Sandricourt and Adorno who held the bridge of Molo while the rest retreated behind them.

Bayard at the Battle of Garigliano

A part of the Spanish vanguard crossed the Garigliano heading toward the French camp. Led by Pedro de Paz, a very brave yet short, hump-backed man, his command held some 120 horsemen each accompanied by an arquebusier on foot. The troop came to the river Molo where a bridge led to the French camp. Initially the Spanish seized the eastern entrance of the bridge and it appeared as if the whole Spanish army was coming, creating alarm and panic. But the Good Chevalier and his companion, the bold Squire Le Basco, Master of Horse to King Louis XII, heard the commotion and arming themselves, they mounted their horses and rode to the cause of the disturbance.

Bayard saw that beyond the river there were some 200 Spaniards thrusting forward toward the bridge. If they crossed and held the bridge, they would disrupt the French forces trying to form. The Good Chevalier called to Le Basco, 'Warn our people to defend yonder bridge or we are all lost! I shall amuse the enemy in the while, but hasten!' Bayard, mounted on his warhorse with his lance at the ready, rode to the bridge's west end, facing the Spanish who were preparing to pass over. But as a furious lion descending against sheep in a fold, destroys, scatters and disperses a flock, so the fearless Chevalier smote the Spanish at the bridge's far end. Two or three Spanish men-at-arms toppled into the swift river, where they stayed, weighted down by their armour. Mounted, Bayard expertly fought with weapon and horse, holding off the advancing Spanish. The angry lion held the bridge, preventing the Spanish host from crossing, defending himself with his sword, fighting, recalled the Spanish, like a demon.

The Squire Le Basco returned and at the head of 200 mounted men-at-arms, charged across the bridge, pushing the Spanish horse back a good mile. They halted their advance when they saw a large body of Spanish horse, some 700 or 800, coming to reinforce their vanguard. Bayard, at the French front, called out, 'Sirs, we have saved the bridge. Let us withdraw in good order.' The formation turned and trotted back toward the bridge with Bayard holding the rear. Whenever the Spanish horsemen came near the French, Bayard turned and pushed them back. All at once, the Spanish men-at-arms rushed the French rear. Striking the French horse, the Spanish dismounted many of their men-at-arms. Bayard fell into a ditch where a large number of Spanish soldiers surrounded him calling out, 'Surrender! Surrender! my lord.' Bayard lowered his arms replying, 'Surrender, I must. I cannot fight all of you!'

Bayard was separated from the withdrawing French formation who had rescued unhorsed men and ridden back to the bridge. They thought the Good Chevalier was with them but suddenly they realized he was gone from their midst. Consternation spread throughout the ranks. The whole company dismounted, and adjusting their horse-furniture, they remounted and moved toward the Spanish in attack formation. Bayard, by this time had surrendered to the Spanish men-at-arms. They remounted him on his exhausted horse and did not bother taking his arms and trappings. They let him accompany them with his sword by his side and his war axe in hand. His captors questioned him about who he was, but Bayard thought the wisest course was to say little and act as if in shock.

The French formation came sweeping down on the Spanish soldiers, yelling 'France! France! Turn Spaniards! Turn! You carry not off our leader!' The larger number of Spanish saw the smaller force charging toward them with astonishment. The Spanish formed up for defence to receive the coming impetuous attack. The clash of arms resulted in many of the best of the Spaniards being unhorsed. When the French attack hit the Spanish,

Bayard was mounted on his tired horse but still armed and armoured. He jumped off his mount and vaulted on a fresh bob-tailed horse which had been the mount of Salvador de Borgia, a brave knight unhorsed by the Squire le Basco. Now well mounted, Bayard launched into battle, crying, 'France! France! Bayard! Bayard! Him let go!' The Spanish, realizing their mistake in not disarming this hero, lost heart and turned and fled the field. Night was falling and the French rejoiced at the deliverance of Bayard, now returned to their camp.

The Spanish Victory

But Andrada's column of Spanish men-at-arms came and drove in the French rearguard. The Spanish horse charged on for miles, passing broken infantry and mired cannon until they reached the walls of Gaeta and met fire from the ramparts. The French lost heart; rather than useless fighting, many surrendered. A body of French horse, riding in from a distance, intercepted by Spanish light cavalry yielded without a blow, although they might have fought their way through. But the question was where they would flee? The French lost some 3,000 or 4,000 dead, all their cannon and baggage, yet even at the end they outnumbered the Spanish, at some 20,000 French to 15,000 Spanish.

On 30 December Gonzalo again reached the hill, Monte Orlando, overlooking Gaeta. Now the hill was empty. He ordered it taken and it fell easily. Once emplaced, his cannon would dominate the whole of Gaeta's fortifications below. That evening, Saluzzo sent a flag of truce offering to surrender Gaeta and storehouses in return for free departure. Gonzalo, building a golden bridge for fleeing enemies, readily agreed. They drew up the convention and signed it on 1 January 1504. One detail he would not accept: Gonzalo demanded to keep as deserters some Neapolitan barons of the old Angevin factions who had surrendered and accepted release on parole. These were members of the houses of Sanseverinos and Aquaviva.

The French officers and their men took ship out of Gaeta's harbour but all the Italians and Swiss had to walk home, and only a few made it. Saluzzo sailed to Genoa but soon died there. Julius II provided food and clothes for some of the defeated armies if they got to Rome. Louis XII was angry at the loss of his kingdom and army: all French commanders were in disgrace. The Bailiff of Caen, who oversaw the commissary, was taken to the gallows.

Conclusion

The French

The French had lost Naples twice. Louis XII was a sound strategist who decided to cut loses. He signed the Treaty of Lyons with King Ferdinand of Aragon on 31 January 1504, ceding Naples *et al* to Ferdinand in return for recognition of the French interests in northern Italy. As a sweetener, Louis signed the Treaty of Blois which stipulated that should Louis die without a male heir, his daughter by Anne of Brittany, Claude of France, would marry Ferdinand's grandson, Charles of Ghent (later Emperor Charles V). Charles would then receive as dowry France's northern Italian dependencies including the Duchy of Milan along with Brittany, Blois and a host of other holdings. As events proved, Louis had no intention of allowing this to happen, but it kept Ferdinand's attention for the moment.

The Italian Wars boiled up again in 1508, in the War of the League of Cambrai and continued for some fifty more years. Louis XII continued ruling France well until his death in 1515. He never recovered Naples and lost Milan in 1512. Anne of Brittany died in 1514, her daughter Claude of France married the heir presumptive, Francis of Angoulême (King Francis I 1515–1547). Louis XII married Mary Tudor, sister of Henry VIII on 9 October 1514 but died on 1 January 1515.

The Borgia

With the death of his father and his continued indisposition, Cesare appeared as powerful as ever, but he knew his position had no foundation. He was floating in air and unless he re-established a solid base, he was going to fall. Remaining in Castle San Angelo during the conclave for his father's successor, Cesare saw to the election of an ally, who became Pius III. But, after twenty-six days, Pius suddenly died. The next conclave promised to be less accommodating to Cesare's interests. On the other hand, the result was not clear for anyone. Cardinal della Rovere approached Cesare with a deal: if Cesare supported the election of della Rovere as pope, then he would confirm Cesare as *gonfalonier* of the church with all his privileges intact. Cesare took the offer; della Rovere became Pope Julius II.

The new pope turned his back on the deal. Cesare found his powers swiftly draining away; he went to his only remaining powerful ally, Gonzalo de Córdoba, who imprisoned him. The papacy resumed possession of all Borgia lands and King Ferdinand sent Cesare to imprisonment in Spain in 1504. He escaped in 1506 and King John III of Navarre hired him as a commander. On 11 March 1507, a band of knights found Cesare alone, killed him, stripped him and left him naked on the ground.

The Spanish

The Spanish victory in southern Italy installed King Ferdinand of Aragon's administration in the Kingdoms of Naples and Sicily. He appointed Gonzalo de Córdoba as viceroy in Naples. The king's wife and colleague as joint sovereign of Spain, Isabella of Castile, died on 26 November 1504. In her will, of 24 October 1504, she designated her daughter, Joanna, as successor to the Crown of Castile, followed by Joanna's son by Philip the Handsome, who was Charles of Ghent. Gonzalo de Córdoba was Isabella's man and a Castilian. Ferdinand initially found himself pushed out of Castilian affairs and he feared Gonzalo might bring Naples to the Crown of Castile.

During 1505–6, Ferdinand, the nobles of Castile, Queen Joanna and her husband manoeuvred and fought for advantage. In June 1506, Philip ascended as King Philip I of Castle but died on 25 September 1506. Joanna believed Ferdinand had him poisoned but Ferdinand claimed that she was mad. In 1507 Ferdinand went to Naples, highly honoured Gonzalo, and retired him to Spain, where honour and retirement continued until Gonzalo's death in 1515 at the age of 62. Ferdinand married again but did not generate an heir. He continued to fight in Spain and Italy. He died in 1516 and his grandson by Isabella through Joanna and Philip became King of Spain, King of Naples and Sicily, then Holy Roman Emperor and much more as Charles I of Spain and V of the Empire.

Bayard

Many of the people we have followed failed in their life's ambitions and some met untimely and nasty ends. Not so Chevalier Bayard. He continued enjoying his celebrity status in tournaments and battles for another twenty years. He was never defeated but, at age a little more than fifty, an arquebus bullet brought him down and he died amidst a crowded death scene worthy of high opera.

Still, he was an anachronism in his own time. He was a great warrior, a leader of men, an exceptional athlete and splendid person but he was no soldier. Fighting in a band of fellows with another band of similarly minded fellows, they all had a great time. That some died merely raised the stakes. For a commander judging the strategic result of an operational manoeuvre, a person like Bayard was difficult because he was just as likely to make his own decision about what he and his band were going to do. In the free-wheeling conflicts of armoured horsemen with no disciplined infantry or forceful missile weapons, such initiative added to the combat effectiveness of an army. No longer: pike infantry, mobile cannon and massed handguns could devastate such undirected wanderings. The chevalier knight was replaced by the cavalry soldier.

The Results of the First and Second Italian Wars

The wars in Italy from 1494 to 1504 did not produce a definite way of war nor any sort of settlement. Rather, the campaigns ripped up the military text-books and rent asunder any possibility of a political settlement. To perceptive people at the time, there appeared many possible outcomes of the chaos King Charles had unleashed upon Italy; none of them were good. Worse, they saw that King Louis' efforts simply deepened the confusion. The future looked dark – and it was.

By breaking the structure of battle and shattering political order, these wars opened up a wide range of possibilities which would change the way people fought, thought, and believed. Different people seized upon different paths as their intelligence and imagination led them and so Europe changed. More important, many Europeans managed to export their ambitions and desires across the globe and so changed the world.

Contemporary Commentators

We perceive the age of the Italian wars differently from the way we perceive the times which precede that period. Medieval chroniclers and historical commentators wrote for a very limited audience because their documents were only reproduced by hand. The emergence of printing reset the whole of the European literary world. As a rising business, book sellers looked for fresh material which would sell. Each of the following authors' materials were found by a book seller who ran or contracted with a printing craft shop to produce a significant run of copies of these works. Then the job was to sell them at profit, in order to cover the loans which provided the capital for their ventures. These authors' works are publishing successes since they were first printed. Because of them, we understand events and people in a particular way. Just as medieval portraiture shows people in a hopefully accurate but two-dimensional way so medieval historical writers can only say so much about personality. But Renaissance paintings reveal a complex three-dimensional portrait of a person, so these writers describe a much more deeply involved sequence of actions making up events.

Phillip de Commines (1447–1511)

Philip de Commines was a member of a noble family of Flanders. His father's death, when de Commines was about six, left him the debt-ridden owner of a noble estate. He grew up in the court of Philip the Good, Duke of Burgundy where he was friends with Philip's son Charles. At 17 the young man was fighting in battle; he became a knight in Charles's household after Philip the Good died in 1467 and Charles became Duke of Burgundy. By 1472 Philip de Commines had had enough of Duke Charles's boldness; he went into the employ of King Louis XI. Angry, Charles confiscated de Commines' property, but Louis XI compensated him with grants of French lordships and marriage to an heiress.

King Louis was long involved with a struggle against Charles of Burgundy and having the personable, perceptive, shrewd and crafty de
Commines in his employ gave the king an advantage. Louis intertwined
Charles the Bold in his web of plots. Striking back, Charles got himself
killed in the Battle of Nancy (1477). Once he was rid of his Burgundian
menace, King Louis didn't particularly need de Commines. After some
disagreements and an accusation of bribery, King Louis sent de Commines
to Italy to handle diplomatic issues. Later, de Commines spent considerable
time performing personal services for the king, much of which was and has
remained secret. De Commines was on the Royal Council when Louis XI
died (1483) and remained there during the early years of Anne of France's
administration.

More attuned to the wants of Charles VIII and the policy of Louis
of Orleans, de Commines supported the opposition to Anne of France.
With Anne's victory, de Commines found himself locked up in a cage in
January 1487. His confinement continued although was considerably eased
until Anne of France gave the reins of state over to Charles VIII, when King
Charles had him freed. Once his confinement allowed, he began writing
his narrative of the events in which he participated or was interested.

A close reading of de Commines' text reveals that underneath the
polished narrative, there are notes de Commines wrote for his own benefit
at the time the events happened. Most probably, de Commines wrote
journals of his everyday experiences, jotting down impressions of people
and their actions for his own reference. In many ways the journals and even
the finished product is a personal discussion of happenings rather than
a formal history. Although he was called back to the royal court, he kept
writing. The main section, covering the reign of Louis XI, was written
during the time 1488 to 1494. After Charles VIII died in spring 1498, de
Commines wrote his account of the Italian War. De Commines produced
these narratives for the interest of friends and colleagues. He never sought
to publish them for a general public. The manuscript remained private
when Commines died in 1511, aged 54. Indeed, the first section, regarding
Louis XI, was not picked up by a printer until 1524. The smaller section
on the wars in Italy was not printed until 1528.

Rather than see de Commines' work as some form of 'modern'
history, we need to understand that these are the impressions of a
busy, struggling world on a perceptive and ambitious individual. De
Commines wrote for himself, so what we see in his text are his honest and

forthright appraisals of people and events. That, of course, is no guarantee of accuracy.

Niccolo Machiavelli (1469–1527)

Niccolo Machiavelli was a Florentine, the eldest son of a successful attorney, of an old and prominent family. Well educated, he found opportunity following the upheavals involved in the fall of the Medici and Savonarola affair. The new administration appointed Machiavelli to an office in the Second Chancery, the secretariat for official documents. Soon he became secretary to the administrative department of interior and war. He also served as a diplomat, representing Florence to many of the leading powers. His reports to the *Signoria* are insightful and interesting.

Machiavelli was also in charge, at times, of the Republic's armed forces. He distrusted the enterprising *condottieri* and supported a citizen's militia. His militia did achieve a number of victories, but as the Italian Wars twisted this way and that, the Medici fought to regain their dominance in Florence. With Pope Julius II's backing and supported by Spanish troops, the Medici retook Florence in August 1512. Once back in power, the Medici threw Machiavelli out of office and in 1513 they accused him of conspiracy against the new regime, throwing him in prison where their agents subjected Machiavelli to the rope torture (binding the wrists behind the back and lifting the subject by the wrists to cause pain in the shoulders and back). Evidently, they gave him only a few yanks because he suffered no permanent injury. They released him after three weeks in the dungeon, but the scare remained. Machiavelli learned the lesson, he retired from politics.

He exiled himself to his rural estate and turned to writing about history and politics. After some time Machiavelli involved himself with intellectual circles in Florence, writing plays which were popular and successful. He continued a correspondence with numerous friends discussing political issues which were widely read. He wanted to get back into politics, but the opportunity never appeared. Nevertheless, as he said, his endeavours in reading the past pushed fear of poverty and death away. Machiavelli died in 1527, aged 58.

He wrote numerous works but most were printed some years after his death, so they had no effect other than through what he said or wrote to his friends. Later generations found his writings illuminating and some of them profound. For our purpose Machiavelli is an interesting commentator on many of the events that make up our narrative.

Francesco Guicciardini (1483–1540)

Francesco Guicciardini was born in 1483 in Florence of an old and aristo-cratic family. For many generations the Guicciardini held high government posts in Florence; they were members of the ruling clique and the Medici political machine. Francesco's godfather was Marsilio Ficino who translated some Platonic dialogues into Latin. Francesco studied the classics, both Latin and Greek. His father sent him to the universities of Ferrara and Padua to study law which he did until 1505. At one time the young Francesco wanted to follow a career in the church, but his father had no use for the corruption into which he saw the church had sunk and convinced Francisco to give up the idea. Instead, the *Signoria* of Florence appointed him a teacher of law.

After some years, the *Signoria* appointed young Guicciardini to lead an embassy to the court of Ferdinand the Catholic, King of Aragon. But the young man was married, had a successful legal career and did not want to leave Florence. His father insisted that the road to prestige often led to distant places where one could represent the honour of Florence. As it turned out, the embassy was a great personal success. Further, Guicciardini experienced the intrigues of the Aragon Royal court. If Florence was sophisticated and politically complex, the court of Ferdinand the Catholic was direct, authoritarian and, at times, harsh even for those times. Deceit, not unknown to the Italian, was a fine art in Aragon.

Soon, the Medici regained power in Florence. Guicciardini quickly requested recall and appealed to Piero de Medici's son, Lorenzo de Medici. Once back, he returned to his practice of law and was soon appointed to the office of internal security and, in 1515, he held office in the ruling *Signoria*. Pope Leo X, Giovanni de Medici, was elected in 1513 and he brought Florence under papal control. Guicciardini impressed Leo X who appointed him governor of Reggio in 1516 and then Modena in 1517. So Guicciardini started a long career in papal administration under Leo X and Clement VII.

Francesco Guicciardini became a great lord with almost sovereign powers. During the wars of Francis I and Charles V he was lieutenant general of the papal army. Guicciardini managed to defend Florence but the imperial army turned and sacked Rome, temporarily breaking papal power. He was arrested by the new anti-Medici republic which declared him a rebel and confiscated his property. The republic fell to imperial troops in 1530 and Pope Clement VII appointed Guicciardini as investigator and judge of those who opposed papal rule. He did his job very well.

In 1531, Pope Clement VII appointed him governor of Bologna, an important position. Clement died in 1534 and Guicciardini resigned from papal service and returned to Florence where he worked for the new Duke of Florence, Alexandro de Medici. The new duke was murdered in 1537 and Guicciardini worked with his successor, Cosimo de Medici. But Cosimo, an older teenager, decided to do without the old warhorse and Guicciardini retired to a rural villa. He died in May 1540, aged 57.

Storia d'Italia

Guicciardini's *History of Italy* was a work of a lifetime. Perhaps because of what he read in Thucydides about writing a work not just to win temporary applause but as a possession for all time, Guicciardini intended his work to explain the Italian Wars in a full and definitive way. Thucydides' long and involved sentences which chew across events, seeing them from this direction and that, are similar to Guicciardini's involved syntax as he explores events from multiple directions. Lorenzo Valla had translated Thucydides into Latin by 1452 and Aldo Manuzio published the first Greek edition in 1502. In his youthful classical studies, Guicciardini with both Latin and Greek at least dipped into Thucydides and the resemblance of his treatment of events shows the same meticulous investigations into the sources of human motivation that makes Thucydides so interesting. That the History of Italy was not just composed in the late years of Guicciardini's life is demonstrated by the fact that the book is 'over-written'. He altered and added to sentences in order to balance different factors, pointing out a more nuanced approach to the narrative. His paragraphs tend to wander through a number of issues as he builds toward a certain point. I speculate that the young Guicciardini, following Thucydides, thought the wars he was witnessing would be very important, started a series of notebooks in which he kept impressions and understandings of events as he heard about them. He then played with his narrative for years as a relaxation from the press of daily business. But, unlike Thucydides, he finished his text before he died.

Guicciardini's work describes the matrixes of events as driven by the dynamos of perceived personal ambitions. All persons see their lives in a singular context which is unique to themselves. Each understands what he or she wants for themselves. As such, this personal interest is what drives their efforts and actions. For elites, rulers, participants in power, those who may command, this observation is critical to understanding why they exorcise the actions they do. This is the *Guicciardinian particolare*. As a principle of observation, it surpasses Machiavelli's and justifies the means because Machiavelli's observation is subsumed under Guicciardini's. Of course, the end justifies the means, if the particular person's interest sees that this course of action is necessary to carry out his personal agenda. And this is the theme around which Guicciardini's history revolves, looked at from many different points of view. He wrote a masterpiece of his time.

Pietro Bembo (1470–1547)

Pietro Bembo was born in the Palazzo Bembo on the Grand Canal in Venice. The House of Bembo, aristocrats of the Most Serene Republic, had long served in the Venetian government. Pietro's father, Bernardo was an ambassador of the Republic and took his young son on his journeys. Pietro loved Florence and her literature. As a young man he studied under the Greek scholar, Constantine Lascaris and attended the University of Padua. Rather than becoming involved with Venetian politics, Pietro Bembo became a poet and musician. Finding a place at the Court of the Este in Ferrara, he knew Ludovico Aristo, who coined the term 'humanism'. There, Pietro wrote his first work, a dialogue on courtly love, *Gli Asolani*. He preferred his poetry read by a woman singer accompanied by a lute. Once the reading was performed by Isabella d'Este. Later in Ferrara, 1505, Pietro Bembo had a torrid affair with Lucrezia Borgia, wife of Alfonso d'Este, heir apparent of Ferrara.

From 1506 through 1512, Bembo lived in Urbino where he worked on music and composed a treatise on the writing in the Italian language, particularly the Tuscan dialect of Petrarch and Dante. Published in 1525, *Prose della volgar lingua* set the standard around which the Italian language developed. Pietro became Latin secretary to Pope Leo X (reign 1513–21) and a member of the Knights Hospitaller. After Leo died, Bembo's health failed; he lived in Padua, working on his composition. In 1530, the Venetian Republic appointed him Official Historian and then Librarian of St Mark's Basilica.

Bembo's *History of Venice, 1487–1513*, is written in two versions, the finest Latin and excellent Italian. In many ways, Bembo's history follows Livy's approach: a detailed *res gestae*, emphasizing Venetian policies and actions. But this is written by a man who had long experience in the affairs of Italy, if not as a direct participant then as an acute observer. Pope Paul III named Pietro Bembo a cardinal *in pectore* in 1538. Bembo came to Rome, entered Holy Orders as a priest and received his red hat in a consistory the next year. He continued to write and study in Rome for the rest of his life. He died aged 77.

The Loyal Serviteur

Published at Paris in 1527, the account of 'The Very Joyous and Very Pleasant Story of the Kind Lord of Bayard' was printed just three years after Bayard's death. The book is authored anonymously; he called himself simply the Loyal Servant. Research over the centuries has identified the archer and friend of Bayard, Jacques de Mailles, as the most probable author. Whoever he was, the author draws a portrait of a near perfect soldier, able and honourable. Like a painting by Botticelli, the figure of the man is idealized and magnified in an artistic context. The subject was attractive to begin with, and the Loyal Servant turned an interesting, if somewhat typical, life of a soldier into a work of art.

Italy in 1490

S outh of the Alps, the fruitful, prosperous Italian lands stretch across well-watered plains and bountiful mountains. Agriculture, trade, manufacturing and artistic endeavour brought wealth and power to the masters of the lands and spread out among the population. Ancient towns, proudly proclaiming their independence, sat behind strong stone walls, guarded by outlying fortresses. Conflict between cities and states, between rulers and ruled, between wealth and poverty was endemic. Main power centres projected their will as they could, dominating lesser centres, which in turn reached out to grab small powers. The whole shifted and coiled as alliances broke and formed anew. In the centre of the Italian boot sat the papacy and the lands of the church; in the north, great mercantile cities struggled over fortresses and borders; in the south, the Kingdom of Naples held sway. There, vast estates, worked by near slaves, supported an unruly nobility, while proximity to the east allowed merchants to act as middlemen between the eastern and western Mediterranean.

Central Italy

Holy Church

The most important power in Italy was Mother Church. At the centre of the peninsula sat the Pope in Rome. By the late middle ages the Latin Church was a mixture of Jewish priestly traditions, Plato's Republic and the New Testament, structured along the lines of the Later Roman administration. Holy Church was a huge organization: every village was part of a parish; most castles had a chapel; many farms belonged to monasteries or convents; each town, besides having numerous parishes, had a head church administrator, the bishop; most bishops recognized an archbishop who oversaw a number of bishops; and all were answerable to the Patriarch of the West, the Bishop of Rome, His Holiness the Pope.

The pope, who holds office for life, appoints the deacons, priests and bishops of the city of Rome. These men are the Roman cardinals who elect a new pope. The pope grants to the Roman cardinals property and income to support their dignity. In the late middle ages, these were often extensive, both in the lands ruled directly by the papacy and in faraway lands which recognized papal supremacy. Since priests and bishops take a vow of celibacy – the office of deacon at that time, was considered a stepping stone to the priesthood – cardinals could not have legitimate children, so property under their control reverted back to the church on their deaths.

However, this did not stop some from having children. By the mid-fifteenth century, many families had occupied church positions for genera-tions. Often, positions passed in succession from uncle to nephew. In reality, this was father to son, the son being described as nephew. At times a prelate supplied dowries to a 'niece'. This, of course, became the scandal of nepotism, the giving of benefits to 'nephews'. Such families of clergy formed factions within the church institutions and often pushed for policies benefiting their geographic base.

One of the main divisions of opinion in New Testament churches was the correct setting for worship. Some view a simple setting, dignified but restrained, as the best place to reflect on the sacred. Others, understanding that now the ascended Christ sits on the right hand of the Father in the heavenly court, desire the setting of worship to reflect the greater glory of God and His creation, as perfect a representation of divine majesty as humanly possible. As the fifteenth century waned and general prosperity grew significantly, many Italians strove to recreate the wonders of the Creation, the world and man, in new representational forms that grandly proclaimed human achievement. Holy Church was often at the forefront of this movement.

Here we need to consider not the artistic wonders of the Italian High Renaissance, but the question of who is paying what to whom. Great buildings, monumental statuary and glorious paintings cost money. But, more important perhaps, than how that money was collected was who spent it. Church officials contracted out their projects and then came the many questions of costs, overheads, kickbacks, donations, gratuities and simple embezzlement. And this is not only applicable to the general contract, but to each of the many subcontracts, not to mention collections, accounting and loans of many types. Holy Church was at the centre of a massive industry producing magnificence and glory and so a powerful centre of patronage.

As head of the Holy, Apostolic and Catholic Church, the pope wielded great power. While that power included both spiritual and temporal instruments, of its own nature that power could fail in the face of forceful and ruthless opponents. As Vicar of Christ on earth, His Holiness was expected to support the general good of all. He was to forgive his enemies and uphold the meek and the poor in spirit. In this real world of humanity that was not always done. If politically some popes seemed a bit beyond acceptable morality, their enemies both outside and inside the church often stopped at nothing. A weak pope was the plaything of powerful ambitious men; so, a certain compromise with the nature of humanity was now and again necessary.

The great medieval papacy had collapsed after the French King Philip the Fair humiliated Benedict VIII (1294–1303). The result was the move to Avignon where the popes were under the direction of the French monarchy (1309–76). While a pope returned in Rome (1376), another pope reigned at Avignon, creating the Great Schism (1378–1417). A third pope appeared as a compromise candidate, but the only result was now there were three popes (1409). The third pope, John XXIII, called for a council, which meet in 1414 at Constance. Emperor Sigismund oversaw the council which defined many issues and ended the schism. Cardinal Deacon Oddone (Otto) Colonna assumed the papal office as Martin V (1417–31).

The new pope was a skilled administrator, pulling together diverse factions and reunited divided jurisdictions with a minimum of complaint from those affected. In many ways he restored the prestige of the papacy. Martin V is considered the first Renaissance pope, supporting humanist studies including art and examining the works of classical antiquity. A member of the powerful House of Colonna, the new pope had a great interest in reviving the city of Rome after the neglect during the Avignon papacy and the Great Schism. Much of imperial Rome had survived the centuries until the earthquake of 1349 brought down buildings that had stood for a millennium. Now much of Rome was a bunch of hovels carved out of ruined splendour but Rome began rebuilding and his was a reign of peace and prosperity. His tomb proclaims, 'His time was happy.'

Martin V's Successors

From 1431 to 1484, there were six popes, each of whom were energetic interesting men, striving to reconcile the world and the divine. Educated and politically aware, each of these popes faced difficult opponents and challenges. The papacy had long held lands around Rome and in central Italy. During the height of medieval papal power, the Holy See ruled these lands through governors who recognized papal supremacy. During the

Avignon captivity and the schism, local potentates gained the lands. While they recognized papal suzerainty, they were unruly and paid nothing in taxes unless an army came to their gates. Moreover, the great families of Rome demanded recognition and power, either in opposition to the papacy or through control of the pope.

These power games intersected with each other and also fed into the conciliar movement. During the fourteenth century, many thoughtful critics advanced the idea that Holy Church should institute a permanent system of councils of bishops and eminent theologians to direct church policy through discussion. One of the decisions of the Council of Constance was the demand that councils become the primary church body. Martin V refused to recognize the legitimacy of that decision, but many churchmen and Italian potentates supported the move. Together with the other concerns, these problems produced a magnificently complex series of power struggles through these six papacies.

Innocent VIII (1484–1492)

Giovanni Cibo, of an important family of Genoa, was educated at Padua and Rome. Made a bishop in 1467, he became a cardinal in 1473 through the support of Cardinal Giuliano della Rovere, nephew of then Pope Sextus IV. After Sextus died in 1484, amidst rioting in the city of Rome, the conclave was seriously fragmented. The Venetian Cardinal Barbo, *Camerlengo* of the Sacred Collage of Cardinals, appeared about to win the election. After the cardinals retired for the night, Cardinal Giuliano della Rovere and Vice-Chancellor Cardinal Borgia sought out a number of important cardinals and secured their votes for Cibo, after they offered assurances about the disposition of certain benefices. Since all the cardinals had signed an election capitulation that held them pledged as pope, to safeguard the personal interests of cardinals, these assurances seemed certain. Cibo took the name Innocent VIII.

The new pope received a strong dominion and smoothly running administration. All his main problems revolved around weak cash flow. There was plenty of wealth in Rome, in the papal lands and in the church, but His Holiness had to watch income diverted into hands not his own. Crime and banditry infected the papal holdings, including Rome, because the local authorities did not have the funds to hire the necessary people to keep the peace. Works of charity and necessary expenses induced Pope Innocent to resume selling church offices to the highest bidder. Also, His

Holiness preached a crusade to recover the Holy Land, always a profitable if not a successful endeavour.

Calls for a crusade were rather constant. Innocent had an advantage in the person of Prince Djem, the brother of the Ottoman ruler and a pretender to his throne. Djem had found refuge in the Christian west and western leaders saw him as a threat to use against the Ottomans. Djem had spent years in the west, five in a pleasant captivity in France. In 1489 Innocent took custody and thought to use him as a spearhead to launch a crusade east. A main obstacle arose when King Ferrante of Naples raised objections. Innocent issued a call for King Charles VIII of France to come and regain his inheritance, the Kingdom of Naples.

All of this, however, became moot when the Ottoman Sultan Bayezid concluded a secret agreement with Innocent in December 1490, in which the Sultan pledged not to attack Rhodes, Rome, or Venice and also to pay 40,000 ducats for Djem's allowance to Innocent directly as long as His Holiness kept Djem in custody. With a crusade on the horizon, Djem's allowance flowing into his treasury, Innocent remained a major player in the Italian games of power.

Northern Italy

Lombardy

The ancient towns of northern Italy had welcomed the Lombard invaders who conquered northern Italy by 570. Displacing Eastern Roman administrators and taxes, the Lombard commanders split the lands up into 'duchies' that rested lightly on the inhabitants. The Lombard kings took as a symbol of their authority the Iron Crown which contained, we are told, a nail of the True Cross. The rule of the Lombard kings was loose and light on nobles and towns. Desultory war was constant; usurpations and treachery the order of the day.

The Frankish king, Pepin the Short, son of Charles the Hammer and so the first Carolingian king, received royal unction from the Archbishop of Mainz in 751. At the request of Pope Stephan II, Pepin went to war against the Lombards, forcing them to relinquish lands the Pope saw as belonging to the Church. These lands were known as the Donation of Pepin and founded the temporal power of the popes. Pope Stephen II travelled to Paris in 754 and anointed Pepin a second time, anointing his two sons, Charles, 12, and Coleman, 3, also. This is the first time the pope installed and recognized temporal rulers. After Charles and Coleman became kings of the Franks, a new pope, Adrian I, requested help to defend papal lands from Lombard encroachment. Charles descended into Italy in 773, dealt with the pope and battled the Lombards. After the siege of Pavia, Charles assumed the Iron Crown, adding the Lombard realm to the Frankish monarchy. The Frankish king and the papacy drew close, so much so, that during a political crisis in Constantinople, Pope Leo III crowned Charles Roman Emperor.

The elevation of Charlemagne to emperor changed the political landscape of Western Europe. Northern Italy, instead of being an independent land was now stretched between two poles: the emperor to the north and the pope to the south. During the period of imperial and papal weakness following the disintegration of the Carolingian state, the cities of northern Italy revived. The restored Ottonian dynasty (919–1024) and the early Salian dynasty (1024–1075) rested easily on Northern Italy. The strength of the Ottonian – Salian Empire depended on the Imperial Church, the lands held by the Archbishops of Mainz, Cologne and Trier, along with their sub-bishops. The emperor appointed the bishops to these and other important sees.

In 1075 the new pope Gregory VII issued the *Dictatus Papae*, a manifesto of church reforms intended to eliminate secular corruption in the affairs of the church. Gregory VII maintained that the pope was superior to the emperor and was the source of legitimate political power. In addition, a council in Rome decreed that the pope alone appointed bishops and assigned them to their see. Emperor Henry IV (1056–1105), battling rebels in Germany, saw these decisions as a serious weakening of imperial prerogatives and he fought against their imposition in Germany and Italy. This started the great Investiture wars. From 1075 to 1250 emperors and popes fought each other, using whatever weapons came to hand.

The struggles between emperor and pope spread across Italy. Particularly in northern Italy, which was the road between Germany and Rome, different towns joined one faction or the other; in each town there was a papal party and an imperial party and many families split over the issues involved. Eventually each faction was assumed under the names of Ghibellines and Guelph. The Ghibellines, an Italian slang name for a castle belonging to the Hohenstaufen who were the most powerful imperial dynasty, supported the emperor. The Guelph, a slang version of Welf, the most important German family who were opponents of the Hohenstaufen, supported the pope. Everything else also fell into this mix. The Ghibellines supported strong authority, the wealthy and hierarchic government. The Guelph supported the less wealthy, popular and often republican government.

In 1490 the northern Italian cities were all self-governing, contentious, independent states. Some were military despotisms; others, oligarchies; still others, popular republics. Many had experienced all three types of government within a lifetime. They are all important and interesting but for the purpose of this narrative, we will deal with three: Milan, Florence and Venice.

Milan

A former capital of the Later Roman Empire, Milan commands the Lombard plains and has long been a major trade centre. The city had a full complement of imperial monumental buildings and solid fortifications. While often misused and badly damaged by war and earthquake, many buildings which look fairly modern have late Roman structures masked by later additions and repairs. During the struggles of emperors and popes, Milan was Guelph. After the collapse of the Hohenstaufen dynasty (1250), local Guelphs fought bitterly over control of the city. Pope Urban IV made Ottone Visconti Archbishop of Milan in 1262; Raimondo della Torre, Bishop of Como, opposed him. After a decade of violent civil war Ottone Visconti won the Battle of Desio (1277), pushed the della Torre out of the city permanently and founded a dynasty that held Milan until 1447. The Emperor Wenceslas raised Gian Galeazzo Visconti to Imperial Duke of Milan in 1395. The state well-managed prosperity and power through the years of Visconti domination.

Among the powers in Italy at this time, there were entrepreneurs who rented the use of professional armies to those states which preferred not to use their own citizens or subjects as soldiers. *Condottieri* (contractors) ran these mercenary armies as a business and as a political-military force. Successful *condottieri* could become great lords or even independent rulers. Francesco Sforza (1401–1466) was one of the most successful 'venture captains'. Son of a *condottiere*, Muzio Attendolo, a rural Lombard noble (called Sforza from *sforzare* to exert or force) and his mistress, Francesco was strong, able to bend metal bars with his bare hands; he handled weapons well and was an exceptional strategist. Francesco was working in his father's enterprise until Muzio was downed in battle when the younger Sforza was 23. Then he set himself up as an independent *condottiere* after avenging his father's death.

Francesco Sforza played the *condottieri* game very well, fighting for Naples, the papacy and Milan among others. The Duke of Milan, Filippo Maria Visconti, thought highly of Francesco but, business being business, Sforza generally took the highest bid, and so for twenty years he fought for and against Milan, usually winning. In 1433, he was betrothed to Bianca Maria, age 6, illegitimate but only child of Duke Filippo Maria. He married her in 1441, when she was 14; despite the age difference Bianca and Francesco were a very successful couple. When Filippo Maria Visconti died in 1447, he named the King of Naples, Alfonzo of Aragon as successor. Local factions in Milan founded the Ambrosian Republic and named Francesco Sforza as Milan's captain general. Sforza expected to become ruler of Milan, but leaders of the republic resisted his efforts and Venice saw an opening to weaken Milan. The republic made peace with Venice in 1449, without reference to their Captain General. Sforza, supported by some factions in Milan, blockaded Milan causing famine, unrest and upheaval. The senate of Milan recognized Sforza as duke and on 26 February he entered the city as ruler.

The House of Sforza sat firmly on the throne of Milan because of military force. However, the appointment by a secular body did not grant legitimacy; neither pope nor emperor confirmed the appointment and so many began investigating records to find a legitimate reason to displace the Sforza. Peace became the objective of Sforza's government. Bianca Maria managed administration and appointments with a sure hand. She saw that no internal threat to Sforza rule appeared. Francesco allied with Cosimo de Medici of Florence; their alliance balanced the alliance of Naples with Venice, creating the conditions for a half century of relative peace in Italy. As Francesco grew older and became ill, Bianca Maria took over the running of the government.

Francesco Sforza died in 1466; Bianca took over the regency and recalled their eldest son, Galeazzo Maria Sforza from France where he was serving Louis XI in that king's war with Charles the Bold. Galeazzo came quickly and initially worked with his mother. The new duke was not about to submit to anyone for long. Cruel and sadistic, Galeazzo Maria assumed that everyone was his enemy. Only torture brought truth and the duke enjoyed working his own torture chamber to find the truth for which he was looking. In 1468 Bianca died, rumour said she was poisoned by her son: Galeazzo did use poison to rid himself of those he disliked. Wives of nobles, merchants and any lady who struck his fancy accepted invitations to his bed or their family suffered. A silent conspiracy formed and after a mass in 1476 a group of nobles stabbed Galeazzo Maria to death.

Milan remained under the control of the Sforza; Galeazzo Maria's wife, Bona of Savoy, took power as regent for her 7-year-old son, Gian Galeazzo. She had a rival: Lodovico the Moor, fourth son of Francesco and Bianca Maria. As the young duke's uncle, Lodovico saw himself as more worthy of power than the foreign-born woman. As fourth son, Lodovico's mother ensured he was educated in the arts of the new humanism, including painting, sculpture and letters, along with government and war. Later in life he personally worked with Leonardo de Vinci as a painter. Brilliant, shrewd and bold, Lodovico struggled with Bona of Savoy until his final victory in 1479.

Once in undisputed power, Lodovico worked to improve Milan's economy. He poured money into more efficient agriculture, breeding horses and cattle. He supported the metal industry and the manufacturing of arms and armour. He oversaw the expansion of the canal network and improved Milan's fortifications. He kept his nephew, the duke, in custody while he ran the duchy as ruler. In 1490 Milan was doing well, as was Lodovico, but there were clouds on the horizon.

Eventually, Gian Galeazzo, now 21, would want power. Even if Lodovico managed to control him, other Italian powers would become more interested in his welfare and status. Then, the whole question of Sforza power was questionable. The Sforza title came from the city, not from either pope or emperor. The old claims of the Visconti were alive and well in many different lands, including Naples and France. Lodovico looked to the future with apprehension.

Florence

Florence is a city in Tuscany, the land of the ancient Etruscans. The city is not particularly ancient but, so we are told by the medieval chroniclers, was based on a Roman camp founded after Catiline's defeat in 63BC as a garrison. The old Etruscan mountain top town of Vipsul (now Fiesole) served as a base for some of Catiline's forces and the Romans forced the defendable site evacuated and settled the inhabitants near the Roman garrison on the Arno. Through the time of the Roman Empire, Florence was a substantial but unremarkable town. As a settlement, Florence barely endured during the upheavals of the early middle ages, only reviving with the establishment of the Carolingian kingdom of the Iron Crown. By the time of the Investiture controversy, Florence was again substantial, under the direction of imperialist nobles, but with the collapse of the Hohenstaufen power (1266), the Florentine Guelphs gained control, throwing the Ghibelline nobility out of the city.

The city guilds formed the basis of policy and administration, but they were divided into the greater and lesser guilds, the greater guilds handling imports, exports and wholesale merchandise and the lesser guilds handling retail. The greater guilds represented larger, richer, and more profitable enterprises. The Great People controlled the greater guilds; the Little People ran the lesser guilds. Besides this split, the Guelph faction split between the Black Guelphs and the White Guelphs. The Blacks supported more authoritarian government and the interests of the larger businesses; the Whites worked toward more open government and the interests of skilled workers and smaller businesses. The old nobility, the dissatisfied and those looking for trouble all threw themselves into the struggles between the many sides. At times the violence was extreme; the city burned now and again; many died either by the sword or execution; yet, wealth increased, power grew and Florence flourished.

In 1348 the Black Death swept across Europe. For a horrid five months, three-fifths of the Florentines died, including the chronicler Villani and Petrarch's Laura. The city was devastated. Slowly, Florence recovered wealth and power, but the republic was ever riven by factions. Pope Gregory XI returned to Rome in 1377 as Florence had re-established her predominance. Catherine of Siena implored this pope to come with the Cross in hand like a meek lamb. Instead Gregory hired foreign *condottieri* to bring those lands he saw as belonging to the Roman See under control. War burned across northern Italy. Florence rose in power as fierce factions tore at the republic.

By the early fifteenth century the struggle morphed into the battle of the palace against the piazza, the rich and powerful against the poor and struggling. Into this swirling maelstrom came the money men, the bankers. Investments require stability; business needs predictability. Money conquered where mere force simply created chaos. With proper direction, force would bring profit and so increase wealth. The banks, of course, were not autonomous things but the personal interests of their owners. The most successful bank belonged to the House of Medici.

Giovanni di Bicci de Medici, Giovanni son of Bicci, of the Medici family, transferred his bank from Rome to Florence in 1397. The Medici were an old and prominent north Italian family and branches of the family were members of the Florentine *Arte del Cambio*, the centuries old guild of money changers and bankers. Giovanni and his brother Francesco were managers, then partners, in their relatives' banks before Giovanni established his own business. This business prospered and in 1420 Giovanni retired, leaving the bank to his sons, Cosimo and Lorenzo di Giovanni de Medici. Cosimo was the public face of the Medici bank, while Lorenzo (the Elder) handled technical issues.

The business Cosimo took over was wealthy and powerful with branches across Italy and Western Europe, wool and silk workshops in Florence and high-ranking customers. While Cosimo did not seek political office, his influence managed much of the republic's policy. But after disastrous wars with Milan and Lucca, many blamed Cosimo for the resulting high taxes. He was arrested on 7 September 1433 and sentenced to death. Instead, he, his brother and many family members were exiled to Venice. As often with Florentine politics, the tide turned and the republic soon recalled the Medici. Cosimo took the hint: for his safety and his business's security, he had best manage the republic.

The recurrent unsuccessful wars led Cosimo to find reliable military investments; one investment was Francesco Sforza. During the 1440s Cosimo made sure that Sforza had sufficient business and funds to keep his company going. After Filippo Maria Visconti died in 1447 Cosimo backed Sforza's efforts to gain power in Milan. The resulting Medici – Sforza alliance became one of the axes around which Italian diplomacy revolved. Florentine politics remained as contentious as ever, but always working behind the scenes, Cosimo maintained pre-eminence by out manoeuvring or bullying opponents, if necessary, by calling in Milanese mercenaries to quieten the streets. Cosimo died in 1464, his only living son, Piero, succeeded him.

In his late forties when he became head of the House of Medici, Piero suffered from gout which was probably a symptom of more complex health issues. Moreover, Cosimo had sacrificed Medici business interests to political goals and the Medici bank was in a weakened position. Piero had to retrench. He relegated some branches into receivership thus contracting operations and calling in old outstanding loans initially given for political advantage rather than sound practice.

The chief debtor, Luca Pitti and others began plotting to get rid of the Medici. Allied with the Duke of Ferrara, the conspirators staged an uprising in Florence but, despite the presence of Ferrara's troops, the Florentines would not support them and the coup collapsed. Piero also organized an efficient mercenary army to fight a war with Venice which tried to take advantage of the instability in Florence. In the winter of 1469, Piero died and his son, Lorenzo, ascended to head of the house.

The Magnificent, as Lorenzo was known in his time and ever since, was political boss of Florence until he died in 1492. He was tough and ruthless; he made his enemies' suffering a warning to any who might think of opposing him. The republic continued as usual but with more stability and direction. He hid his iron fist in a velvet glove of show and art. Lorenzo provided work and money for Leonardo da Vinci, Michelangelo di Lodovico Buonarroti Simoni, and Sandro Botticelli. He not only supported them at times, he advanced their careers by paying them to provide entertainment for the Florentine people. Da Vinci made fireworks, Botticelli painted what amounted to bill-boards, and Michelangelo sculpted public monuments.

Beyond the art and style, at which Leonardo did so well, there was murder, bribery and coercion. For business, prosperity and popular happiness, the Magnificent needed peace. Allied with Milan, first with Galeazzo Marie Sforza and, after his assassination, with Lodovico Sforza, Lorenzo maintained good relations with the King of Naples, balancing any combination Venice might make. The answer to the problems of politics for Lorenzo was power. He was a Machiavellian prince.

Venice

The Most Serene Republic of Venice started as a collection of refugees from the chaos of the barbarian invasions of Italy. At noon on Friday, 25 March AD 421, imperial authorities from Padua established a trading post in the lagoons. A collection of little communities grouped around the trading post. Even after the Lombard invasion, the lagoon settlements viewed themselves as subject to the Caesars in Constantinople as the population increased with more refugees. At the beginning of the seventh century, Byzantine authorities organized the communities as an outpost of the empire under the command of an imperial general (*dux*) with consular power (*hypatos*). The emerging new state could choose their leaders and imperial recognition of them would follow.

In the local dialect *dux* (duke) became doge, chosen for life by the community. A line of doges continued through the centuries as Venice formed as a formidable power. After Charlemagne became emperor, a long-standing dispute in the Venetian state erupted between those who wanted to remain loyal to Byzantium (an emperor further away) and those who saw the Carolingian Empire as more attuned to their interests (an emperor close by). After upheaval and war, the Venetians repulsed the Carolingians. Charlemagne, facing a protracted fight with the new eastern emperor Nicephorus I, negotiated an agreement with Constantinople, the *Pax Nicephori* (803) which brought order to relations between the empires and recognized Venice as under the suzerainty of the eastern Caesar with trade rights in Italy.

As a distant outpost of the Byzantine Empire, Venice slowly grew in strength. In 991, Doge Pietro Orseolo, shifted focus from mainland Italy toward the Adriatic Sea. The Venetian fleet drove pirates and hostile forces away from the coastal towns, opening up and securing trade routes. While the Venetians brought order to the Istrian and Dalmatian coast, the Byzantine Emperor, Basil II, was conquering the Balkan interior in the Bulgarian Wars. Basil II found the alliance with the Venetians useful. He awarded the doge of Venice the title and responsibility of *Dux Dalmatia*. This did not surrender the Adriatic to the Venetians, but rather recognized the Venetians as part of the empire. The emperor recognized this new status with an imperial pronouncement, the *Grisobolus* (Golden Bull). To celebrate the new orientation of the Venetian community, Orseolo performed the 'Marriage of the Sea' ceremony. This ritual takes place once a year and continues to this day.

As the military hold of the later Macedonian dynasty on the imperial frontiers weakened, the Venetians paid less attention to Constantinople, strengthening their own holdings and extending their trade routes east and west. In the disastrous Battle of Manzikerk (1071), the Seljuk Turks broke the imperial armies in the east. Soon, all sorts of different potentates in the eastern and western Mediterranean saw the Byzantine state collapsing; they sought to profit from the imperial misfortune. The Norman Kingdom in southern Italy launched a strong attack against western Greece. The Seljuks occupied Anatolia. The Byzantines needed troops quickly; Emperor Alexius called on Western Christendom to send help. The same upheavals that struck the Byzantines descended on the Levant. The Christian communities in and near Jerusalem had a somewhat tempestuous co-existence with the ruling Moslems and the ongoing disruption became worse.

Pope Urban II, building on the spiritual revival following the investiture controversy, combined the call for help from the east and the interruption of the pilgrimages to the Holy Land into a vast social movement called, by later ages, the First Crusade (1096–99). The Venetians found the First

Crusade and those that followed, the path to profit and power by transporting goods and peoples to the eastern Mediterranean. To facilitate transport, the Venetians built fortified bases which became trade centres. They directed crusaders to areas where they wanted more influence, even directing the Fourth Crusade to take Constantinople and establishing a 'Latin' as opposed to a Greek empire.

Genoa, Pisa, and various local powers battled the Venetians for control of bases and trade routes. Despite those struggles, by 1300, Venice sat at the nexus of trade routes that extended across Eurasia both by land and sea. Wealth poured into Venice and from Venice spread across Western Europe. Marco Polo's travels illustrate the extent of the routes – through Central Asia to China, then south by sea through the Spice Islands, thence to India and the Persian Gulf. A series of naval bases protected Venetian shipping through the Adriatic into the eastern Mediterranean. To hold the bases, the Venetians seized their hinterland, extending their frontiers to defendable boundaries. The routes, bases and defensible frontiers all added up to a large but dispersed empire. The Venetians believed ships, trade, bases and empire should pay for themselves, which meant that their subjects paid the bills. The Venetian Empire was powerful but not popular.

Through the fourteenth century, the Venetians fought Austrians, Hungarians, Greeks and especially their Italian competitors who supported any Venetian enemy. Islands and bases were lost and regained and lost again, but Venice thrived. They raised soldiers, built ships and put sailors in them. When armies lost, the Venetians raised new ones. When commanders failed, they hired different commanders. But always, determined in the corridors of power, the leaders of the Most Serene Venetian Republic pursued their policies with consistency and imagination.

By the end of the fourteenth century the *Signoria*, the collective ruling group of the republic, decided that they would do well to extend their holdings in northern Italy. Previously, the Venetians did their best to ignore events in Italy, because they depended on their connections to the east. With the resurgence of Islamic power in the east, however, the Serene Republic now saw their trade and supply routes threatened. By building a substantial dominion in northern Italy, they would acquire a source of supply and manpower to defend their empire and that dominion would pay for itself.

Hungarian instability led, in 1408, to the full recovery of Dalmatia. By 1410 Venice had 3,300 ships, manned by some 36,000 sailors; their new Italian domain included both Verona and Padua. Wars continued with Milan, Florence and other north Italian powers: some the Venetians won, others they lost. Under the administration of Doge Francesco Foscari (1423–57) Venice reached the apogee of its power, but their eastern empire began to collapse with the fall of Constantinople in 1453. Their diplomats negotiated trade treaties with the Turks but the Venetian bases and outposts in the east fell slowly to Turkish forces. By 1470 the Turks launched a massive offensive capturing more Venetian bases and ravaging parts of Dalmatia. Diplomats negotiated new trade treaties, but the trade was less and less. Of course, prices went up and customers were not happy.

In 1490, the Venetians faced difficulty on two fronts: in the east, holding on to their trade empire and attempting to increase if not trade, then profit, and in Italy, holding or expanding their territorial holdings in order to increase their resources.

Southern Italy

The Kingdom of Naples

The Emperor Justinian's conquest reunited Italy and Sicily with the empire but the war's devastation and high imperial taxes precluded social recovery. Commerce ended and production failed. Invading in 569, the Lombards swept across Italy, advancing south of Rome. While the northern Lombard holding coalesced into a kingdom, in the south, the Lombard lords built a series of loosely organized commands based on fortified hilltop towns. Here, the empire still held most ports and large cities with the Lombards gaining the hinterland as all concerned fought for advantage. Beginning around 840, Lombard lords hired Muslim mercenaries to fight in the never-ending wars. The soldiers of Islam, having seized Sicily, established bases in Southern Italy. The Lombards and East Romans, joined in alliance under the direction of Pope John X, defeated the Moslem forces at the Battle of Garigliano in 915.

For the following years of the tenth century, the East Romans strengthened their Italian holdings on one side and the Western Empire began extending influence south of Rome on another side, putting pressure on the lands of the southern Lombards. Both East Romans and Lombards looked for support from freelance soldiers, hiring them as needed, letting them go when possible. Beginning around 1000, Norman freelances became common. The successful Norman man-at-arms, Rainulf Drengot became an independent lord, Count of Aversa and Duke of Gaeta. In 1038 William Iron Arm and his brother, Drogo, eldest sons of Tancred of Hauteville a minor Norman nobleman, landed in southern Italy, hoping to repeat

Rainulf's achievement. They soon established their own dominion in the former East Roman lands of Apulia and Calabria.

The youngest son of Tancred of Hauteville, Robert, landed in southern Italy in 1047. Later generations knew Robert as 'Guiscard,' the wily or the fox, a most apt description. By the time of his death in 1085, Robert ruled most of southern Italy and Sicily. His successors built the domain into a kingdom which was well run, prosperous and joined together people of Italian, Byzantine and Islamic ways of life. By the 1150s the situation in Italy had changed. The rising power of the House of Hohenstaufen brought new strength to the western empire, now becoming known as the Holy Roman Empire. Emperor Frederick I Barbarossa descended into northern Italy to bring the virtues of imperial order. In campaign after campaign he battered at the Lombard cities. The Norman kingdom in southern Italy and Sicily struck him as an important base from which to unify all Italy. He had his son and heir Henry marry the heiress of the Norman domain.

After he became Emperor, Henry IV gained control of southern Italy, using the kingdom as source of supply and manpower. He intended on making the German, Italian, and papal realms into a hereditary monarchy. His wars were hard and expensive, his wife turned against him and he died in 1197. His son, however, eventually picked up all his titles. He became Emperor Frederick II, the most powerful of medieval rulers. Frederick organized the south Italian Sicilian kingdom into a well-run state; he founded centres of learning, encouraging commerce and production. He also fought against the northern Italian cities and the papacy. The wars were implacable and both sides fought without ceasing. Frederick remained undefeated but he died in 1250.

Enemies of the Hohenstaufen, enemies of Frederick, supporters of papal power and those looking to despoil the defeated, all joined together to destroy all Hohenstaufen imperial forces. The result was that the pope declared the throne of Naples vacant and awarded it to Charles of Anjou, brother to the French King Louis IX. Charles, in return, recognized papacy over lordship and agreed to substantial payments to His Holiness. By 1266 Charles held the kingdom and publicly executed the last male heir of the Hohenstaufen in the public square of Naples in 1268. King Charles I of Anjou was a harsh ruler. He needed money to pay those who financed his expedition, to pay the pope and to keep up a strong military presence in order to hold his throne.

On Easter Monday 1282, an insurrection started to sweep across Sicily, resulting in the killing of 4,000 Frenchmen and the repudiation of Angevin rule. Sicily became independent of Naples as the Kingdom of Trinacria under the House of Aragon. Separated from Sicily, the Neapolitan kingdom continued as an Angevin dominion until the reign of Queen Joan I (born 1338, ruled 1343–1382). She was the last direct heir of the Angevins of Naples, however, there were many other Angevins who each saw themselves as a more suitable occupant of Naples' throne. In the end, a member of a cadet branch of Angevins, the Prince of Durazzo murdered Joan in 1382 and proclaimed himself Charles III.

Now, there were two Angevin lines claiming Naples. Charles III faced a number of competitors during his reign. Unable to generate a legitimate male heir, he left the realm to his daughter Joan II (born 1373, ruled 1414–1435). Joan first adopted Alfonso V of Aragon, then repudiated him; then she chose Louis III of Anjou and finally picked Rene I of the junior Anjou line. Rene I succeeded Joan and, in many ways, united most claims of the different Angevin branches. What the Angevins did not expect, however, was Alfonso V's invasion and conquest of the kingdom in 1442.

Alfonso united Sicily, and Aragon in one realm but when Alfonso V died in 1458, the Kingdom of Naples went to his illegitimate son, Ferrante, who was still ruling Naples in 1490. Alfonso assigned the Kingdom of Sicily to his brother, John II King of Aragon, who passed Sicily to his son and heir of Aragon, Ferdinand the Catholic.

The Empire

The Holy Roman Emperor claimed what were called the imperial regalia rights in Italy. Since Charlemagne, emperors had descended into Italy to secure their just dues: the Ottonians (936–1014), the Salians (1024–1099) and the Hohenstaufens (1138–1254) had all fought in Italy to secure their imperial rights. The destruction of the Hohenstaufens led to the Great Interregnum, the time without a generally recognized emperor (1254–1273). The great houses then contended for the imperial office (1273–1440): these were the Hapsburgs, the Wittelsbachs and the Luxembourgers. During this time the most successful house was that of Luxembourg. Of particular importance, the Emperor Charles IV reformed imperial administration in the Golden Bull of 1356, issued by Reichstag and Kaiser. The Golden Bull established the collage of Elector-Princes, the rulers of the seven most powerful landed states of the empire. The electors chose the emperor in a set due-process scheme.

The Holy Roman Empire became a confederation of dependent states, a realm directed by the emperor (*Reich und Kaiser*). Emperors continued to descend into Italy to secure recognition of the imperial regalia, but the struggles were never again as harsh as those of the Hohenstaufen. Usually, the emperors came to Italy at the behest of some Ghibelline faction in order to stifle some Guelf faction. The last Luxembourg emperor, Sigismund (ruler of empire 1410–1437) was an important potentate in western European politics, calling and presiding over the Council of Constance that ended the Great Schism in the church, crusading against the Turks, suppressing heretics and furthering peace where possible.

The House of Luxembourg failed to produce an heir for Sigismund and the Hapsburgs won the imperial election of Albert II (1438–1439) and then again in the election of Albert's successor, Frederick III the Peaceful (1440–1493). The long reign of Frederick III was a time of contention, but the affairs of the empire continued to bring stability to a chaotic polity. Frederick's son, Maximilian, was an energetic and perceptive ruler. His enemies made fun of his peripatetic way of dealing with issues and later historians faulted him for not building a German nation. Of these criticisms, Emperor Maximilian was innocent. He knew how to make the most of slim resources and he knew nothing of nationalism, supporting, instead, the ideal of a universal realm of all good Christian people. Maximilian sponsored significant reforms in the imperial constitution which were quite successful. They allowed the imperial structure to survive the upheavals of the Reformation during the reign of Maximilian's grandson, Charles V.

Appendix III

ehind the princes and republics, the armies and fortifications, the peasants, workers, churchmen and nobles, there existed a whole world that is rarely seen and often purposely ignored. Behind the manoeuvres and successes of the powerful and the struggles and suffering of the rest, there was the world of money. This is a subject about which everyone knows something but in its totality is very complex and controversial. Those who truly understand money and its manipulation usually have access to a great deal of it. Most of those who have limited access to money generally distrust those who control a lot of money. The systematic study of monies and the economies in which they function suffer from the same problem of perspective. Each person relates to the world in which they live differently and so views of economy and money, both in a micro or macro scale differ greatly. Further, different ideas of what economic structures should do lead to very different understandings of how they function.

Since the beginning of the sixteenth century, the Europeans managed to expand their influences throughout the world. While many commentators have given reasons for this, from guns and germs to courage and love of conflict, the basic fact remains that the main difference between the developing European society and all the other societies was money. Ming China was wealthy, perhaps in total wealthier than Europe, but the Ming Emperors could not mobilize the amount of cash in hand of each major European power. The question is how did the Europeans come into such a different way of handling wealth?

This European world of money was only a few centuries old in 1500. There had been a moneyed world 1,000 years before, during the Hellenistic-Roman ages. A shard of that world survived in the lands surrounding Constantinople, shorn of great power, stripped of world empire but still a moneyed society swirling around the urban society of the great city. The lands to the east, the Islamic world, used coins, but the whole structure of interest-paying banks was not allowed. Such institutions were not acceptable to the governments in India and China. Nor were they acceptable in Europe. But, in Europe a constellation of factors coalesced into a pattern that led to the rise of massive capital-intensive institutions that smoothly handled a great number of transactions and were able to invest massive amounts of money in profitable establishments. These methods of handling money emerged by 1300. European monetary development revolved around three types of activity; their combination together emerged as a unique and different economic system that subsequently spread throughout the world. The three activities are coinage, commercial instruments and methods of keeping track of transactions.

Coinage

During the High Roman Empire (96–180) the economy of the imperial east was monetized, but not so much in the west. With the rise of the western successor kingdoms, coins became more important as status symbols rather than actual economic tools. But the old Roman money structures remained in place, even if not very functional. Coins in the west were silver rather than the more valuable gold. The main unit of account was a pound of silver, the liber: 240 silver coins, the denarius (so denari) added up to a silver pound. Twelve denari made a solidus and 20 solidi made a pound (consider traditional English money, 240 pennies made a pound, 12 pence made a shilling and 20 shillings made a pound).

In the east which retained a monetized economy, the base coin was the *nomisma*, the coin Constantine I made for his economic reforms. With gold of 24 carats, the coin had a weight of about 4½ grams and remained the same for centuries. Also called the bezant, the Islamic powers copied it as the dinar. The upheaval striking the Byzantine Empire in the mid eleventh century caused the imperial administration to debase the *nomisma* but Emperor Alexius I, after he put the empire on a stable footing, issued a new coin in 1092, the *hyperpyron* (the very pure). This coin also weighed about 4½ grams but was 20½ carats. The Fourth Crusade shattered the Byzantine state and the *hyperpyron* slowly lost gold content until in the late thirteenth century, it became next to worthless. The commercial Italian city-states needed sound coins to transact their business and decided to produce them.

The Florin: in 1252, the Florentine Republic began minting the florin, the first European gold coin for commercial use since the Later Roman Empire. The coin's value was to equal that of the money of account, the lira, the Florentine accounting term for a pound of silver. The coin had a little better than 3½ grams of high-grade gold. Immediately successful, the florin replaced the half pound silver bars, the mark, that were being used. The Florentines maintained the integrity of the florin until 1533.

The Ducat: The Most Serene Republic of Venice used Byzantine currencies until Emperor Michael VIII Palaeologus greatly debased the *hyperpyron*. In 1284, the Grand Council ordered the minting of a pure gold coin, the Doges' coin, the ducat, of over 99 per cent purity, weighing about 4½ grams, slightly more than the florin. The ducat continued as designed until the fall of the Republic in 1797.

With the emergence of sound and trustworthy currency, the economic growth of the thirteenth century continued through the disasters of the Black Death and even accelerated. In time, other powers also minted sound currencies and found them necessary to economic activity. The whole of European commerce relied on these currencies.

Development of Commercial Instruments and their institutions

Knights Templar

The European economy passed from low level activity toward greater monetarization with the Crusades. Besides increased trade, the movement of people, animals and ships required liquid wealth. The Italian and Rhineland towns profited mightily. Many interests involved themselves in satisfying the need for the transfer of liquid wealth. The most successful interest was the order of Poor Fellow-Soldiers of Christ and of the Temple of Solomon, that is, Knights Templar for short. The fighting knights founded the order in 1119, and papal authority recognized the order in 1139 as a charity. Each member knight took a vow of poverty, giving his wealth to the order and official recognition brought many donations. In the Levant, the order possessed castles and estates; in Europe, they provided for the transport of people and supplies to the Holy Land; they developed an efficient and widespread network, handling money to accomplish their goals.

Pilgrims, crusaders and people with money used the Templars' network to facilitate the transfer of funds from one area to another through the order's management of credit and loans. People would deposit title to their property with the order before they set out to the Holy Land and the Order would oversee and protect the property while the traveller could draw on his wealth in distant lands by presenting documents to local chapters of the order. Expanding an old idea used by numerous small-scale merchant houses, particularly in the Levant, the Templars devised Bills of Exchange. This instrument allowed the circulation of paper instruments that transferred significant amounts of money without need of transporting coins or bullion. While charging interest was forbidden, especially by a Church institution, the Templars charged 'rent' for the monies tied up in the credit instruments. Moreover, since the Templars were pledged to poverty, their overhead was very manageable. The Knights Templar Order became rich and powerful.

As rich and powerful as the order was, it was not able to accomplish its main objective: protection of the Christian kingdom in the Holy Land. The Saracens took Jerusalem in 1244; despite great efforts, Acre, the last Crusader base in the Holy Land fell in 1291. The wealth, power and influence of the order became very irksome to many in the European kingdoms. King Philip IV the Fair of France, after he had found loans from the order most useful, arrested all members of the order in France in the morning of Friday, 13 October 1307. The French authorities put them all in prison and tortured them to gain confessions of terrible doings. France's neighbours followed suit and the order collapsed. Finally, in March 1314, Philip the Fair burned at the stake Grand Master Jacques de Molay and three other high officials of the order. We are told that the Grand Master, dying in the flames, brought down a curse upon Philip and his house.

While that may be, as it was, the monetary functions of the order lay in ruins. But in the handling of money, the Templars had competition. The grain trade, growing, harvesting, and selling of grain, often required a loan to support the producer during the time it took to grow the grain. In Italy, this function was originally handled by Jewish merchants who loaned to farmers against crops in the field and so secured grain sale rights against the coming harvest.

Early Banks

Some merchants found a good business providing the services of holding and securing notes of debt (*billette*), converting currencies of different types and transferring funds from one place to another, at an agreed-upon price, of course. Local merchants often filled this function, slowly restricting Jewish trade and forcing the Jews out of major transactions. These financial businesses worked off tables set up in the market soon known as counters or benches, whence *banca*, 'bank'. They became centres for holding currency against a *billette*, a letter of formal exchange or a bill of exchange. While they held currency to settle bills of exchange, they lent money on the basis of those deposits. Unfortunately, every so often a bench was caught short, and could not deliver currency when requested; when this happened, people said the bench was broken, *banca rotta*, bankrupt.

While the Templars dominated money exchange and transfer in Europe, there were interests who preferred to trust their funds to other hands, in particular the Venetians who distrusted the Templars in the Levant. With the support of the Republic, Venetians founded an early bank in 1157. The Venetian Republic guaranteed the bank while at the same time raising a forced loan to support the Republic. Serving the interests of Venice and Venetians, the bank spread throughout their empire.

Never to be outdone by the Venetians, Florentine families founded numerous banks. Bankers were members of the *Arte del Combio*, the Guild of the Money Changers. When the Templars collapsed, the most powerful Florentine banks quickly expanded. These included the Acciaiuoli, Mozzi, Bardi and Peruzzi families, each developing branches across Western Europe. More speculative than the Templars, the Florentine bankers often over extended and then collapsed. But, of course, to the financially adept, a bankruptcy was just another way to make money. When one bank failed, there were always more to pick up the pieces, and so the Lombard bankers flourished.

The Templars had transferred money through a written financial mandate in the form of a letter. The letter guaranteed payment to the bearer in remote Templar houses. The letter stipulated payment in weight of gold or silver, not in the face value of coins. The Lombard bankers adopted this method of money transfer and circulation in the form of the bill of exchange, a contract of money transfer. The Templar financial mandate implied two parties: the owner of the coins and his bank. The bank granted payment of the amount specified in the document. The Lombard letter of exchange implied three parties: the coin owner, the bank and the beneficiary of the letter. The beneficiary simply signed the letter of exchange as drawee and the representative of the bank counter-signed the letter, thus executing an exchange of funds without any coins in hand.

Many other developed societies had similar instruments, but what made the Lombard banking unique was the fact that they could draw letters of exchange without actually having the coin reserves to pay them all off at once. They began balancing accounts by exchanging the letters themselves.

Based in weights of gold and silver, the letters were mutually exchangeable so the debts of one paid off the debts of others. And, of course, at each stage a fee for service and a rent for the money generated further funds. Slowly, the amount of money in circulation expanded significantly beyond the amount of coins or bullion at hand. Now and again a bank or group of bankers over-extended their credit and the system collapsed. But there was enough wealth in the economy to allow recovery and continued expansion.

In practical application, these banks started to come into their own in the late thirteenth century. In Italy, the Hohenstaufen power revived after the death of Emperor Frederick II with the ascent of Manfred to the Kingdom of Naples. The new pope, Urban IV elected 1261, invited Charles of Anjou, brother of Louis IX, to remove Manfred and take over Naples as his kingdom. Since Charles needed money, Pope Urban threatened to release debtors of Florentine banks if they did not look favourably on Charles's enterprise (in secret, those who did loan substantial funds to Charles were except from such an eventuality). As part of Florentine internal politics, twenty-one Guelf companies pledged significant support for Charles and the destruction of Hohenstaufen rule in Italy.

The result: the bankers provided Charles with interest-bearing loans, secured by specific ecclesiastical taxes, mainly in France. Also, Urban declared Manfred a Muslim and so the campaign officially became a crusade and so crusader taxes applied. Those responsible for the taxes, who were prelates and ecclesiastical institutions, did not have ready cash on hand so they borrowed from the same Florentine banks at a goodly interest rate. These gave the Florentine bankers a double profit: loans to Charles and loans to those paying Charles. But the really important fact is that the money was available to pay for Charles's expedition. Previously, such largess was simply not possible. By 1267, King Charles of Anjou was the strongest ruler in Italy.

The other side of the coin for Florence was the financial collapse of 1343–46 when over-expansion, low cash reserves and unsettled conditions brought down large banks and their many invested partners. The commune itself was deeply in debt and high taxes exacerbated class differences. Nevertheless, after some years, Florence recovered and became richer than ever.

Counting and Accounts

Dealing with money in any form means questions of amounts. Counting coins of different values and understanding how much buying power they represent requires numeration skills. The simplest business analysis is the old three pocket system: how much am I owed? how much do I owe? and how much do I have? In more complex businesses, however, managers need a better understanding of financial activity. Two problems present themselves: methods of keeping track of units of value and calculating amounts. Lines of columns representing incoming and outgoing value, demonstrating balances show business condition and this is achieved by calculating the amounts in the columns. In the Classical Mediterranean, merchants used a simple double entry bookkeeping system. With Greek or Roman numerals (alphabetic numerical systems), the clerk calculated using an abacus. Using a number of pebbles (*calculi*) on a flat surface with a number of horizontal lines, the merchant added, subtracted and multiplied in a number of ways. Pope Sylvester II (reign 999–1003), a noted scholar before he became pope, popularized an abacus using beads on wires instead of pebbles on boards.

The lines on the abacus represented the Roman numbers: fives, tens, fifties, hundreds and so forth. Still, unless the person doing the calculations had a facility with arithmetic, the work was very difficult. The merchants who dealt with Muslim vendors saw them using a different numeration system than either the Greek or Latin methods. While many merchants had different approaches to the Arabic numeral system, Leonardo da Pisa (1170–1240, later known as Fibonacci) described best practices in his books. One of the most important, *Liber Abaci* introduced the Arabic decimal system this way, 'These are the nine figures of the Indians: 9 8 7 6 5 4 3 2 1. With these nine figures and with this sign 0 which in Arabic is called *zephirum*, any number can be written, as will be demonstrated.'

The most important feature of Arabic numerals was the facility they added to arithmetic calculations. Using Roman numerals and an abacus entailed a two-step operation: doing the calculation on the abacus board then writing the result with no record of how the calculation was derived. With Arabic numerals, the calculator used a marker and left a record of calculation process. This made the accounting process much clearer. European universities demanded that records and calculations use Roman numerals, but the nine numbers and zero are a concept not a prescription. With a little facility, it is not difficult to mentally move back and forth between Roman and Arabic numerals, starting with Roman, calculating in Arabic, and writing the answer in Roman. Indeed, using Roman numerals for important dates extends to current times, often seen on official documents and monuments.

The enhanced numerical technology allowed a more complex system of financial analysis. Most major Mediterranean firms used some method of double-entry bookkeeping, developed over the centuries, but by 1300 the Florentine firm of Rinieri Farolfi & Brothers, along with some other companies, had developed specific effective double-entry accounts. There are six essential elements to the double-entry system:.

- First, there is a single accounting entity and that entities' financial relations with others.
- Second, all entries are made in a single monetary unit so entries mesh with each other.
- Third, the system relates the following opposites: increases and decreases in physical holdings of cash or goods, increases and decreases in debts by or to other entities, increases and decreases in the entity own assets and liabilities.
- Fourth, the owner's equity shown as the sum of assets and liabilities.
- Fifth, profit or loss is measured over a clearly defined accounting period.

The book-keeping system, coupled with the more efficient arithmetic methods, resulted in business owners knowing just how well they were doing and sharing this information among partners or clients which allowed a greater degree of trust as now all concerned had a better understanding of business operations.

The New World of Money

These three aspects of economic activity: sound currency, financial institutions operating through paper transference of coins for exchanges or loans, and effective, accurate record keeping, allowed efficient management of money and increased the amount of productive enterprises to an extent not seen in other societies of the time. Money became the main tool of society's masters. This was something very new.

The Greeks and Romans, like the Chinese, Indian and Near Eastern states, financed their operations with hard currency. They minted new coinage from bullion (sometimes diminishing bullion content) and they collected taxes of many kinds from their populace. When the money ran out, they were broke. With the rise of early banks, governments in medieval Europe learned to borrow large sums of money without either new coinage or more taxes.   While interest was condemned, creative financial minds devised all sorts of ways to collect money without calling it interest. Famously, King Edward III of England borrowed most of his war chest to enforce his claim of the French crown and then defaulted on payment. Eventually, the English crown did settle the debt, but Lombard bankers found the experience painful. Governments had to underwrite their loans by pledging the rent of specific land or taxes to cover the loans, which became recommended investments.

The fragmented European political structure allowed all sorts of innovations and experiments dealing with loans, debts and credits. Societies' concept of time and money changed. Human behaviour altered as questions of risk and chance turned on ideas of calculation and probability and the possibility of unbridled speculation. All of these different pieces of economic activity, coinage, exchange letters, book-keeping and everything else involved in the emergence of the new monetary system, were already in use in varying parts of Eurasian commerce. The singular differences in Europe that allowed the emergence of this new system was the confluence of fragmented state control, receptive city-state republics, along with far-flung trade interests.

Innovations came, upsetting age old custom, initiating practices that are maintained today. In 1335 King Philip VI granted the right to Amiens to control city time by bell, calling workers to work in the morning, marking noon and the end of day. In 1370 Charles V standardized time throughout Paris by setting all time according to the clock on the palace on the Île de la Cité. In manufacturing, all sorts of new designs developed. Costume developed fashions which often changed; houses became elegant; armour and weapons improved in quality and there were more for more soldiers; ship building developed new and more efficient types – all this is the result of more money at hand producing more wealth. Of course, this wealth concentrated into few hands: capital concentrations tend to grow while defuse money dissipates.

The scramble for cash intensified and interested parties devised methods to admit more people into the world of money while making some cash for themselves. Particularly in Italy, new educational enterprises sprang up, including the Abbaco Schools. Intended for the sons of merchants and artisans, these schools accepted students at age eleven, teaching them reading and writing in the vernacular, while also including Arabic numerals and arithmetic in their curriculum. Some of these schools appeared by 1290; in 1338, Florence had six Abbaco schools. Textbooks for these schools, written in the vernacular, include rules for solving business questions such as discounting, partnership divisions and value exchanges between currencies and goods.

The emergence of the money men also drew attention to intellectual issues which appealed to them, particularly interest in the secular world of the Greeks and Romans. The old literature, descriptions and discussions of politics, society, philosophy and the natural world became popular and sold well. Questions of mathematics beyond arithmetic intrigued and inspired new ways of viewing the physical world. Their interests were not those of warrior horsemen, but questions of power remained an important concern. They were Christians who believed in the church, yet who had questions about church management. Leonardo da Vinci put the issue succinctly: the good painter paints two things: man and ideas in men's mind.

Appendix IV

The Development of Gunpowder Weapons

Along the courses of the Huang Ho and Yangzi Rivers, arose a sophisticated, complex civilization: these are the lands of the Central Realm, which we call China. Their scholars investigated the nature of humanity, the functions of human institutions and proper ways of managing society. State-supported schools and learned societies emphasized human relations as the centre of educational concern. Intellectual developments blossomed in the Age of the Warring States (480–230 BC), followed by the unification of the Chinese world under the Qin Dynasty (230–221 BC). The Qin Empire lasted from 221 to 206 BC and was followed by the Han Dynasty (221 BC -220 AD).

Manufacturing, crafts and trade boomed in the age of civil peace during the Han Dynasty. The imperial state kept a close eye on economic activity through a well-developed bureaucracy and worked to maintain order according to Ruists (Confucian) principles. In the urban centres, there were numerous groups of people who made a good living in different crafts and trades. Working in an intellectual tradition that mixed different forms of magic, mysticism and practical trial and error, these people found new ways and new materials to produce things. These different 'ways' are parts of the Dao (The Way), a series of idea formations different from and not necessarily consistent with the 'official' understandings. The literature produced by these 'Daoists' was not quite accepted and could lead to severe punishment when the political winds shifted.

Western understandings classify many of these writings as alchemy. In China, one of the trains of thought involved the mixing of opposites to produce a harmonious whole. Chinese cuisine provides a good example: different textures, colours and tastes are mixed together, particularly opposites like sweet and sour, meat and vegetables and so on. The intricacies of materials fascinated these investigators, connecting their ideas about such things with mystical texts of the Zhou Yi and the I Ching (the Zhou Yi was an early form of the I Ching.) Like a puzzle of many pieces, different materials fit together, especially when exposed to water or fire. The results were many trials, many conclusions, many mistakes and many discoveries.

The first mention of a gunpowder-like compound appeared in Wei Boyng's treatise, *Can Tong Qi*, (Kinship of Three.) Here, Wei describes a mixture of three powders that violently 'flew and danced'. His account comes from about 150 AD, during the later Han Dynasty. Exactly what this stuff was, is not clear but gunpowder is the only explosive mixture that is made from three powders. A hundred and fifty years later, Ge Hong's book, *Bao Pu Zi* (Master of Basic Understandings) records the results of his work with heated saltpetre, pine resin, charcoal, and other carbon substances. With these Ge Hong produced explosions. This is the earliest record of a form of gunpowder.

In the later years of the Tang Dynasty, a formula and a warning is found: six parts sulphur, six parts saltpetre, to one part birthwort herb is the formula and the warning, 'Some have heated together sulphur, realgar (arsenic disulphide) and saltpetre with honey: combustion results so that hands and faces are burnt, and even whole houses burn down.' The Chinese investigators called these mixtures *houyao* (Fire by complex mixture – *yao*, 'pharmaceutical' as in medicine can also refer to any complex concoction made to accomplish a specific result).

Fire was always an important weapon in Chinese military history. Explosive fire became even more important. A record of how far the technology had developed by the time of the Northern Song Dynasty is contained in the military manual, *Wu Jing Zong Yao* (Comprehensive Compendium of Military Classics) published, 1044 AD. This book contains the earliest known chemical formula of gunpowder. In the following years, gunpowder weapons proliferated using all kinds of creative designs. By tinkering with formulae, designers produced results from smoky hot fires to large explosions. We still can see some of their results in modern fireworks, including smoke bombs, Roman candles, sky rockets and the many types of fire crackers. Of course, the weaponized results produced bodily harm or material damage, as modern fireworks easily do when mishandled.

A main difference between gunpowder devices was their method of delivery. Pictures in the source material show all sorts of things with poetic names. Between 1044 and the 1200s there were arrows that burned with gunpowder flames, hollow sticks that shot fire, sometimes mixed with stones or pellets, and bombs little and big that exploded with the sound of thunder, spreading missiles in all directions.

Invention of Guns

The development of concoctions that explode was important. However, it's called gunpowder not only because it explodes but because it pushes hard objects out of tubes so that they hit and destroy things. This tube machine, the gun, is equally important. What appears to be the oldest known gun is the Wuwei bronze cannon. A unique bottle-shaped tube, unevenly cast, some 14 inches long, weighing 7.5 pounds, appears from context to be from around 1220. Another cannon, much smaller, about 3.3 pounds, was found in a similar context. However, there is a sculpture among the Dazu Rock Carvings that shows a man holding a gourd-shaped hand cannon. This sculpture ensemble was completed after the fall of Kaifeng to the Jin Dynasty, by 1128. Interestingly, the shape of the hand cannon is similar to the earliest European guns. The oldest securely dated gun is the Xanadu Gun, found in the remains of the Mongol summer palace in Inner Mongolia, a little better than a foot long and more than 12 pounds. Not only was the context in which the gun was found clear, but the weapon was inscribed with a serial number and manufacturing information with a date that is Gregorian calendar 1298.

Guns first appear during the wars of the Northern Song Dynasty and their Jin conquerors (1125–9). Developments continued during the Southern Song-Jin wars (1152–1224) and the Mongol-Jin wars (1211–1234) and then during the Mongol conquest of the Southern Song Dynasty (1234–79). The Mongol armies appear to have adopted guns into their armouries. Since they willingly accepted anyone into their service who would help their military efforts, the Mongols swept up Chinese, Turks, Iranians and others into their armies. Makers of gunpowder, metal fabricators and cast makers found ready rewards from their Mongol overlords.

Spread of Firearms

While specific evidence is lacking, it seems reasonable to see the initial spread of gunpowder and guns as part of the Mongol conquests. From 1210 through 1300, the Mongols directed armies which spread throughout Eurasia. By 1300, all along the frontiers of the Mongol dominion, societies began manufacturing and using gunpowder in battle. These weapons were of different types, but all worked in a manner similar to the early Chinese weapons. In Central Asia, Iran, and the Near East, the ideas involved with these weapons found fertile soil in which to grow and change. The ideas also came to Europe and there, they changed even more.

The first mention of a type of gunpowder in Europe is in a letter of Roger Bacon written in 1267. Just a little later, Albert Magnus and Marcus Graecus also give gunpowder formulas. These are all discussions of material interactions not of weaponry. However, illustrations dating to 1326 show black powder guns (*pot de fer* or vase gun). These are very similar to depictions of gourd-shaped guns in the Dazu Rock Carvings. Perhaps they came from China because there are no evidences of older guns in Europe.

Gunpowder itself is the result of tedious and careful processes. The charcoal must have a high degree of purity. Sulphur is unusual in nature, found for the most part in areas of recent volcanic activity. Saltpetre (potassium nitrate) a complex chemical compound, is fairly common but requires complex processing methods. Making gunpowder in pre-industrial societies was labour intensive and very expensive. A single craftsman, knowledgeable about the product and skilled in the operations needed to make the product, could produce in a year maybe 10 or 20 pounds of gunpowder and so about 200 or 300 firecrackers. But the scale of production needed to generate enough gunpowder for military purposes required a hundred or so skilled, motivated people and ready access to the sources of material. In the Near East, guns were in use by the mid-fourteenth century; in India, cannon are recorded in 1366; in Southeast Asia, Dai Viet, cannon were used from at least 1390. Koreans were producing cannon by 1377. And, of course, the Mongol successor states all had the knowledge to produce guns. But none of these weapons were particularly reliable.

The only road to improvement was trial and error. First came the question of gunpowder: the original powder is called rough gunpowder, made by simply mixing the compounds in the correct proportion. Meal powder comes from mixing dry components together and moistening with a 40 per cent alcohol solution and then grinding the mixture up in a mortar and setting it out on trays to dry. Then powder manufacturers can make two variants from this meal: the mixture forms either smaller or larger granules. These granules are known as corns and the process is corning. Corned gunpowder is less susceptible to moisture and is more consistent than rough powder. The manufacturer's process was expensive, finding improvement was more expensive. Then, there is the question of metal processing; the complexities of iron and steel production require special equipment and highly skilled fabricators. To experiment with expensive materials and demonstrate the superiority of a new design over an existing design was also very expensive.

The European Firearm Supremacy

During the fourteenth century, the main areas of Eurasia and Africa were nearly equal in gunpowder weapon technology. By 1500 European gunpowder weapons were more numerous and often much more effective than other gunpowder-using lands. By 1600 Europeans' gunpowder weapons and their manner of use was significantly better than the rest of the world and by 1700, European weaponry was markedly superior and only matched by direct imitation. The question of how this came about is significant. The simple answer is that the Western Europeans had significantly more money to spend on new and better weapons and equipment (see 'Appendix 3 the World of Money'). Because the other great powers of Eurasia and Africa did not have complex banking businesses which charged interests for loans, their state finances were bound to hard currency. They always could debase their currency, but long experience showed this was destructive in the long term. So, if they wanted money, they could tax, control necessary monopolies and confiscate properties of 'corrupt' subjects. Because these methods always took time, most Eurasian and African states stockpiled large amounts of coin or bullion, often in artistic forms. Indeed, the 'riches of the East' that so impressed Europeans were usually collections of valuable goods that were part of the state treasury.

Western European states found a different way to get money. They borrowed it, paying interest on the debt. The lender liked the idea because his contract was backed up by mortgages on specific taxes or a fund-generating mechanism. Even if the state stopped payment, eventually the rulers satisfied these contracts. Edward III launched his campaigns in France on money borrowed from Italian bankers. True, he defaulted on payments but eventually the loan was settled. Moreover, a state contract or the good possibility of one would provide speculative surety for a loan. New products and methods were always a good financial bet. Gutenberg's process of printing was based on lent moneys. His books were profitable but did not met the needs of the lenders and so Gutenberg went broke. Yet he continued working with printing and the book business eventually took off. The costs of faults and failures of inventions and innovations were covered by interest on the loans, so in the long run there were more and better products and more profits. And so, people thought up new and better ways to make things that would sell.

This was particularly important in the weapons industries. Once the bankers began lending, although some bad loans happened, in general wealth began developing in the form of improved goods and services. From about 1350 weapons began improving significantly. The heavy cavalry, the manor-born knights, began raising and using better horses, using better weapons and having better armour. The foot now was better fed, practised with the bow and protected by leather armour. Fortifications improved; instead of just the massive piles of stone, strong and formidable, castles began to exhibit specific design elements improving their defences as well as domestic comfort.

The bottom line here – and that is the most important line of all – is that the Europeans had more money with which hundreds, indeed thousands, of ambitious, hardworking, inventive people could become wealthy by borrowing money at interest and developing the type of business that they thought would make them rich. And so European technology expanded while the rest of the great Eurasian societies looked to other matters.

Appendix V

Military Organization

P eople fight, but the difference between a brawl and a war is organization. Military organizations are a matter of numbers and weapons. For centuries, western European armies centred around heavy armoured horsemen with some type of infantry support for flanks and camps. At times, infantry units defeated the heavy horse with pikes or arrows: the Scottish *schiltron*, the English longbows and the Flemish *goedendag* were able to defeat the knights, but units of these weapon holders needed training, discipline and leadership which was often lacking. Farsighted commanders often found ways to circumvent these weapons systems. However, significant new units appeared in the Italian Wars that changed the face of combat. Here I will describe some of these main developments as they appeared in Italy. We will look at the military organization of the French, the Swiss and the Spanish.

France Military

The French army in 1490 excelled in organization, weaponry and tactics. The efforts and achievements of the French monarchy laid foundations for this excellence after the collapse of French forces in the Agincourt War (1415–29). The revival of the French state under Charles VII the Well-Served brought a new sense of national purpose and new ways of raising armed forces. Of particular importance in the revival of the French state was the career of Jacques Coeur (c. 1395–1456, in power 1436–51). Coeur was a merchant financer who had been in the Near East where he dealt with the merchants of Damascus and Alexandria. His business dealings were widespread and profitable. King Charles VII appointed him superintendent of royal finances and minting. Coeur brought the French economy from chaos to prosperity. In the process he made enemies who finally colluded to bring him down, but his work, a prosperous and economically powerful France, endured.

Charles the Well-Served initially collected fighting forces from any source he could. The appearance of Joan of Arc gave his efforts a great impetus, and the money Coeur raised kept his forces going until the French expelled the English. Charles utilized a large number of different types of forces, some feudal lords, some urban militias, spearmen, swordsmen and crossbowmen among others.

Charles and his son did not agree on much. Prince Louis fled from Charles to the court of the Dukes of Burgundy. There, he became friends with Duke Philip the Good's son, later known as Duke Charles the Bold. When the prince ascended to the French throne as Louis XI (reign 1461– 83), he brought order to what he saw as chaos in his father's administration. Among his reforms he brought order to French armed forces. Instead of relying on different bands of horsemen and foot, Louis XI employed noblemen dependent on himself to raise companies of horse and foot for which the royal treasury paid the bills, with sufficient funds left over so the noble captain would find the endeavour worth his while. Louis XI found the cash nexus a far greater inducement to loyalty than feudal sentiment.

Louis' son, Charles VIII, took the royal army as he found it. As an instrument of war, the army was superior and more loyal than its opponents. The royal French army was organized into different arms – heavy cavalry, spear and pike infantry and artillery. The basic cavalry units of organization were the *companies d'ordonnance*. The cavalry company held 100 lances. Each lance was an armoured mounted man-at-arms supported by two or three mounted archers. The retinue included a groom, cook, armourer, at least two warhorses, along with horses for everyone and some spares. So, in actuality, a company of lances might approach 1,000 people including camp followers. The king also raised royal companies for his personal guards and uses. The leaders of these were royal favourites and their troops, the elite soldiers of the kingdom. During campaigns, the royal administration accepted the services of adventurers, experienced military leaders who raised companies on their own initiative in order to receive payment from the king.

The foot was organized along the same lines as the horse. Louis XI fought a number of wars with Charles the Bold and Charles's Swiss pikemen impressed him. Building with Swiss mercenary companies, Louis built a standing force of 6,000 Swiss pikemen. Louis also paid noblemen to raise companies of foot swords and spearmen.

Charles the Well-Served invested in the artillery works of Jean Bureau (d. 1463) and his brother, Gaspard. Experimenting with different metals, types of gunpowder, and design configurations, the brothers produced the weapons which blew down English walls. Louis XI continued to employ

Jean Bureau and after he retired, continued investing in cannon and guns. When Charles VIII organized his Italian expedition in 1494, he had a long train of large and small cannon. Most cannon were cast of bronze and drawn by horses on carriages and so kept up with marching soldiers. These carriages also served as firing platforms and easily changed direction and elevation. Everyone else's cannons were cumbersome, slowly drawn by oxen and needed emplacements dug and prepared in order to fire. Charles's guns are described by a contemporary:

'The French are taking with them a numerous artillery, all on carriages. The guns are not too big, being of one hundred to three hundred pounds; the balls are of iron, which weighs more; the guns are made very heavy in the breech, where the powder is put; and then they taper off into a narrowish mouth. In the centre are supports for making them fast on the carriages. Each gun has its carriage, gunners, and balls, with a great number of charges of powder suited to the gun.'

'Who have seen the guns with their own eyes, tell you things about them that make your flesh creep.'

Florentine ambassador

The Swiss

High up in their mountain fastness, the peoples of the high Alps had developed a viable polity by 1353 which became known as the *Eidenossen* (comrades by oath, in English the 'Confederation') usually identified with the name of the core community, the Canton of Schwyz. The high country was not a good place for many horses, so the Confederates armed them-selves with crossbows and stout spears. These lands, consisting of deep river valleys and mountain meadows did not allow the growth of large estates but favoured small, independent communities and small towns. These people fought off outside enemies and each other in never ending small squabbles. They fought well; they were independent and while they rarely agreed on most issues were all agreed on maintaining their independence.

Independence was good but prosperity was also nice. The Swiss produced wool, cheese and animal-hide goods but real money would be better. They found out they could rent their strong young men to neighbours who paid very well, but their pay depended on their success as soldiers.

So, the Swiss united their strength with their organizational skills, along with their ability for rapid movement into a powerful irresistible infantry. All the Swiss formations had to do was win battles; always, regardless of conditions. They sought to instil fear and hatred in those they fought and those for whom they fought. Deliberate and cold-blooded cruelty marked their passage. On the battlefield, there were no better disciplined troops; after the battle, they plundered and murdered those in their way.

The Swiss units formed in large squares, their main weapon was the pike, shaft made of ash, eighteen feet long with a long steel head adding another foot. Using two hands at extended holds, the pikeman poised the shaft at the shoulder with the point slightly lowered at a downward thrust. The points of the soldiers in front extended out from the square, those of rows one through four. The face of the square was an impenetrable hedge of sharp points. The soldiers whose pike heads did not extend beyond the square's front held them perpendicular. In the square's centre, older more experienced soldiers carried halberds. These weapons were eight feet long, sharp point on top, axe blade on front, hook on back. Wielded by two strong experienced arms, the weapon cleaves through plate armour and mail. If the pike wall of the square front failed, the halberd men moved out front, slashing right and left, breaking horse legs, cleaving through armour and detaching arms, legs and heads.

The whole square, a moving forest, approached the enemy rapidly. Above the formation flew many flags, pennons of districts, towns, guilds, along with banners of cantons and once in a while the standard of the High German League, a white cross on a red background. The soldiers stood with kin and neighbours under the banner of their community. Each unit was recruited in a single area and the soldiers elected their officers. Town and district councils appointed commanders.

The soldiers wore coloured uniforms but no armour except perhaps a helmet; the commanding officers were armoured and rode horses as they oversaw the line of march but when battle came, the officers dismounted and fought among their soldiers. The Swiss's main force were the pike squares, but they also utilized light troops to screen the squares. The light troops were anywhere from a fourth to a tenth of the Swiss contingent, armed with crossbows (later they used firearms). Spread out in front of the Swiss squares, they softened up the enemy with missile fire and drew fire in return. When the pikemen came up, they retired into the spaces between the pike squares and became rearguards.

Swiss Tactics

The Swiss squares worked in a simple tactical system. They marched directly toward the enemy without regard for conditions. They did not take prisoners so there was never an argument over ransoms. At dawn, they settled on the composition of the squares and immediately moved off to battle. They marched fast in solid masses, in perfect order and deep silence. They moved straight at the enemy; just before they struck, a loud war-cry burst out as one voice.

Each Swiss band had one commander, the *haupman*; his second in command was the *venner* who was also the standard bearer. Also, there was an *untervenner*, a clerk, a quartermaster, two horn blowers and an executioner. Each district had a flag bearer, who was the commander of the district contingent. There were no underofficers, sergeants, or corporals. The first man who clearly panicked was immediately handed over to the hangman.

All bodies of Swiss mercenaries in one location divided themselves into three square units. They always deployed in echelon. The first square, *vorhut* (vanguard) drove for a point in the enemy line. The second square, *gewaltshaufen* (bunch of violence) advanced parallel to the first unit on either the right or left rear. The third square, *nachhut*, (rearguard) held back from the first two units until the results of the attack were evident. In their attack formation, the three Swiss squares always left clear space behind each unit so that, if repulsed, it would not disorder the rest of the force. While this sequence of manoeuvre was usual, given different conditions, the centre might attack first or both wings hit together at the fighting onset.

The Swiss mercenary formations were almost irresistible in the field. They drew their strength from the simplicity of their structure and singleness of purpose. The soldiers simply had to fight, to push their pikes and kill those who opposed them. Their commanders did not have to balance different arms or complex manoeuvres, all they had to do was accompany their formations as the large juggernaut strode across the field. No matter how disorganized in camp, a powerful Swiss battle unit fell together because each man knew what he had to do. Each soldier depended on his confidence in himself and his brothers-in-arms. If the commanders erred, hard fighting solved the problem. Whatever the situation, the Swiss thought the answer was to rush to fight. Mercenary war was the main

Swiss industry and despite many internal differences they always fought as one.

Spanish Military Organization in Italy

Initiative and Innovation

King Ferdinand of Aragon sent Gonzalo Fernandez de Córdoba to southern Italy in order to counter King Charles's conquest of Naples. An imaginative commander, Gonzalo had fought for years during the war for Granada. His dress, always fancy, his posture, always grand, his movements, always dramatic, drew to him the name, the Great Captain. When he arrived in Italy, he received only a few troops and few supplies. He faced the armed might of France and he beat them.

The Great Captain returned to Spain in 1498. Joining with the *Condottiere* Pedro Navarro, he fought for the Venetians in the Adriatic islands against the Turks during 1500. When King Ferdinand the Catholic partitioned the Kingdom of Naples with Louis XII, the king sent Gonzalo back to southern Italy. Arriving in 1501, Gonzalo experimented with different unit formations, drawing on Spanish practice and his experiences in the war for Granada and the war against Charles VIII.

Having met the massed Swiss pikemen, Gonzalo organized a formation to take advantage of their weaknesses. He developed close ordered units of crossbowmen, arquebusiers and swordsmen who were protected by their own pikemen. The shooters blew holes in the opposing formation, withdrawing to reload under cover of their pikes. Then the swordsmen charged into the gaps and slashed away at the opposing pikemen, disordering ranks and breaking their formation so that men-at-arms could disperse them. If enemy men-at-arms approached, the Spanish horsemen could find cover in the infantry formation.

This was the first pike and shot formation. Called a *coronelias*, the formation was commanded by a coronel ('colonel' – this is the first use of this title). The *coronelias* consisted of twelve companies (*capitania*) of 500 each: 200 pikemen, 200 swordsmen, and 100 arquebusiers. The total number of men in the infantry of the *coronelias* was 6,000 soldiers and attached to the formation were 300 heavy cavalry and 300 light horse. Two *coronelias* made an army under a captain general. In different situations, the formation proved its worth. In actual practice, the numbers worked well as much smaller units.

The mixed formations were useful on almost any field. In time they spread north to France, Germany and England as local versions of the Spanish *tercios*. But even more important, these are the formations that the Portuguese brought to the Indian Ocean and Cortez brought to Mexico. The one thing that these formations had that their opponents outside Europe did not was money for supplies, weapons and manpower. Of course, their objective was to gain more money to pay the loans that launched them in the first place.

Appendix VI

Pope Alexander VI in Church History

The social world that existed in the time of the Italian Wars is long gone. The Italian city republics, the north Italian states, the southern Italian kingdoms, the Kingdom of France, the Holy Roman Empire are all gone. Knights and pikemen, nobles and serfs, peasants and independent mercenary captains, also have gone. And yet, one major part of that social world remains: popes, cardinals, bishops, the structure of the Holy and Catholic Church. Just after the time covered in my narrative began that revolt in which a good part of Western Europe broke away from the Catholic Church in protest against perceived shortcomings. Many people at the time said the popes were a significant cause of the emerging Age of Reformation. This brings up the interesting question: what are the opinions and explanations in the modern Roman Catholic Church regarding the colourful Pope Alexander VI Borgia?

This pope in the years covered in my narrative had bad press from the time he ascended to the office. Alexander VI Borgia was the subject of condemnation and disapproval in his time and ever after. Certainly, I am not interested in making an argument for rehabilitation. One redeeming quality was a perceptive insight into artistic achievement, creating as a patron some of the greatest artistic works in human history. However, as Vicar of Christ, his political and military deeds are troubling, to say the least.

To find out how the modern Catholic Church sees the papacy of the Renaissance Popes, I discussed this question with the Reverend Martin Zielinski, MDiv, PhD, Associate Professor in the Department of Church History at the University of St Mary of the Lake Mundelein, Illinois.

My conclusions, in light of what Professor Zielinski has indicated are as follows: the papacy has periods of vitality and weakness. The church is a central hierarchic administration with very many local centres; when the centre weakens, the strength in the peripheries gathers and reinvigorates the centre. Also, the winds of change over time sweep around the church and her peoples, altering conditions and understandings. In this mixture of sacred purpose and human desires, the involved personalities intersect with events in many ways. After the decline of the Carolingian imperium, the papacy reach nadir under dominion of the House of Theophylact, Counts of Tusculum, who installed family members as popes and used them as adjuncts to their power. The decadence in the Roman papacy evoked reform movements, particularly the Benedictine reforms, in good part centred on the monastery at Cluny.

Some of the results of these reforms appeared in 1059, when Pope Nicholas II decreed that henceforth the suffrage in papal elections was limited to the College of Cardinals. Behind the reforms as a driving figure and militant supporter stood Hildebrand of Sovana who became Pope Gregory VII (1073–85). From this foundation rose the Great Medieval Papacy of the High Middle Ages (1073–1257). But eventually political instability and doctrinal disagreements began weakening church institutional structure and prestige. In 1303, French King Philip IV the Fair sent his henchman to assault Pope Boniface VIII and then by 1309, the papacy moved to Avignon, near France (Babylonian Captivity 1309–77).

Cardinals opposed to dominating French influences in the papacy elected a pope from Naples who took the name Urban VI and set up residence in Rome. In reaction, the French cardinals elected a pope who took the name Clement VI in Avignon. So began the Great Schism; two competing successions of popes, each claiming universal obedience but neither actually able to achieve it (1478–1417). A group of cardinals formed a council at Pisa in 1409; they claimed to depose both the Avignon and Roman claimants to St Peter's throne and elected another man pope. The scheme fell through and by 1410, there were three rival popes. The failure of the papacy in the tenth century was poor quality of individuals; in the fourteenth century, the failure was the poor quality of administration.

The duty of the pope is to guard the Throne of St Peter. His main question is how to support the spiritual Throne and its message in the material world. To operate in the world, to broadcast the message of the Gospels and minister to God's people, the administration of the church needs financial resources and authority. However, when financial resources and authority become the end of administration rather than a means to the general good, then there comes a crisis of leadership.

Disappointment, anguish and outrage had simmered for years in the European lands over the disgraceful condition of the papacy. In 1414, the Pisan pope called for a council to resolve the issue. Support came from Emperor Elect Sigismund and the pope in Rome to assemble the council at Constance. The results of the Council of Constance included a number of significant reforms and the resignation of both the Pisan and Roman popes. Martin V was elected pope and while the line of Avignon popes continued to 1429, unity returned to church administration.

The early fifteenth century saw the flourishing of a new worldliness in the revival of Greco-Roman literature and thought which greatly contributed to the understandings of the natural world and representations of that world. In the later years of the fifteenth century, the trajectory of church reform and re-establishment of papal power came to form the Renaissance papacy, which invested heavily in the new thought. Here, we should see that the worldliness in the spirit of papal actions at this time was a reflection of the age, a symptom, not a cause. Despite this fact, we cannot ignore the weakness inherent in these popes' personal ambitions, materialism and emphasis on worldly domination. These men did not become pope by virtue of their grasp of Christian truths or their abilities of spreading spiritual grace. They schemed, plotted and fought for the position by any and all means at hand. Once in power, they became even more unscrupulous to keep power. By the same note, we must see their outstanding material contributions to the church.

In the late fifteenth and early sixteenth centuries, the ancient patterns of life shattered in the storms of technological and social innovation. People, including committed Christians, were faced with unprecedented and challenging questions concerning their roles and purposes. Some found deeper spirituality; some simply became confused; some eagerly jumped into the worldliness. Pope Leo X said: let us enjoy the papacy. The Renaissance popes ended up disassociating the pope from the church, not wholly but in good part. Renewed vitality emerged from the periphery: renewal in religious orders, the emergence of saintly men and women, reforms beyond Peter's Throne.

Of significance at this time were happenings during the Fifth Lateran Council opened in 1512 under the papacy of Julius II. Giles of Viterbo, Prior General of the Order of St Augustine, the most celebrated preacher of the time, delivered the opening address. He announced that the recent defeat of the papal army at Ravenna was a sign from God to show that the church should be defeated when she leaned on inappropriate arms. The church ought to return to her own weapons, to religion, veracity, prayer, to the armour of faith and the sword of light. The revered preacher described the profound corruption of the time and the priesthood. The call for the reform of the church in head and members had echoed throughout Christendom since the early fifteenth century.

In an age of spectacular technological and social transformation, the church was similar to all institutions and, indeed, all individuals, in that the only way to find their way, was to experiment, to explore possibilities, to see what might be done before they understood what should be done. This is the path of human development and the people who strive to find their way in the unknown make all sorts of choices, some good, others the opposite.

Appendix VII

Poison in the Renaissance

The stories of people using poison pervade the Renaissance. Elaborate rings with a top that pops off and allows someone to surreptitiously pour poison into a glass of wine, poison in the communion cup, poisoned pages in a book, all these stories are part of a stock-in-trade of Renaissance literature. Guicciardini and many of his contemporaries were in no doubt that poison ended the careers of many people. In this book, I identify at least two important figures who died by secret poisonings: Charles VIII and Alexander VI. True, this is controversial. In the late nineteenth and early twentieth century historians and most people became more aware of the nature of diseases.

The nineteenth century was an optimistic age, looking toward the progressive perfection of human society. Most historians of that time were very willing to give the benefit of the doubt to what could not be proven. Lord Acton in his essay, 'the Borgias and their Latest Historian', a review of Gregorovius' *History of the City of Rome in the Middle Ages*, volume seven, brings up the fact that Ranke and Gregorovius both accept the story that Alexander VI died by poison, only to pull a minor source out to find a contradiction and then dismiss poison. Of course, the whole point of poison is to murder without personal blame.

Recently, a couple of interesting cases have come to hand. In an interesting study published in 2006, Francesco Mari, Aldo Polettini, Elizabetta Bertol, forensic toxicologists, and Donatella Lippi, Professor of the History of Medicine, describe the results of a study of the remains of Francesco I de Medici Grand Duke of Tuscany (reign 1574–87) and his wife, Bianca Cappello (d. 1587). Both fell violently ill on 9 or 10 October and, while seeming to begin recovering, they relapsed and died within five hours of each other that day. Many at the time were of the opinion, based on circumstantial inferences, that they were poisoned, but the official story was they both died from malaria. The study by Doctor Mari et al seems conclusive. They died because of arsenic poisoning. The perpetrator is fairly obvious and the suspicions of the time seem correct.

Another interesting case is the discovery of poisoned books in the old book collection of Southern Denmark University. There are three books, Polydorus Virgil's Latin text, *A History of England*, published in 1570, a double volume containing information on Bohemian anti-Catholicism, 1575, and a German text of the controversial Protestant theologian, George Major, published in 1604, reprint of a work originally published in 1544. All three books fit together in a private library and probably in England, in say 1610. The poison, inorganic arsenic, was impregnated into the book covers. Simply having it smeared on somebody's hands would not produce a permanent fix but there were other uses.

Speculating: the arsenic was smuggled into the house in the books and enough was put in food or drink to accomplish the job. Rather than destroy the books, the perpetrator sold the books out of the country. Of course, the academics did not see the diabolical nature of the phenomena and concluded that early nineteenth century restorers used paint made of Paris Green to repair the covers. For many reasons, this is very unlikely.

Bibliographic Notes

The Renaissance

People living in the age we call the Renaissance were aware of their time's uniqueness. Their writings tell us about this at some length. The Florentine, Leonardo Bruni (1369–1444), used the phrase, *studia humanitas*, the study of human life, which is the source of the term humanist. He made many translations of ancient Greek authors and was actively involved in Florence's politics. His *History of Florence* was written over the years, 1429–39. In his book, Bruni talked of the ages of history, ancient, medieval and modern, identifying his own time as the beginning of the Modern Age. Many writers and artists talked of their time as a rebirth of ancient wisdom, a move away from a time of darkness and ignorance, away from an age of Gothic Barbarism. Vasari was particularly insistent about this. In his 'Preface to the Lives', he makes the statement that art in his time is a manifestation of a second birth demonstrating a true perfection in the spirit of humanity. In northern Europe, besides humanism, many people worked toward reconstructing Christ's Church as it was originally. They saw their 'Cleansing of the Altars' as a rebirth of the Church.

The achievements of the late fifteenth and early sixteenth centuries continued to inspire people through the eighteenth century with images of rebirth and innovation. In the nationalistic churnings of the nineteenth century, the age acquired a name. The French national historian Jules Michelet titled volume eight of his *Historie de France, jusqu'au XVIe siècle*, 'Renaissance' (1855), and so added a word to the historians' lexicon. The word was repeated by the Swiss historical writer, Jacob Burkhardt in his 1860, *Die Kultur der Renaissance in Italien* (ET Civilization of the Renaissance in Italy 1867). Burkhardt's book is a marvel, still in print and well worth reading, he draws together politics, art, thought and actions in a finely constructed narrative, firmly based on primary sources.

With the emergence of Liberal Arts Education in Victorian Britain and late nineteenth century United States, questions of how to present history developed into the New Social Studies Movement. The answer came with the work of Lord Acton who inspired a generation of historians interested in education. He established the English Historical Review in 1886 after a political career. Regius Professor of Modern History at Cambridge and Fellow of All Souls at Oxford, his pedagogical approach to the subject of Modern History was as a continuing growth of liberty from the 'discovery of the individual' in the Renaissance to the growth and flourishing of the nation state. The vehicle for the presentation of this curriculum was a series of volumes recounting the history of Europe and European dependencies from the Renaissance (vol. I) to the Latest Age (XII) with two more volumes containing the index and an atlas. The work was the result of objective, detailed and collaborative scholarship. Lord Acton died in 1902 but the project moved on and was completed in 1912. This is the *Cambridge Modern History*.

A more important publication in the academic history business is hard to imagine. After the First World War, which was a terrible shock to everybody, educators designed social studies' curricula around the problem of understanding war and peace in the modern world. And so came the course: Modern European History. Textbooks were made aplenty, each one being a personalized abridgement of the *Cambridge Modern History*. This course is now called Western Civilization Since 1500. As an interesting side note, to up-date a credential, I took this course in a Junior College just a few years ago. I had taken the course some sixty years before and I have taught the course over the years. Indeed, it is still the same course, updated to be sure, but Lord Acton's vision still shines brightly.

The first volume of both the original *Cambridge Modern History* and the *New Cambridge Modern History* (1957 rev. 1961) starts with the Renaissance and so does every modern history textbook. With the Renaissance so front and centre, there is no surprise that new books and articles appear through the twentieth century and into the twenty-first. Biographies, specific cities, artistic analysis, economic understandings, general histories keep coming. In the second decade of the twenty-first century, two fine general studies came out: Guido Ruggiero, *The Renaissance in Italy* (Cambridge UK, 2015) and Carlos Eire, *Reformations, the Early Modern World, 1450–1650* (Yale, 2016). Both books are excellent. There is a fine current overview of the renaissance, Gordon Campbell (ed), *The Oxford Illustrated History of the Renaissance* (Oxford, 2019).

Italian Wars

The Italian wars attracted great attention while they ground on and have forever after. With the rise of modern historiography, the wars found important interpreters. Leopold von Ranke's first book was his *History of the Latin and Teutonic Nations* (1824). When the book was first published, both Germany and Italy were collections of independent states and Ranke was exploring the nature of nationalities in micro-states or multi-national states. While his analysis of nationalism seems quite dated, his narrative of events (1494–1515) is clear and objective.

As part of French history, these wars have drawn a large number of fine accounts in French. Jules Michelet's monumental *Histoire de France volume IX*, gives an energetic and dynamic account as also Francois Guizot's multi-volume *Popular History of France volume III*. A number of works combine and discuss contemporary chronicles. One of the best is Leon Pelissier, *Louis XII et Ludovic Sforza, volumes I and II* (Paris, 1896). Here, the details of Louis XII struggles with Milan are very detailed.

For Italian involvements, none have done better than Ferdinand Gregorovius, 'Geschichte der Stadt Rom im Mittelalter' (1858–72), ET Anne Hamilton, *History of the City of Rome in the Middle Ages, vol. VII pt. I; VII pt. II; VIII pt. I* (London 1909–12). Gregorovius has a particularly perceptive account of political manoeuvring. John Bridge, *A History of France from the Death of Louis XI, volume II, Reign of Charles VIII; volume III, Reign of Louis XII* (Oxford 1924–9) recounts the wars from both a French and an Italian perspective, including a detailed military narrative. An excellent summary of military technology is given in F.L. Taylor, *The Art of War in Italy* (Cambridge 1921). A more inclusive and detailed account: C.W.C. Omen, *A History of the Art of War in the Sixteenth Century* (London, 1937), is probably the best single volume on the subject.

After the Second World War, the academicians told us war was obsolete and we did not have to bother with past wars because they all were won by economic forces (despite all the small wars which ground on through the fifties, sixties, and seventies of the twentieth century). The late twentieth and early twenty-first century have seen a resurgence of fine works on the subject, including David Nicole, *Fornovo 1495* (Osprey, 1996) and Stephen Turnbull, *The Art of Renaissance Warfare* (Yorkshire, 2006). Pride of place, however, goes to the series, *War, State, and Society in Early Modern Europe* Michael Mallett, Christine Shaw, *The Italian Wars* (New York,

242 The First and Second Italian Wars 1494–1504

2012 First Edition), Shaw, Christine, Michael Mallett, *The Italian Wars* (New York, 2019 Second Edition). As a compendium of the Italian Wars, it is unexcelled at this time.

The Borgias

Bold audacity marked the Borgias' path through the reign of Pope Alexander VI. Most public figures find upset and affront qualities to avoid, but a few relish and exult in the amount of outrage they generate. The Borgias held to the maxim, 'There is no bad publicity!' The family of Rodrigo Borgia created scandal and rumour from the beginning of Pope Alexander's reign and the talk still continues. Commines, Machiavelli, Guicciardini and Bembo all have a lot to say about the Borgias as also Paolo Giovio (Pauli Jovi), *dell Istorie del Suo Tempo*, the Diaries of Johannes Burchardus and many others. The accounts continue through the centuries, such as Alexander Gordon, *The Lives of Pope Alexander VI and his son Cesare Borgia* (London, 1729). Of the many works in the early twentieth century, I find William Woodward, *Cesare Borgia a Biography* (London, 1913) particularly good on military matters and anyone interested in the subject should not miss the excellent works of Sarah Bradford, *Cesare Borgia, his Life and Times* (London, 1976) and *Lucrezia Borgia* (New York, 2004).

Gunpowder Weapons

In the second half of the twentieth century careful scholarship unearthed the beginnings of gunpowder weapons. Hans Delbruck, in the early twentieth century, was unclear about where gunpowder and guns came from. He suggested, in his volume on modern military history, a number of European sources, based on Greek Fire, but he was not sure. In the later twentieth century, the studies of Joseph Needham confirmed the Chinese origins of gunpowder and guns, in *Science and Civilization in China, Vol. 5, Chemistry and Chemical Technology, Pt. 7, Military Technology the Gunpowder Epic:* Cambridge UK, 1986 (available as PDF). The best overview of the emergence of gunpowder weapons from China to the rest of the world, that I have seen, is Tonoi Andrade, *The Gunpowder Age* (Princeton NJ, 2016). For further descriptions and fine illustration, Steven Turnbull's Osprey New Vanguard, *Siege Weapons of the Far East (1), AD 612–1300*, is very good. Details of European developments are described in detail in Bert Hall, *Weapons and*

Warfare in Renaissance Europe: Gunpowder, Technology, and Tactics'(John Hopkins, 1997) and Chase, Kenneth, *Firearms* (Cambridge UK, 2003).

Money and Economics

When we are speaking about money and banking in the Late Middle Ages and the Renaissance in Europe, we are discussing the rise of Capitalism. Because our society revolves around money, questions of finance and credit become very personal. The continued developments of banking and commerce have inspired many people to create theories regarding deep mystical human interrelations which follow some predetermined path of development explaining the social structuring of human societies. But, beyond the fact that, like many mammalian societies on the earth, humans reveal inherent hierarchical patterns of ordering themselves, there is no evidence that we are dealing with anything other than multiple choices by large numbers of individuals which may lead into any number of directions.

The Dismal Sciences of Economics may leave many of us bewildered but books about money are interesting and plentiful. First, for our book-keeping brothers and sisters, you will find J.B. Geijsbeek, *Ancient Double-Entry Bookkeeping*, Lucas Pacioli's treatise (1494) with Commentaries (Denver, 1914), utterly fascinating (available on Internet archive). Then, Raymond de Roover, *The Rise and Decline of the Medici Bank* (Harvard, 1963) is a very interesting description of a bank at this time along with an insight into Renaissance Italy. Also see Richard Goldthwaite, *The Economy of Renaissance Florence* (Baltimore, 2009).

For money, see Jack Weatherford, *The History of Money* (New York, 1997); Glyn Davies, *A History of Money* (Cardiff 2002); Niall Ferguson, *The Ascent of Money* (New York, 2008); Felix Martin, *Money* (New York, 2014); and William Goetzmann, *Money Changes Everything* (Princeton, NJ, 2016). As a general overview, I highly recommend, Fernand Braudel, *Civilization and Capitalism, 15th-18th Century: volume I The Structure of Everyday Life* (New York, 1981); *volume II, The Wheels of Commerce* (New York, 1982); volume III, *The Perspective of the World* (New York, 1984)

The Military Revolution

The term revolution as applied to major historical events was popular in the middle of the twentieth century. V. Gordon Child spoke of the Neolithic Revolution and the Urban Revolution in his works on *How*

Man makes Himself (1936; 1951) and had many imitators. The idea that society developed by a series of quantum leaps and these leaps were 'Revolutions' was an accepted principle of historical analysis. Typical was Crane Brinton's *The Anatomy of Revolution* (1938, revisions, 1952, 1965), in which he compares and contrasts the British Civil War (1642–1660), the American Revolution (1776–1790), the French Revolution (1789–1799) and the Russian Revolution (1917–1922). His book is interesting, to be sure, but whether he identifies an archetypical pattern in human development is open to debate.

And so, in this milieu was born the 'Military Revolution'. British historian Michael Roberts delivered his lecture, 'The Military Revolution, 1560–1660' at Queen's University of Belfast on 21 January 1955 (presented in its final form when published in 1967). His thesis runs thus: military technical developments exert lasting influences on society at large. The innovations of Maurice of Orange, inspired by the ancient writings of Vegetius, Aelian and Leo VI, replaced the Spanish *tercio* and Swiss square with linear formations. The linear techniques found initial perfection under the offensive tactics of Gustavus Adolphus. This generated a profound influence on future events.

As a matter of fact, the military historian, Theodore Dodge, explored these profound tactical developments during the first half of the seventeenth century in his study, *Gustavus Adolphus* (1890). His work is a detailed narrative and examination of tactical evolutions. From the eclipse of horsemen by infantry in the sixteenth century, he follows Gustavus Adolphus' campaigns from 1611 through the Thirty Years War until his death in the Battle of Lutzen, 1632. Then, he continues through the rest of the Thirty Years War and narrates campaigns of Cromwell, Turenne, Condé, Montecuculi, Eugene, Villeroi, and Marlborough. Dodge does not use the term 'revolution' but does find significant results from technological and tactical change.

Actually, Charles Oman was one of the most important commentators about these developments. His *Art of War in the Middle Ages AD 378–1515* (1885) followed by an expanded edition, *The History of the Art of War in the Middle Ages*, volumes I and II, (1898, new edition, 1924) and *A History of the Art of War in the Sixteenth Century* (London, 1937), remain basic statements of medieval-early modern tactical systems. Omen's theme was the rise and decline of the armoured horseman. The major change in warfare was the emergence of pikemen, supported by arquebusiers and backed up by mobile cannon. Properly employed, these inevitably defeated the armoured horse. All that followed, the *tercio*, linear volley firing, cavalry formations, were developments of the initial gunpowder tactical system.

Hans Delbruck, in his '*Geschichte der Kriegskunst im Rahmen der politischen Geschichte*' Volume 4 (ET *History of Warfare in the Framework of Political History* volume 4) first edition 1908, followed the same general scheme. Delbruck was an insightful historian, both he and Oman looked at the evidence and both described, each in his own way, what the evidence says.

My conclusion is that the rise of gunpowder armies was the most significant development. While Michael Roberts and Theodore Dodge are right about the importance of early seventeenth century developments, these improvements were the elaboration of guns and gunpowder techniques. The consequence is this: fighting power before gunpowder was muscle power. Swords, lances, and bows depended on human or animal muscles to generate force and shock. Metals enhanced force by concentrating or dispersing it. Fire was often a useful adjunct to muscle force, but fire was a commonplace tool not understood but controlled and well-managed, most of the time. Gunpowder produced energy by chemical reaction and so was a unique method of applying force in combat, as Charles Oman and Hans Delbruck so well pointed out.

Still, gunpowder was a common possession of the major Eurasian societies. How did western European potentates develop the ability to generate more powerful forces than the other major societies? My answer is the fact the western European potentates could control more money through loans from private interests than other powers. Innovators, fabricators and manufacturers found their efforts richly awarded. Ready money in great amounts paid for guns, uniforms, soldiers, military experts and so forth. True, the debt level went up significantly, but since money was a business in itself, soon more wealth came about, taxes increased and so larger loans were made. As long as commercial and military interests led to more profitable outcomes, the force structures improved.

There are a number of interesting books about the 'Military Revolution'. Four of these are: Clifford J. Rogers (ED), *The Military Revolution Debate* (New York, 1995) which contains twelve important articles which discuss aspects of the topic, including Michael Roberts' original essay. Geoffrey Parker, *The Military Revolution and the Rise of the West (1500–1800)* (Cambridge UK, 1988) describes changes from the perspective of the Habsburgs. Jeremy Black, *Beyond the Military Revolution* (New York, 2011):

narrates and analyses world military developments during the seventeenth century. Peter A. Lorge, *The Asian Military Revolution, From Gunpowder to the Bomb* (Cambridge UK, 2008) describes weapons development in east and south Asia from the Southern Song to the twentieth century. All these works are very much worth the reading.

Bibliography

Note: all books published before 1923 are available for free downloading on the Internet Archive. Using a PDF app on an iPad, the works are very accessible. I find the books from the John Adams Library particularly well done.

Acton, John Lord, (John Figgis ed.), *Lectures on Modern History*: 1906, many printings

Andrade, Tonoi, *The Gunpowder Age*: Princeton NJ, 2016

Arnold, Mathew, *The Life and Times of Rodrigo Borgia*, New York 1912

Arnold, Thomas, *The Renaissance at War*: Harper, 2006

Auton, Jean d', *Chroniques de Louis XIII*, Paris 1889–95

Benner, Erica, *Be Like a Fox*: New York, 2017

Berville, Guyard de, *The Story of the Chevalier Bayard* (ET Edith Walford): London, 1869

Bowd, Stephen, *Renaissance Mass Murder*: Oxford, 2018

Bradford, Sarah, *Cesare Borgia, his Life and Times*: London, 1976

Bradford, Sarah, *Lucrezia Borgia*: New York, 2004

Bridge, John, *A History of France from the Death of Louis XI, volume II, Reign of Charles VIII; volume III, Reign of Louis XII*: Oxford, 1924–9

Browning, Oscar, *The Age of the Condottieri*, London 1895

Burchardus, Johannes, *Diarium*, Paris, 1883–5

Campbell, Gordon, *The Oxford Illustrated History of the Renaissance*: Oxford, 2019

Chase, Kenneth, *Firearms*: Cambridge UK, 2003

Cole, Alison, *Italian Renaissance Courts*: London, 2016

Commines Philip de, (ET edited Andrew Scoble), *Memoirs*: London, 1877

Dobson, Chris, *San Romano, the Art of War*: Hempstead, 2013

Duffy, Christopher, *Siege Warfare*: New York, 1979

Eire, Carlos, *Reformations*: New Haven, 2016

Fyvie, John, *The Story of the Borgias*: London, 1912

Geijsbeek, J.B., *Ancient Double-Entry Bookkeeping*, Lucas Pacioli's treatise (1494) with Commentaries: Denver, 1914

Giovio, Paolo, *dell Istorie del Suo Tempo, Prima Parte*: Venice, 1608

Goldthwaite, Richard, *The Economy of Renaissance Florence*: Baltimore, 2009

Gordon, Alexander, *The Lives of Pope Alexander VI and his son Cesare Borgia*: London, 1729

Gregorovius, Ferdinand, (ET Annie Hamilton), *History of the City of Rome in the Middle Ages, vol. VII pt. I; VII pt. II; VIII pt. I*: London 1909–12

Guicciardini, Francesco, (ET and editor Sidney Alexander) *The History of Italy*: Princeton N.J. 1969

Guicciardini, Francesco, (ET Austin Goddard), *The History of Italy*: London, 1753–56

Guicciardini, Francesco, (ET Geffray Fenton) *The Historie of Guicciardini*: London 1599

Guicciardini, Francesco, *Storia d'Italia*, Bologna, 2010

Guizot, Francis, *Popular History of France volume III*: New York, 1870

Hall, Bert, *Weapons and Warfare in Renaissance Europe: Gunpowder, Technology, and Tactics*: John Hopkins, 1997

Jones, Jonathan, *The Lost Battles*, New York, 2010

Larchey, Loredan, (ET), *History of Bayard*: London 1883

Lev, Elizabeth, *The Tigress of Forli*: New York, 2011

Machiavelli, Niccolo, *Collected Works*: Kindle Delphi Classics, 2017

Mallett, Michael, *Mercenaries and their Masters*: Barnsley, 2009 (reprint from 1974)

Mallett, Michael, Christine Shaw, *The Italian Wars*: New York, 2012 (First Edition)

Mclachlan, Sean, *Medieval Handgonnes*: Osprey, 2011

Meyer, G. J., *The Borgias*, New York, 2013

Michelet, Jules, *Histoire De France*, volume IX: Paris 1876.

Needham, Joseph, *Science and Civilization in China, Vol. 5, Chemistry and Chemical Technology, Pt. 7, Military Technology the Gunpowder Epic*: Cambridge UK, 1986

Nicolle, David, *Fornovo 1495*: Osprey, 1996

Omen, C.W.C., *A History of the Art of War in the Sixteenth Century*: London, 1937

Omen, C.W.C., *The Art of War in the Middle Ages*: Oxford, 1885

Pelissier, Leon, *Louis XII et Ludovic Sforza*, vols I and II: Paris 1896

Purcell, Mary, *The Great Captain: Gonzalo Fernandez de Córdoba*: Garden City, 1962

Ranke, Leopold von, *History of the Latin and Teutonic Nations*, (first edition, 1824, ET, revised edition Bohn 1887)

Rogers, Clifford J. (Ed), *The Military Revolution Debate*: Westview Press: 1995

Roover, Raymond de, *The Rise and Decline of the Medici Bank*: Harvard, 1963

Ruggiero, Guido, *The Renaissance in Italy*, Cambridge UK, 2015

Shaw, Christine, Michael Mallett, *The Italian Wars*: New York, 2019 (Second Edition)

Shellabarger, Samuel, *The Chevalier Bayard*: New York, 1928

Simms, Gilmore, *The Life of the Chevalier Bayard*: New York 1847

Sismondi, J.C.L., (ET and editor William Boulting), *History of the Italian Republics in the Middle Ages*: London, 1906

Strathern, Paul, *Death in Florence*: New York, 2015

Strathern, Paul, *The Medici*: New York, 2016

Taylor, F.L., *The Art of War in Italy*: Cambridge 1921

Turnbull, Stephen, *The Art of Renaissance Warfare*: Yorkshire, 2006

Unger, Miles, *Machiavelli*: New York, 2011

Unger, Miles, *Magnifico*, New York, 2008

Vasari, Giorgio, *Lives of the Most Eminent Painters, Sculptors, and Architects in ten volumes*, (ET Gaston Du c. De Vere): London, 1912–14

Vasari, Giorgio, *The Lives of the Artists* (ET Abridgement Julia Conaway Bondanella and Robert Bondanella): Oxford, 1991

Woodward, William, *Cesare Borgia a Biography*, London, 1913

Index